Compa
Revised Com

7. Mining th_____ng

Year B

Michael J. Townsend

Companion to the Revised Common Lectionary

7. Mining the Meaning

Help in Sermon Preparation

Year B

EPWORTH PRESS

Copyright © Michael J. Townsend 2002

British Library Cataloguing in Publication data

*A catalogue record of this book is available
from the British Library*

0 7162 0560 2

*First Published 2002
by Epworth Press
4 John Wesley Road
Peterborough, PE4 6ZP*

*Typeset by Regent Typesetting, London
Printed and bound in Great Britain by
Biddles Ltd, Guildford and King's Lynn*

Contents

General Introduction to *Mining the Meaning: help in sermon preparation, Year B*

For almost twenty years Epworth Press has offered *Companions to the Lectionary* as an aid to preachers and worship leaders. The majority of the material has been prayers in various styles and for different purposes.

The *Companion to the Revised Common Lectionary* (from 1998) has already broken new ground with material for All Age Worship for Years A, B and C, but now Epworth offers aids to reflection and thought for those who will be preaching on the appointed lections.

The three volumes in the *Mining the Meaning* series, of which this is the second, will follow the Lectionary for the Principal Service for the day, as it is set out in the *Methodist Worship Book* (1999). This is virtually identical to the ecumenical *Revised Common Lectionary*, authorized for use in a number of major denominations. We offer this series, like its predecessors, to all who are called and appointed to preach.

The *Mining the Meaning* volume for Year C of the Lectionary has already been commissioned.

Gerald M. Burt
Editorial Secretary

Introduction

The purpose of this book is to help busy preachers, lay and ordained, to prepare sermons which take the lectionary readings seriously. It is not, of course, a book of sermons: if they are to have integrity we must write our own. I have had two aims in mind. The first was to offer the kind of comments which might provoke a train of creative thought for a reader and thus provide a 'way into' a sermon on the reading. The second was to try and summarize some of the best of contemporary biblical scholarship with regard to the lectionary readings, and to interpret what others are saying to us. Our busy lifestyles mean that, with the best will in the world, we who preach do not always have the time or opportunity to consult all the major commentaries on the biblical books. As this book has been written during a three-month sabbatical I have been able to do so. My debt to such professional scholars is everywhere evident. Space does not permit much singling out of this indebtedness, but I want to pay tribute to the late F. F. Bruce who first opened my eyes to the excitement of biblical studies when I was a student at Manchester University. His work on Hebrews, Ephesians, Paul's letters to Corinth and the Johannine epistles has been regularly and profitably consulted. In Year B of the Lectionary most of the Gospel readings are drawn from Mark. Of the dozen or so commentaries on Mark against which I regularly checked my own work I have found that by Morna Hooker (A. & C. Black, London, 1991: ISBN: 0-7136-3284-4) the most consistently helpful and illuminating. For readers who want to explore the Marcan readings in much greater depth than is possible within these pages it would seem to be an essential purchase.

I have deliberately tried to write the comments in a variety of styles. Some of them make brief but direct suggestions on how a sermon might be preached from a lection. Others begin from contemporary life and, as it were, move into the lectionary reading. Yet others, perhaps most, offer a kind of 'running exposition' of the main thrust of the reading, leaving it to the reader to pick up ideas and engage in his or her own reflection on how to use the material in preaching. What I hope all of them do is to take the biblical text seriously, but the reader must be the best judge of whether or not that is the case.

Most sets of comments include a number of cross-references, both to other parts of the book from which the lection is taken, and to other biblical writings. Insufficient space prevented printing these passages in full, but I strongly urge readers to look these references up; they are an important part of the commentary. This also encourages what is, in my judgment, a very sound exegetical principle; that where possible, scripture should be interpreted by scripture. Also for reasons of space, where lections occur a second time I have (with only very few exceptions) referred the reader to the previous occurrence rather than writing a fresh set of comments.

The authorship of some writings is a matter of scholarly dispute. However, it would waste precious space to refer to this on every occasion. I have therefore simply used whatever term expresses what I personally judge to be the case. So, for example, comments on passages from the Letter to the Ephesians refer to Paul as the author since (unfashionably) I judge Ephesians to be Pauline. But comments on the Pastoral Epistles refer to 'the writer' since (rather more fashionably) I do not think Paul wrote them. Readers whose views differ from mine on such disputed matters will doubtless make appropriate adjustments.

The *Revised Common Lectionary* (RCL) is a very serviceable piece of work, but it is not perfect, nor is it sacrosanct. From time to time I have found it necessary to criticize where particular lections begin or end, even to suggest different starting or finishing places. I always give my reasons for this and, if the reader finds them persuasive, there is no reason why the reading should not be adjusted accordingly. If the lessons are to be read by someone other than the preacher, some appropriate liaison will be required.

Readers who use the Church of England's Principal Service Lectionary for Sundays (*Common Worship*, Church House Publishing, London, 2000, pp. 542–578) will be aware that there are a number of 'Church of England variants'. To be precise: in Year B there are five Sundays on which the Gospel is different, five Sundays on which the Epistle is different, five Sundays on which a different Old Testament lection is specified, and four Sundays on which the Continuous Old Testament reading is omitted. It has not been possible to take account of these variants in the present book. A number of Sundays have slightly different titles. More significantly, this version of the Lectionary uses 'Ordinary Time' only as a general designation, individual Sundays within it being referred to as 'Propers'. It also recognizes four Sundays of an Epiphany Season and four Sundays before Advent. For the convenience of those who use the Church of England version, where there are significant differences the titles used in that version are printed in brackets immediately after the title used in this book.

For many years most of the major Protestant denominations in these islands used lectionaries derived from those produced by the Joint Liturgical Group. During that period we became accustomed to having a 'theme' for each Sunday. Looking for the links between the readings (even if they did not always seem immediately obvious) was a fruitful way to prepare a sermon. It is quite crucial to realize that the *Revised Common Lectionary* does not use that principle. Preachers can sometimes be heard to grumble that they cannot find any obvious links between the Lectionary readings. The answer will often be: 'That is because there aren't any'! However, sometimes there are. Broadly speaking, we should look for links between all the readings when we are in a *season* (Advent, Christmas and Epiphany, Lent and Passiontide, Easter), and on specific *days* (Pentecost, All Saints etc.). Sometimes these links will be fairly direct, at other times they will be more in terms of mood or 'feel'. Those Sundays which are outside a season are called 'Ordinary Time'. There is always an intended link between an Old Testament reading and the Gospel on Sundays in Ordinary Time. Since only one Old Testament reading is normally provided for the first eight Sundays in Ordinary Time this is straightforward. However, from the Ninth Sunday in Ordinary Time (Proper 4), two Old Testament readings are offered. One is designated *Related*, which means that it is related to the Gospel for the day. The other is designated *Continuous*, which means that it is unrelated to any of the other readings for that day, but it is related to the *Continuous* Old Testament reading for the previous Sunday, or the following Sunday, or both, because it is taken from the same book of the Bible. Strictly speaking, RCL follows a *semi-continuous* pattern, since it omits some portions of all books, but that is a technical matter. The Gospel in Year B is usually from Mark, supplemented by John, which appears in all three years of the Lectionary. In Ordinary Time the Epistles are read *continuously*. Set down like this it seems extremely confusing, but in practice it is not so. Most of the time preachers can get by on two simple rules: (1) in *seasons* look for links between all the readings; (2) in *Ordinary Time* look for links only between the Old Testament reading – the *related* one if there are two – and the Gospel.

We may very well take the view that the whole of the canon of scripture is important. But that does not mean that all of it is equally important to Christians in all times and in all places. Any lectionary is selective, but even so it may not be obvious that every passage the lectionary offers is immediately relevant to Christian congregations in Britain in the twenty-first century. So for example, passages about how Christians cope with persecution and martyrdom do not speak directly to our condition. They have certainly spoken to Christians of previous generations. Sadly, they may still speak directly to Christians who are our contemporaries in other parts of the world. Conceivably, they may speak to Christians in Britain in future generations, but the fact remains that they do not do so in the present moment. They need to be read, because they are part of the universal Church's understanding of discipleship, in which we share. It is less obvious that they should be preached on. When the lectionary offers us readings which fall into this category I have tried to expound and explain them, but I have not tried to find a 'relevance' which does not exist.

Those who devise lectionaries are conscious that they are part of a great tradition. That tradition, like liturgical work in general, is usually (and in my opinion rightly) conservative. In some cases lectionary passages have been associated with each other for many years, even centuries. But the reasons why they were originally brought together may reflect an understanding of how to use the Bible which we do not hold today, and perhaps have not held since the rise of modern biblical scholarship. In such instances it has seemed right not to force the interpretation of one passage to fit another, but rather to outline as best I can what we may reasonably understand the passage to mean. There are occasions when this rather undermines some of the links the compilers of the lectionary had in mind: a good example is the relationship between the Old Testament and the Epistle on the First Sunday in Lent.

This is the second of three projected volumes under the title *Mining the Meaning*. Generally speaking it follows the pattern set by Henry McKeating's first volume, for Year A of the Lectionary. However, there is one significant difference. The version of the Lectionary printed in *The Methodist Worship Book* includes additional readings for six special occasions (p. 600). These lections are common to all three years. Comments on them are included here, though they were not in the volume for Year A. There is a simple explanation: Dr McKeating wrote to a strict publishing deadline which did not allow him to tackle the additional readings. This volume was written well in advance of the publishing deadline and so I was able to include them.

For many years I have been totally committed to the use of 'inclusive language'. I find it frankly astonishing that at this date there are still some people who can assert that words such as 'man' and 'mankind' do not necessarily exclude women. However, a problem of a different order and magnitude arises when we come to language which refers directly to God. It is unarguably the case that God is neither male nor female, but beyond gender. We are then faced with the difficulty that the biblical writers invariably refer to God as 'he', not because they actually thought that God is male as opposed to female, but because they desired above all else to stress that God is *personal*. In the context of their various cultures they conceived of the masculine as 'the norm'. We, I hope, do not, though we can understand why they expressed things in that way. However, it remains essential that we too think of God as personal, otherwise much of the Christian gospel becomes incomprehensible. So how do we express this in English which (unlike some other languages), only has the personal pronouns 'she' and 'he'? I experimented with writing 'God' every time a personal pronoun hove into view and the result was frankly unreadable. I tried writing 'he' and 'she' alternately when referring to God, but found the effect very self-conscious, though I recognize that others might not do so. Using 'Godself' in place of 'himself' appears to depersonalize God. I have therefore avoided personal pronouns for God as much as possible, but where one seemed unavoidable I have, with some reluctance, used the masculine. If any readers are offended by this I apologize. Future years may bring us better solutions!

The comments in this book are based on the New Revised Standard Version (Anglicized Edition) of the Bible. Other translations are referred to by the following abbreviations: AV = Authorized Version; GNB = Good News Bible; JB = Jerusalem Bible; NEB = New English Bible; NIV = New International Version; NJB = New Jerusalem Bible; REB = Revised English Bible; RSV = Revised Standard Version.

YEAR B

FIRST SUNDAY OF ADVENT

Isaiah 64.1–9

The prophet has been recalling the story of God's dealings with Israel, a story of gracious deeds and mercy in the face of rebellion and disobedience (63.7–14). This forms a striking contrast with how things are now. The nation has behaved as though it is no longer God's people. They are punished by the triumph of their enemies, and even more seriously, by the absence of God (63.19). The possibility that life might continue like this is almost unbearable and so the prophet calls on God to return in a theophany (vv. 1–4), reminiscent of the time he descended on Mt Sinai (Exodus 19.18ff). Yet even as this plea is made, the prophet hardly dares hope that it might be answered. How can sinful and unclean people meet with a holy God (vv. 5–7)? Only by recognizing what God requires, remembering God and doing right (v. 5), and by throwing themselves on the mercy of God who, though he cannot be presumed upon, is nevertheless their Father (v. 8 – see 63.16). It is part of our Christian experience that we both desire the presence of God and fear it at the same time. The coming of a holy God into our lives shows up our shabbiness. We may want to do what is right but also fear the necessary transformation. And if our assurance is that God is our Father, we cannot rush too quickly to that claim or presume upon that relationship. Advent is a time of self-examination which searches out whether we really mean what we say when we call upon God to be 'God with us'.

1 Corinthians 1.3–9

In accordance with the letter-writing customs of the time, Paul's letters usually begin with thanksgiving concerning the recipients. However, it is surprising to find it here, because Paul will go on to say many very hard things to the Corinthian Christians about their character and behaviour and about their misuse of their spiritual gifts. We learn from Paul's letters to them that 'speech' and 'knowledge' were among the gifts they most prized, so Paul picks out those things for thanksgiving, not doubting their reality even if he will later question the way they are exercised (v. 5). Yet at the same time as he affirms the reality and value of their faith (vv. 4–7a), he also tells them that they have not yet fully arrived, they must 'wait for the revealing of our Lord Jesus Christ' (v. 7b). He reminds them too, that if they are to be saved on the last day it is not because they are clever but because God is faithful (v. 9). No doubt this passage is included in today's readings to remind us that we too must 'wait' and not think we have fully arrived. It also offers us an oblique but necessary reassurance. When we are tempted to dismiss the Church because of its failure, weakness or petty-mindedness, it is important to remember that it is the faithfulness of God, not the perfection of our fellow believers, which ultimately matters.

Mark 13.24–37

Perhaps the real problem with this passage for most of us is not so much that it offers a happy hunting ground for religious cranks (though it does), but that in relatively stable Western societies we have little recent personal experience of living through cataclysmic events. Even increased floods due to global warming hardly count as that. Those who live in long-standing war zones, or under religious or political persecution, find Mark's language resonates with their experience. In fact v. 24 marks a decisive time shift in Mark's 'Little Apocalypse', moving from persecution, destruction and flight to what will come 'after that suffering'. Morna Hooker rightly notes that 'commonsense questions about what will actually happen are out of place, for the language is the language of myth.' We are looking forward here to the time unknown (v. 32) when the Son of Man will return to gather his 'elect' (vv. 26–27). However we choose to interpret this, it is part of Mark's good news, intended to sustain persecuted believers. The parable of the man who goes on a journey (vv. 34–36) draws the appropriate lesson: we are to be vigilant. In Lamar Williamson Jr's words this is 'especially pertinent for those who have forgotten to expect anything at all'.

SECOND SUNDAY OF ADVENT

Isaiah 40.1–11

To those who have been exiled in Babylon the unknown prophet brings a message of joy and hope. Human beings are inconstant (vv. 6–7) but God is faithful. The time of punishment is past (v. 2), that which was thought impossible, a new Exodus, is about to happen. What counts most is that the covenant relationship still endures; sinful people are still 'my' people, says God, and those who know they have no claim on God will hear him described as 'your' God (v. 1). The prophet depicts this faithful God travelling back from exile with his people (v. 10), which C. R. North contrasts with the picture in Ezekiel 11.22–25 of God's earlier solitary departure from doomed Jerusalem. This return cannot be concealed; rather, all are invited to 'see' God who, of course, cannot be seen (v. 10). But the invisible God can be seen in effects on human lives, in this instance as people experience the combined gentleness and strength displayed in the picture of the shepherd at lambing time (v. 11). Those who have experienced this good news must share it loudly and confidently so that others whose lives are dominated by fear and despair may hear it too (v. 9). Sharing what God has done for us is a key element in Christian mission and it is something we can all do.

2 Peter 3.8–15a

The writer is responding to 'scoffers' who call Christ's return in question by saying that 'everything goes on exactly as it always has done since the world began' (2 Peter 3.4, REB). However, that is also our experience. The saviour of the world came among us over two thousand years ago and although the first Christians were much exercised about when and how he would return, the Church as a whole no longer finds it helpful to think like that. Our response to the writer's argument that God's sense of time is different from ours (vv. 8–9) might well be: 'Fine, but we still experience things going on as they always have done!' This does not make us cynical scoffers. We are called to vigilance by the imagery of the unexpected thief (v. 10), here as elsewhere (Matthew 24.43–44; Luke 12.39–40; 1 Thessalonians 5.4). Each generation of Christians is called to live 'as if' Christ will return unexpectedly. Speculating about the manner and time of that is simply a distraction. But our writer does point to a basic aspiration of the human heart, the desire for somewhere where 'righteousness is at home' (v. 13). Many people, including those who would not think of themselves as religious, share that longing. The writer of 2 Peter suggests that the character and conduct of ordinary people such as ourselves has a part to play in helping to bring it to fruition (vv. 11b–12a, 14). This gives purpose and direction to our daily living.

Mark 1.1–8

In 1.1 Mark makes plain that this is the beginning of a new creation story no less momentous than the first. Yet it is also continuous with God's activity in the nation's past. What is to take place is 'as it is written' (v. 2). And although the centre of this story is Jesus, we first meet John, who prepares the way for him by appearing in the wilderness and preaching a unique baptism of repentance. He says two things about the one whose way he prepares: he is greater than John himself (v. 7) and he will baptize people with the Holy Spirit (v. 8). It is sometimes questioned whether John could have talked about baptizing with the Holy Spirit, but Donald English's suggestion, that a prophet who had meditated on Ezekiel 36.25–28 could well have done so, repays reflection. The phrase is not a reference to a specific action that Jesus will perform, but to the way in which his life and work will bring people into a new relationship with God. When the first Christian Pentecost comes (Acts 2) it will only be possible because the ministry of Jesus has been brought to fulfilment. After this proclamation Mark views John's work as accomplished. His task is not to draw attention to himself, but to point to Christ. This is how it should be for all who are heralds of Christ – not just those with formal preaching responsibilities, but all who bear his name.

THIRD SUNDAY OF ADVENT

Isaiah 61.1–4, 8–11

The opening of this passage resonates in our minds as the words on which Jesus preached his sermon (his 'manifesto' as some have called it) in the synagogue at Nazareth (Luke 4.16ff). Here the prophet reveals that it is the manifesto of a God who is always concerned with justice, freedom and right dealing. Some of those to whom the good news will come are experiencing physical distress: they are the oppressed and the captives. Others are experiencing spiritual distress: they are the broken-hearted and the mourners (John Sawyer points out that the Hebrew original of what NRSV translates as 'release to the prisoners' in v. 1, really means 'opening of the eyes', as in the NIV footnote, so a release from spiritual bondage is there in view). God is concerned with all kinds of distress, not just those we call spiritual. God loves justice and hates wrongdoing (v. 8) and so will act to put things right. And when God has acted, the righteousness and praise which the final hymn of thanksgiving sets out will be a demonstration to the whole world of how things should really be (v. 11b). The prophet thus reminds us that all kinds of oppression, cruelty and evil are equally intolerable to God and when we do something towards ridding the world of any of them we do God's work.

1 Thessalonians 5.16–24

It would be better to choose v. 12 as the starting point for this lection. Verses 12–15 do not appear elsewhere in RCL, and the whole passage is about mutual relationships in the church, including the congregation's relationship to its leaders (vv. 12–13) and the leader's care for the congregation, especially those who struggle (v. 14). Many of these exhortations are familiar to us from elsewhere in Paul's letters, but this particular collection is offered against the hope of the coming of Christ (v. 23). We may note that rejoicing, giving thanks and praying, are grouped together as commendable in all times and circumstances because they are the will of God (vv. 16–18). Paul does not mean that we should always be on our knees or perpetually have a smile on our faces. Rather, Christian life is to be lived in an attitude of prayer, thanksgiving and joy (the last of which is different from mere happiness), because it is rooted in gratitude for

what Christ has done for us and comes from the Spirit who is given to us. It would be easy to pass over v. 19, and the two subsequent verses, which qualify it. In some churches (Corinth in particular), Paul had more than his share of trouble with those whose joy in the Holy Spirit led them into excess. But sometimes the institutional church has been guilty of allowing no room for the Spirit and playing it safe. While paying attention to the caution to 'test everything', we need also to allow the Spirit to move and change us through those to whom this gift is given.

John 1.6–8, 19–28

One consequence of having four Gospels and a three-year Lectionary is that the Johannine material has to be inserted at appropriate points, resulting in Gospel readings on John the Baptist on two successive Sundays in Advent. However, John's material is significantly different from Mark's. Most importantly, there is the Baptist's own repeated emphasis that he is not the light of the world/Messiah/Elijah etc. (vv. 8, 20–21), though the denial that he is Elijah needs reading alongside Mark 9.13. His repeated insistence that he is not the light, and the evangelist's avowal of the same thing (*a* light but not *the* light, as it were) in vv. 7–8, have led to speculation that there was a group which looked to John the Baptist, rather than Jesus, for its origins and inspiration. However that may be, the Johannine record (in the verses excluded from today's reading) is emphatic that the true light of the world lay elsewhere. Significantly, the persistent questioning of the Baptist by the religious authorities (vv. 19–25) indicates that what is taking place in the Christ event will not be universally understood or welcomed. One of the many lessons which can be drawn from this is the endemic resistance of religious institutions to new things which God may be doing, and what this might say to the traditional churches today.

FOURTH SUNDAY OF ADVENT

2 Samuel 7.1–11, 16

Once David had been anointed as king of all Israel, had defeated the Philistines and brought the ark of the covenant to his new capital Jerusalem, his mind turned to the possibility of building a 'house' (temple) for God. But God told the prophet Nathan that it would be, in one sense, the other way round: God would build a 'house' (dynasty) for David. The promise in v. 16, known as the Davidic covenant, came to assume great importance for Israel. The dynasty lasted physically for four hundred years. After it ended, the hope of its restoration through a Messiah figure offered hope in times of difficulty (e.g. Isaiah 11.1–5, 10; Jeremiah 23.5–7). That Jesus was – through Joseph – of the house of David, was of great importance to the first Christians. It shapes the purpose of Matthew's genealogy (Matthew 1.1) and Luke's infancy narrative has four references to it, including two in today's Gospel reading. The title 'Son of David' is used for Jesus throughout the Gospels; even a roadside beggar knows this much about him (Mark 10.47). It might at first seem that for Gentile Christian communities in the Western world this has little immediate relevance, but both the Epistle and Gospel for today suggest otherwise.

Romans 16.25–27

If this doxology is not by Paul it is by someone who understood his thought. The 'my gospel' of v. 25 refers to the good news of salvation in Christ which Paul sets out so thoroughly in this letter. This was a 'secret' in the sense that God did not reveal it until the right time, but now it is no secret at all. Indeed God now commands that it be offered to everyone in order to bring them to faith (v. 26). There are no apocalyptic images here, but because glory is to be given to God through Jesus Christ 'for ever' (v. 27) there is a clear looking forward to the consummation of human history when, as Paul says elsewhere, all should acknowledge the Lordship of Christ (Philippians 2.11). What began with God's promise to an Israelite king ends with God bringing to completion what has been promised.

Luke 1.26–38

There are many possible themes in today's Gospel reading. But given the other Lectionary passages for the day, the best choice is the fulfilment of God's promise in the Davidic covenant. Luke states this by tracing Joseph's descent from David (v. 27), as he will do again later in the Gospel (3.23–31). Even more significantly, it forms an important strand in Gabriel's announcement to Mary (vv. 32–33). Yet we must face the fact that it sounds very odd to us (which may be why we often ignore it). The idea that Jesus will 'reign over the house of Jacob for ever' seems more like the mistaken ideas about his messiahship held by some of his contemporaries than it does of the sort of kingship Christians think of in connection with Jesus. So how do we work with this? Some help may be found, perhaps unexpectedly, in Luke's account of Paul's sermon in the synagogue in Antioch (Acts 13.16–41), which repays careful reading. The sermon involves a telling of 'salvation history' in which the Davidic covenant and its continuation in Jesus play an important part (Acts 13.22–23). But it goes on to major on the resurrection and to contrast David and Jesus (Acts 13.32–37). It is because Jesus is now the risen Lord that his reign, seen as a bestowal of forgiveness and new life, knows no end (Acts 13.38–39). Whatever is sometimes said about the authenticity of the sermons in Acts, this fits perfectly with what Paul elsewhere says about Jesus being Son of David 'according to the flesh', but declared Son of God because of the resurrection (Romans 1.3–4). We may ask what immediate relevance all this has for us, but perhaps immediacy is not the point. Advent is a time for looking beyond the immediate to the sweep of God's action in human history. That story is not finished yet and we, like Mary, have a part to play in it. If, as may be the case, today is the day for the nativity play (or even the carol service!) some less demanding theme may have to be chosen, which would be a pity.

CHRISTMAS DAY: SET I

Isaiah 9.2–7

This passage, possibly originally an independent poem, was probably written for the accession or coronation of an Israelite king, probably Hezekiah. It was not, of course, originally intended as a prophecy about Jesus, but that need not worry us unduly. The plain fact is that as Christians have read the text it has seemed obvious that the prophecy was fulfilled well beyond the original writer's expectation. In turn, centuries of reading the text in this way have contributed to the rich meaning that it now has. The poem is in three stanzas. Verses 2–3 express a transformation of the nation's fortunes, a joy that comes suddenly and unexpectedly and could only have come from God. Verses 4–5 indicate that the reason for this is the overthrow of an unendurable oppression, a miracle as great as when 300 men under Gideon routed a vast Midianite army (Judges 7). Verses 6–7 express the qualities the nation hope for from their new ruler. 'Wonderful Counsellor' points to one whose wisdom is something to marvel at. 'Mighty God' is a translation of the Hebrew rather heavily influenced by its Christian interpretation; 'God-like hero' would be better. 'Everlasting Father' points to one whose care for his people is unfailing. 'Prince of Peace' simply speaks for itself. Most importantly, the one with these qualities has been 'born for us' and 'given to us' (v. 6). Salvation is always the gift of God, something we could never have done for ourselves, as the incarnation supremely demonstrates.

Titus 2.11–14

This short passage is packed with theology. It begins by insisting that the grace of God has become manifest in human history, a clear reference to the birth of Jesus. The purpose of its appearing is to bring salvation for the whole world. For those who are saved by God's grace there are then consequences which go rather beyond going to church once a year to sing carols. Negatively, God's grace itself trains us to 'renounce' things contrary to God's will (v. 12a). Positively, because we are living in the 'present age' our lives should be marked by those things which are pleasing to God. The reason for this emerges in v. 13b, which says that we are waiting for the glory 'of our great God and Saviour, Jesus Christ'. Commentators are

fairly evenly divided as to whether this, or the NRSV footnote translation, 'of the great God and our Saviour' is correct. Even if divinity
is not here directly attributed to Jesus, it is still a very remarkable
statement that what Jesus did for us through his earthly ministry
(described in v. 14) is indeed the work of God. These, as other
passages in the Pastoral letters, 'encourage people who have been
saved by God through Christ Jesus to pursue an active life of justice,
mercy and love', as Margaret Davies puts it.

Luke 2.1–14 (15–20)

There is little new to be said about this passage, but Christmas Day is
not the time for novelty. Our task is to make a familiar story live in
contemporary Christian experience. The difficulties involved in
Luke's historical information are well known, but need not bother us.
We may, however, note the contrast drawn between the wider world
in which this story takes place, with its mention of the emperor, the
governor and officialdom, and the particulars of the story which
involve an ordinary couple, humble circumstances and yet humbler
shepherds. The wider world does not know – yet – what has
happened to it. Keith Nickle has helpfully drawn attention to the
significance of the manger. In v. 7 it is merely the receptacle for the
infant Jesus. But in v. 12 it is a part of the angelic announcement
to the shepherds, something of special significance. Then it is
mentioned again in v. 16, when it need not have been. Does Luke
intend us to remember Isaiah 1.3, where the animals know their
master's crib but the people do not know, or understand? It is an
attractive suggestion, which points to the way in which now the
Messiah has come, people are invited to come to the manger and
know the character of their God. What do we see in the Bethlehem
manger? A child at the centre of an attractive if slightly sentimental
scene, or the God who has come to be like us in order that we might
become like him?

CHRISTMAS DAY: SET II

Isaiah 62.6–12

Other than for its general air of rejoicing it is not obvious why this passage has been chosen for Christmas Day in preference to say, Micah 5.2–4. It is one of the oracles addressed to the desolate city of Jerusalem (Zion) during the hard years of the people's exile in Babylon. In it, God promises to restore and establish the city and make it renowned throughout the earth. A distinctive, though not unique, feature is the solemn promise that when this is done it will be for ever (v. 8). A link with the incarnation might perhaps be made from v. 12, since those who respond to what God has done through the birth of Christ will indeed be those whom the Lord has redeemed and who are called to be, in Christ, a holy people (1 Peter 2.9).

Titus 3.4–7

The 'but' with which v. 4 begins is a direct contrast with what has come immediately before, and if that is not being read it would be better to begin, 'When the goodness . . .' This is a reference to the incarnation through which, the writer says, God saved us. We should certainly note the two phrases 'God our Saviour' (v. 4) and 'Jesus Christ our Saviour' (v. 6). They do not intend a distinction between God and Jesus, but v. 6 is clear that the Spirit has been given to us by God, through Jesus. It would be anachronistic to draw conclusions about trinitarian theology, still less the *filioque* clause in the Nicene Creed. The point is that 'Jesuology', rather too prevalent in churches in Britain today, can be dangerous. The salvation which Christians experience comes from God. Jesus matters, if we may so express it, because he is the revelation of who God is and what God is like: God is incarnate in him. The Jesus of the Fourth Gospel frequently makes this point using varied imagery (e.g. John 3.10; 5.19; 6.46–47; 7.16 etc.). Christmas is a good time to reflect on this. The centre of the story is not so much the child in himself, as what God is doing in and through him. And that, this reading tells us, is nothing less than the water/washing of rebirth (which may be a reference to baptism), renewal through the Holy Spirit, justification in God's sight and, finally, the offer of eternal life. It seems a pity not to read v. 8a, with its proper insistence that this teaching is very important.

Luke 2.(1–7) 8–20

As far as v. 8 the story is told with great economy and simplicity. Anybody who had never heard about the events narrated in Luke ch. 1, would find this a straightforward enough story with nothing very remarkable about it. Over the generations, the Christian imagination has elaborated it and the elaborations appear in most nativity plays (and George Mackay Brown's wonderful poem 'The Lodging'). There is much that is right about that, but a congregation might be helped to stand back from the nativity play approach and sense the simplicity and ordinariness. This is by way of contrast with what happens next. From v. 8 there are moving responses to amazing events. The first response is that of the shepherds to the unexpected appearance of first one, and then a multitude, of angels. They are terrified, just as Zechariah (Luke 1.12) and Mary (Luke 1.29–30) were. When the frankly supernatural bursts in on daily experience fear is an appropriate reaction. But once they have been given the message that this is about 'good news of great joy for all the people' (the 'all' is important; this is not just for the elite of the land), their response is quite different. They believe what they have been told and therefore want to see for themselves – without delay (vv. 15–16). When they have seen, they cannot keep it to themselves but must tell others (v. 17), and those who are then told have yet another response – 'amazement', which implies acceptance (v. 18). The final response is from Mary, who treasures what has happened, reflects upon it and makes it an inward experience of growth and development. Here we have a range of possible responses to the incarnation: delighted belief in it, the sharing of its message, the dwelling on its meaning and significance. All are appropriate responses for Christian worshippers today.

CHRISTMAS DAY: SET III

Isaiah 52.7–10

John Sawyer suggests that this hymn is reminiscent of the enthrone-
ment Psalms (e.g. Psalms 93, 95–99) celebrating God's victory over
the powers of chaos. It certainly captures the imagination. We
can picture the messengers running across the mountains to the city
with their good news that liberation is near. Concentrating on the
messengers, however, rather misses the point. Rejoicing is appropriate because God has (a) comforted his people and (b) redeemed
the holy city (v. 9). The consequence is that this salvation will be seen
throughout the world (v. 10). It is sometimes asked whether it is not
insensitive for Christians to rejoice in a world so full of pain and
misery, oppression and injustice. Indeed, is it possible for us to
rejoice fully until such things are finally vanquished? As a South
American Christian once posed the question: how can we share the
bread of the Eucharist (thanksgiving) until all have bread to share?
That is a proper question; each of us must find our own answer. Part
of our thinking might be that any genuine response to the redemption
God offers through the incarnation will commit us to the struggle for
justice throughout the world.

Hebrews 1.1–4 (5–12)

The Letter to the Hebrews is a difficult document for a contemporary
Gentile Christian to understand. The longer version of today's reading (which ought really to finish at v. 13) involves an extended comparison between Jesus the Son of God and the angels, the latter being
more of a reality for the first readers of the letter than for most of us
today. If it is used and is to be preached on, then the central point the
writer makes is that Jesus is not only more than just another human
being, he is more than just another angel. He is therefore the supreme
source of help in spiritual matters. One way into this seemingly
intractable material is to think of some of the ways in which people in
our society today do turn to secondary sources of help (e.g. astrology,
the occult and wicca). However, vv. 1–4 may suffice – they are
astonishing enough! They acknowledge that God's revelation of himself has been known before Christ (v. 1) but claim that what God
has done through Jesus is qualitatively different (v. 2). He is the
'reflection of God's glory' (v. 3) which means, in F. F. Bruce's

words: 'Just as the radiance of the sun reaches this earth, so in Christ the glorious light of God shines into the hearts of men and women.' Christ is also 'the exact imprint of God's very being' (v. 3); imprint, as in the way the image on the coin corresponds to the die. Is there a higher Christology in the New Testament than this? Our congregations might be invited to consider not so much 'and is it true?' (to use a phrase from John Betjeman's Christmas poem) as, 'if it is true, what then?'

John 1.1–14

What can possibly be said of this reading which has not already been said a thousand times? Two things must suffice here. First, John's presentation points up strongly the claim in v. 9 that Jesus is 'the true light'. We must ask what the phrase, 'which enlightens everyone' actually means. After all, it does not say, 'which has the potential to enlighten everyone'. The second-century apologist Justin Martyr argued that whenever people in any age have apprehended truth, only Christ can have been its source, even though they did not (indeed could not) know it. If he was right, this has significant implications for our attitude to other world faiths. And yet, almost immediately, we have the statement that when the Word came into the world, 'the world did not know him.' We cannot avoid wrestling with this in a multi-faith world as we celebrate the incarnation. Second, the climactic verse is 14, and the word 'flesh' cannot be overemphasized. Too many contemporary Christians think of Jesus as if he were God wandering around Palestine in a kind of 'spiritual' body. Or as one young preacher was reported as saying: 'Jesus was God, therefore he could do anything.' Too many contemporaries who would not claim to be Christians think of Jesus as just a great religious teacher. John allows us neither option, but makes us wrestle with what it means for God to take flesh.

FIRST SUNDAY OF CHRISTMAS

Isaiah 61.10–62.3

The passage begins by repeating two verses from the Old Testament reading for Advent 3, and then, with ch. 62, moves into a new oracle of salvation for Zion. However, the original oracle appears to run as far as v. 5. The total effect of the reading is to emphasize that God's salvation brings observable results and responses. One response is that those who have experienced it are filled with a deep joy (61.10). Another is that God's righteousness will grow naturally, like plants from seeds (61.11). Indeed, what God will bring is far more than mere restoration of their previous fortunes. They will have a new name, given by God and everyone will know of it (62.2). All these ideas are applicable in a general way to those celebrating the incarnation. It is worth pausing on 62.1, where the prophet is so moved by the nation's plight that he can no longer hold back his good news. There are examples of this sort of involvement elsewhere in scripture (a lovely one occurs in Zechariah 8.21, where either the prophet, or perhaps a scribe copying the text, is so moved by its vision of peace and prosperity that he adds a note about his own intention to participate). We might ask ourselves whether we are so moved by (a) the state of the world in which we live and (b) the story of God's salvation which we celebrate at Christmas, that we are spurred into sharing our good news.

Galatians 4.4–7

This short reading spells out what we might describe as the consequences of Christmas. Paul makes it clear that the incarnation was no accident. It was part of God's plan, as 'the fullness of time' (v. 4) indicates. Jesus was 'born of a woman', a phrase which affirms his full humanity, neither supporting nor denying Virgin Birth. He was also 'born under the law', which also affirms that he experienced human life in its particularity. Then Paul gives two reasons why the incarnation took place. The first is that so that those who were 'under the law' (which, strictly speaking refers only to Jews) might be saved; the second that 'we' (now including Gentiles) might be adopted as God's children (v. 5). The rest of the passage spells out some of what it means to be children of God. The Holy Spirit (not distinguished here from the Spirit of the Son), enables us to call God by the intimate name which Jesus used (see Mark 14.36), which Aramaic word did indeed pass into the language of Christian prayer (Romans 8.15). We are therefore not slaves, we are children of God. The consequences of Christmas are huge, not least in an age when people search endlessly for a sense of identity and belonging.

Luke 2.22–40

In this reading there is material to feed many sermons. Though Luke does not explicitly state it, vv. 22–23 are about the circumcision of Jesus, giving a link with Galatians 4.4 from today's Epistle. Luke concentrates on his naming, forming a link with the Annunciation at 1.31. Jesus is indeed going to be a saviour, and the two stories which follow explore some of the implications of that. Simeon belongs to those who are waiting for the Messiah (v. 26) and we may assume the same of Anna. In the Nunc Dimittis (vv. 29–32) Simeon is supernaturally enabled to know that this child fulfils all his hopes and he can die happy. Here, at the centre of the Jewish religion, Jesus is proclaimed as the saviour for Gentiles too. Although the early church struggled with this, Luke wants us to understand that God always intended it. In Acts he will tell the story of how the church worked it out in practice. Anna is a respected figure of deep piety. She too supernaturally and immediately discerns who Jesus is (v. 38). Yet this passage brings the first hint that the Messiah's mission will run into difficulties, that there will be division because of him (vv. 34–35). Luke writes with just as much hindsight as we find in John 1.11, but wants us to understand that opposition to Jesus from within his own people does not invalidate his messiahship. A sermon could be preached exploring how v. 35b would change and deepen what is described at 2.19. Faith is not just about pondering beautiful and amazing things. It can bring pain.

SECOND SUNDAY OF CHRISTMAS

Jeremiah 31.7–14

This passage comes from what is sometimes known as 'The Book of Consolations'. It is probably from more than one author and, though short, falls into two distinct parts. The first, vv. 7–9, is a song of joy because God's people, scattered to the ends of the earth after their crushing defeat by the Babylonians, are to be brought back to the promised land (v. 8a). A journey even greater than their delivery from captivity in Egypt centuries before is here in mind. Unlike the privations and difficulties of that journey, when they wandered in the wilderness for forty years, frequently disobedient to God's command, this journey will be smooth and straight (v. 9b). Professor Robert Davidson has drawn attention to the contrast between the attitudes the people displayed before they went into exile (see Amos 6.1–7), with those they will display on their return. True, they have the title 'chief of the nations' (v. 7), but this is only because God will make them so. They will come back as a 'great company' including those in great need (v. 8b). More, they will return with weeping and with supplications (v. 9a, where 'supplications' is better than NRSV's 'consolations'). They have learned their lesson. The second part is vv. 10–14. The parallels with Deutero-Isaiah are strong (compare v. 10a with Isaiah 41.1; 49.1, and v. 10b with Isaiah 40.11). So too, is the use of the words 'ransom' and 'redeem' in v. 11. Although both these words originated in ordinary life, concerning property or family obligations, they came to be used of what God did in the Exodus (Exodus 6.6; Deuteronomy 9.26) and thus, as Professor Davidson so splendidly puts it, became launched on 'a great theological future'. Although Christians usually associate ransom and redemption primarily with the cross of Christ, reading this passage in the Christmas season reminds us that the cross was not an isolated event, but the culmination of the whole ministry of Jesus and thus of the whole plan of God which began with (or if John's Gospel is right, even before) the incarnation.

Sirach/Ecclesiasticus 24.1–12

'Sirach' is a short version of a fuller title, 'The Wisdom of Ben Sira'. The book is also known in older English translations as 'Ecclesiasticus'. It was written by a pious scribe about 180 years before the birth of Christ. It is accepted as part of canonical scripture by some churches, but not by others. 'The Lord by wisdom founded the earth' (Proverbs 3.19) depicts Wisdom as having a personality of her own or, as we would say, personifies her (see Proverbs 1.20–33; 8.1–9.6). Sirach borrows that idea (and quite a few actual phrases) from Proverbs. This reading is part of a longer poem titled 'Praise of Wisdom'. Although in ordinary speech to say that someone 'sings her own praises' is to cast a slur on that person's character, such a judgment is not intended in v. 1. Wisdom is able to sing her own praises, indeed to do so in the heavenly court (v. 2), precisely because her direct origin is from God (v. 3) and her words are therefore true. Nevertheless, she remains a created being, subject to God's commands (v. 8), though one who is said to have 'held sway' over the sea, the land and every people and nation (v. 6). She is depicted as searching for a resting place, in response to which God told her to 'pitch her tent' with his own people (vv. 7–8). The remaining verses describe how in doing so she has become established and flourished. In some Jewish thought Wisdom is identified with the Law of Moses, and there is an old Jewish tradition that originally the Law was offered to every nation, but only Israel chose to take it. More significantly, we note that in John 1.14, the Greek phrase which NRSV translates 'lived among us' could be literally translated, 'pitched his tent among us'.

Ephesians 1.3–14

To announce a sermon on 'our need for a doxological faith' might be unwise, but this passage positively invites some such approach. Paul here sets out virtually the entire pattern of salvation, but in the form of a prayer of thanksgiving. The six sentences of the NRSV translation have a solemn liturgical quality, capturing the tone of the single sentence of the Greek. 'Blessed be the God . . .' is a liturgical formula familiar to us from the Old Testament, developed in synagogue worship and taken over in Christian tradition. It presents Christian doctrine not as abstract theological speculation, but as the lived experience of Christian believers, prayed through in tones of gratitude. God is to be blessed because he is defined as the 'Father of our Lord Jesus Christ', who, in turn, has blessed us with every blessing 'in the heavenly places'. This is not about remoteness or distance; it is about the way in which Christ has attained supremacy over the forces of evil. As a result, we are blessed in our daily living. This passage is not easy to divide up, but following the initial ascription of praise to God there are, broadly speaking, three sections. In vv. 4–6 there is thanksgiving for what God has done for us in choosing us for adoption as his children through Christ. In vv. 7–12 there is thanksgiving for some of the benefits we have received through this, and three are singled out. First, redemption/forgiveness through the blood of Christ is not something we seek, it is already given (v. 7). Second, we have been given an insight into that great mystery, the will of God, and we know that, to put it simply, we live in a universe which will ultimately find its complete explanation in Christ, not in one which is hostile or meaningless (vv. 9–10). Third, we are not just *called* to live as God's children should do, but actually *enabled* to do so (v. 12). Verses 13–14 give thanks for the work of the Holy Spirit in our lives. As God's adopted children we have been given an inheritance of which the Holy Spirit is a pledge. Above all, this passage encourages us to pray and sing our faith.

John 1.(1–9) 10–18

We turn to the first chapter of John's Gospel for the third time in as many weeks. Just as the Epistle for today has referred to God's 'plan' for humankind as going back before the world was made (Ephesians 1.4), so John's Prologue insists that the Word, now incarnate in Jesus of Nazareth, originates 'in the beginning' (vv. 1–3). We could concentrate today on vv. 10–18, which were included in the third set of readings for Christmas Day, but not in those for Advent 3. Indeed, since congregations are often most familiar with the Prologue through hearing it read at carol services, where it usually finishes at v. 14, it may be profitable to explore vv. 15–18 in particular. Verse 15 is probably an insertion (though an important one) which explains vv. 6–8. Verses 16–17 expand on what it means to say that the incarnate Logos is 'full of grace and truth', and they do so by testifying that we have now received 'grace upon grace'. The generous love of God (which is what 'grace' means) has always been poured out upon humankind but now, in Jesus Christ, it has been received in full and inexhaustible measure. John is probably not intending to disparage the Law of Moses in v. 17, only to point out that the generous love of God which came to people in that way is now even more freely available in Christ. Verse 18 begins with a statement with which few people would argue. Even the greatest of figures from Israel's past had not been able to see God (Exodus 33.18–23 is a good story to tell in this context). But, says John, what God has done through the incarnation is a making known every bit as real as a physical sighting would be; more so indeed, for this revelation is of God's character and nature. It comes about because 'God the only Son' (this, the more difficult reading, is to be preferred to the NRSV footnote alternative) is the bosom companion of the Father and is therefore uniquely able to disclose what the Father is like. Precisely how the Son will set about making this disclosure, John will go on to narrate in the rest of his writing. We often talk about humanity's search for God, but the story of the incarnation and all that follows from it is more properly understood as God's search for us. What difference might that understanding make to the way we live?

THE EPIPHANY

Isaiah 60.1–6

This is another of Deutero-Isaiah's prophecies of the restoration of Jerusalem after the exile, several of which have been read during the Advent and Christmas seasons. Here the restoration is depicted as the city which welcomes the light of God's presence. The distinctive note is that Jerusalem itself must 'shine' (v. 1) in response to God's light. Verse 3 is one of those significant moments in Old Testament literature when the nation is reminded that it possesses the privileges of being God's chosen people in order that it may in turn become a light by which other nations may live (compare Isaiah 49.6). This alone makes this an appropriate reading for Epiphany. Verses 4–6 present a scene of great joy, with the returning exiles gathering the wealth of the nations to be their inheritance. What makes this reading irresistible for Epiphany is the reference to gold and frankincense being brought from foreign lands (v. 8). It is not a prophecy of the story Matthew will tell (in any case, myrrh is missing) but is a happy verbal link with the Gospel for the day.

Ephesians 3.1–12

In Ephesians 2.11–22 Paul writes to Gentile Christians about the wonder of how God has made them sharers in the covenant promises once reserved exclusively for the Jewish people. He then turns to the 'mystery' which has only now been made clear (v. 5). What is this mystery? We need to remind ourselves that the Jewish tradition had always taught that one day the special blessings which they had received from God would be shared with all humanity. That much is clear as far back as the promise to Abraham (Genesis 12.3b). As today's Gospel reading says, with the birth of Christ that day had arrived. What had not been so clearly understood was that God would go further and, in Christ, would make the two groups one (v. 6, see 2.15). In a society which divided people into either Jews or Gentiles, and dealt with them accordingly, this is a staggering claim for the inclusiveness of the Christian good news. The Feast of the Epiphany is a good time to reflect on the divisions which are rife in our society and on how the good news of Jesus nullifies them all, no matter how deep-seated. We are called to be an inclusive community. In this the Church should lead the way by deeds and not just words.

Matthew 2.1–12

If Luke's birth stories have been subject to much imaginative embellishment, how much more has Matthew's narrative about the magi. They were probably included in the nativity play (before Christmas!) as if they arrived at Bethlehem hard on the heels of the shepherds. Carols will have been sung calling them 'kings', though Matthew calls them magi, which originally referred to a priestly caste of the Medes, but by this time meant astrologers, or those who studied the stars, thus wise men (the tradition that they were kings is probably derived from Isaiah 60.3). They may even have been given names, though that tradition is unknown before the sixth century. Other carols assert that they 'followed the star wherever it went', though v. 9 makes it plain that having seen it at its rising they did not see it again until they left Jerusalem. It would probably not be wise to try having two or five magi in the nativity play, even though Matthew nowhere tells us how many there were, and the tradition that there were three derives entirely from the number of gifts they brought. It is good for a congregation to see the embellishments for what they are, in order to recapture the essence of the story, which is, in the fine phrase from *The Book of Common Prayer*, the 'Manifestation of Christ to the Gentiles'. Matthew's story makes the same point that Luke makes a little later in the infancy narratives: right from the start Christ is recognized as the saviour of the whole world, he is the light of revelation to the Gentiles (Luke 2.32 – see, again, Isaiah 60.3). But Matthew has already made it clear that it is Israel's own saviour whom the Gentiles seek (1.21). In the light of the way Christians have usually treated Jews subsequently, a reminder that we all owe our salvation to the Jewish child of a Jewish mother is not out of place.

SUNDAY BETWEEN 7 AND 13 JANUARY

Sunday after Epiphany
First Sunday in Ordinary Time (The Baptism of Christ)

Genesis 1.1–5

It is easy to become sidetracked when preaching on the story of creation. We may feel a need to justify the Genesis account to those who hold a scientific world view. Or we may be aware that some of our hearers could be biblical literalists who will insist that this passage recounts how creation actually happened and may be offended if we do not affirm it. Either way, we can miss dealing with the main thrust of the passage, which can be summarized as: 'In the beginning, God'. For the biblical writers there was no question of choosing whether or not to believe in God. Choosing to obey God was another matter, but in obedience and disobedience alike, God was, and that was all there was to it. Without God there would be nothing. That was not a philosophical statement but a description of how things were. We, of course, live in a very different world. But Genesis's first word to us is still the same: In the beginning, God. And therefore, God alone is supreme and to be worshipped. However, this passage also tells us something about the nature of God. It is notoriously full of translation problems, but NRSV makes v. 2 a description of how things were *when* God created, rather than a description *of* God's creation. This fits well with Isaiah 45.18, whose writer also knew that God is a God of order and the work of creation is essentially that of bringing form and order out of chaos. A sermon on this reading might well explore some of the ways in which God has continued that work until today.

Acts 19.1–7

This passage relates a unique story in which Paul encounters a group of 'disciples' (v. 1) whose discipleship must have struck him, for some reason, as defective. He learns in response to questioning that they have only received John's baptism (v. 3). Whether they received it from John in Judaea twenty or more years previously, as described in today's Gospel, or whether from some continuing activity of John's followers, we are not told. However, they have therefore not received, or even heard of, the Holy Spirit (v. 2). Paul then instructs them and they receive Christian baptism from him (v. 5). When Paul laid hands on them they received the Holy Spirit in true pentecostal fashion (v. 6). John's baptism was of preparation, but Christian baptism was of fulfilment, and the fulfilment had taken place. Luke seems to see the story as descriptive of how those with a loose association with what had happened in Judaea and Jerusalem during the ministry of Jesus (perhaps because they had been visitors there during that time) are brought into communion with the apostolic Christian Church after Pentecost. This is the only instance in the New Testament of anybody being re-baptized, and it happened only because their first baptism was not a Christian baptism (i.e., 'in the name of the Lord Jesus', v. 5). For some younger Christians in particular, there is an issue around re-baptism, and it might be pastorally helpful to reflect on this story bearing that in mind.

Mark 1.4–11

The story of the baptism of Jesus is the climax of the Epiphany season and is itself an 'epiphany' (a showing forth). It has always been a slightly problematic story. Matthew adds extra material (Matthew 3.14–15), probably to deal with the question of why John should baptize Jesus if Jesus was the greater. Luke slides over it as something which has already happened (Luke 3.16), probably because he was unsure how to deal with the question of why a sinless Jesus should be baptized at all. John does not mention it. Mark recounts it very simply and the descent of the dove and the voice from heaven which follow are inward experiences, personal to Jesus. We, the readers, know of them through Mark's writing, but would not have experienced them if we had been there. Both are a declaration from God of Jesus' identity, intended to 'show forth' to us who he really is. The voice will be repeated on another critical occasion when the disciples need to be reminded of this (Mark 9.7). As we follow Mark's Gospel through this Lectionary year, we must hear the stories he will tell in the light of it.

SUNDAY BETWEEN 14 AND 20 JANUARY

Second Sunday in Ordinary Time
(The Second Sunday of Epiphany)

1 Samuel 3.1–10 (11–20)

The story of Samuel's call is credible and interesting, and is skilfully told. It begins long before today's reading. How Samuel came to the shrine at Shiloh is significant. 1 Samuel 1 relates his birth to Hannah in answer to prayer, and how she then gave him back to God. It is Samuel's natural destiny to serve God; 1 Samuel 2.26 prepares us for this. The call comes to Samuel three times so that there can be no doubt about it. The narrative is structured so as to prepare us for the downfall of the old priest Eli and his house (1 Samuel 2.22–25). Yet, in a beautiful touch, it is actually Eli who recognizes who it is who is calling Samuel, and he who tells the boy how to respond (vv. 8b–9). The shorter version needs nothing more than an imaginative retelling, inviting the hearers to reflect on how and when we hear God's call in daily living. The longer version has more to offer. Whereas most prophets stood outside the power structures of their day, for Samuel to follow God's call meant becoming his nation's leader, with all the responsibilities that entailed. Verses 15–18 relate how soon his first big challenge came. To hear the call of God may be one thing: to shoulder the responsibilities involved may be another.

1 Corinthians 6.12–20

Christianity is associated in the popular mind with repressive, legalistic and moralistic attitudes to sexuality, so we fight shy of preaching about it. Yet this passage has things to say which we need to hear. There was a group in the Corinthian church which held that Christian faith was a purely spiritual matter and so what a Christian did with his or her physical body was immaterial. Paul challenges this attitude, briefly in relation to food, then in relation to sex. For Paul, 'body' – used eight times here – meant more than just the physical body. Nigel Watson's 'the person as capable of relationship' defines it well. This is why Paul can argue that as 'persons' we are members of Christ (v. 15). It also explains his emphatic insistence that sexual relations are about more than the satisfying of a physical need or desire. The sexual act is undertaken by 'persons', not just bodies. Our culture in contemporary Britain is so permeated by the notion, reinforced by television soaps and lifestyle magazines, that the only question we need to ask about sex is 'How was it for you?' that Paul's insistence that casual uncommitted sex is harmful will scarcely be heard, let alone understood. We cannot give up on it on that account. Whatever our views about particular expressions of sexuality, there is nothing repressive or moralistic about saying that relationships need to be loving, caring, non-exploitative and committed. For Christians, there is the additional consideration that only those kinds of relationships glorify God (v. 20).

John 1.43–51

So rich and dense is this passage that no single sermon could do justice to all it contains. Indeed, it demands to be explored in a study group with all the resources that the commentaries can provide. But a sermon might just begin to unpack a few of its riches, so two comments, differing in magnitude. First, we may note that when Jesus has found Philip, it is Philip who finds Nathanael (vv. 43–44) just as, earlier, Andrew has been found and in turn finds his brother Simon (John 1.41). And when Nathanael is sceptical, Philip does not argue with him, but says, in effect, 'come and see for yourself' (v. 46). This is how church growth mostly happens, as recent studies of the church in Britain have confirmed, and every member of a congregation needs to know this. Second, the dialogue in vv. 47–50 superficially suggests a clever Jesus who knows things which astonish Nathanael supernaturally, and who chooses Nathanael as his disciple because he is worthy. Since when did Jesus choose disciples because they were worthy? Kenneth Grayston's penetrating insight must give us pause: 'Jesus is a saviour, not a management consultant.' Nathanael, then, appears for other reasons. He is the best kind of Jew/Israelite, contented with God and with his lot (see Micah 4.3–4). But he must be shaken out of his contentment (v. 50b), as must we.

SUNDAY BETWEEN 21 AND 27 JANUARY

Third Sunday in Ordinary Time (The Third Sunday of Epiphany)

Jonah 3.1–5, 10

'For the love of God is broader/Than the measures of man's mind' wrote F. W. Faber. The novella or extended parable which is the book of Jonah was written to bring home that point to those who so cherished their status as God's people that they couldn't believe God would save anyone else, and perhaps did not want God to do so. Jonah represents them, pagan Nineveh represents the wider world that God loves, though we sometimes doubt it. Today's reading begins after the story of Jonah's encounter with the great fish. The reluctant prophet, back on dry land, is beginning to learn that when God issues instructions it is best to obey them. The word of the Lord which comes to Jonah is the same as the first time round (compare v. 2 with 1.2), and this time Jonah sets off in the right direction. The storyteller exaggerates the size of Nineveh (v. 3b) to stress the point that Jonah's preaching begins in the suburbs (v. 4). The response is both immediate and universal (v. 5) and the result is that God changes his mind about what will happen to the city (v. 10). The story still stands as a rebuke to us when we limit God's love and concern to people like ourselves.

1 Corinthians 7.29–31

Paul may be writing here about the effects of living in the last days. On the other hand, he says that the 'present form' of this world is passing away, rather than that the world itself is doing so, so the passage may be referring to a time of impending or present crisis in Corinth (see 7.26). The heart of the matter is Paul's teaching about how Christian people should relate to their families, personal circumstances, possessions and daily routine or work (vv. 29b–30). These are very important things. Paul recognizes that they are important, but insists that they do not have ultimate importance. In Jean Héring's phrase, 'the Christian must not become once again a slave to the world, its possessions and its passions.' We find this relatively easy to understand (though not to do) with regard to possessions or work. It is harder with regard to families and relationships. Those who say, 'my family means everything to me' are counted virtuous, in the Church as in wider society. Should it be so? What do we make of the calling out of family relationships in today's Gospel reading, or passages such as Luke 14.26 and Mark 10.28–30? Can relationships also be idolatrous? To put it another way: if our relationships, along with the things mentioned in v. 30, were taken away from us, what would we have left? Paul elsewhere answers that question by saying, 'the surpassing value of knowing Christ' (Philippians 3.8). Can we even begin to think in these terms today? And should we?

Mark 1.14–20

Mark's summary in vv. 14–15 shows Jesus beginning his ministry in Galilee, not then a quiet backwater, but a busy, cosmopolitan and semi-pagan region. His message concerns the 'kingdom of God', but 'kingdom' is an unsatisfactory translation implying, as it does, something both territorial and static: 'reign of God' would be better. Jesus proclaims this reign of God as having 'come near' with him. The call is to 'repent' (compare Mark 1.4), but the consequences are now that people should 'believe the good news' which is about to unfold before them. Mark moves straight to the call of the first disciples. Jesus' demand, 'follow me' – literally, 'come after me' (v. 17) – suggests his authority, as does the immediacy of the responses (vv. 18, 21). What is involved in this response? The phrase, 'I will make you fish for people' is obviously appropriate, given their occupation. It also suggests that right from the beginning this is a call not just to discipleship as a process of learning and following, but to some personal involvement in the mission of Jesus. In some churches today will be 'Vocations Sunday' and this reading is clearly appropriate. However, by associating it with a call to particular vocations we may miss the point that for the first disciples the call to follow Jesus, and to what he will then make them, is about life's loyalties. That, surely, is true for us too as we share in Christ's mission.

SUNDAY BETWEEN 28 JANUARY AND 3 FEBRUARY

Fourth Sunday in Ordinary Time
(The Fourth Sunday of Epiphany)

Deuteronomy 18.15–20

Moses reminds the people about the time they asked him to bring God's words to them (Deuteronomy 5.22–27), saying that as a result, God decided to continue prophetic witness into the future (v. 18). Over time, some people came to expect one prophet in particular, a 'second Moses', to usher in a new relationship between God and humanity. In the sermon reported in Acts 3.22–23, Peter refers to Deuteronomy 18.15, saying that the promise has now been fulfilled in Jesus. The significant and repeated admonition in today's reading is that people must 'heed' the authentic prophets because their words come from God. There is a clear link with the Gospel reading and the 'authority' which people perceived in the teaching of Jesus (Mark 1.22–27). It is often said that in contemporary Western society we are very unwilling to accept that anything is authoritative for us unless we have discerned it for ourselves. If so, what effect does it have on Christian witness and mission?

1 Corinthians 8.1–13

This passage has a narrow setting, and thus a narrow application, though a general principle runs through it. The setting is a meal in a pagan temple (v. 10). Could a Christian share in such a social gathering, knowing the meat had been sacrificed to the pagan god (idol) concerned? Clearly some Corinthian Christians had done so without being troubled and, when challenged by others who found it scandalous, pointed out that since the idols were not real gods they 'knew' it was harmless. Paul agrees in principle (v. 4), but points out another consideration. If there were fellow Christians ('the weak' of v. 9b, 11), unable to distinguish between sharing in the meal and sharing in the pagan worship which was the occasion for the meal, they might lapse back into the pagan worship from which they had come and be destroyed (v. 11). Paul's sense of both the unity of the Christian family, and of that between Christ and his Church (v. 12) leads him to insist that those who 'know' taking part in such a meal is harmless should actually live by another and more important principle, which is love for others (v. 2). Such love would, in this instance, involve abstinence. It is hard to find a parallel in modern Britain, though in a multi-faith setting we rightly encourage friendship and contact between people of different faiths. On occasions social events take place which may involve elements of worship. 'Strong' (or liberal) Christians must then take account of the consciences of their 'weak' (or conservative) fellow believers. However, to compare major world religions to Corinthian idols is not helpful, and in any case the presence of converts to Christianity who would be thereby tempted to relapse is unlikely. The general principle, that we act with love towards the 'weak', remains true.

Mark 1.21–28

Jesus' teaching activity and the exorcism are deliberately woven together in Mark's account in order that the exorcism is understood as part of his proclamation of God's reign as surely as is the teaching. Nothing is said about the content of the teaching, presumably given at the invitation of the synagogue president. Much is said about the reaction to it and the astonishment it gave rise to on account of its authority (v. 23). The preaching of the scribes (v. 22b) consisted of much quotation from others, with an 'on the one hand this, but on the other hand that' tone to it. Jesus' teaching was the opposite, which means it was direct and clear and given on his own authority. Demon possession was not an issue for Mark. In this instance, the demon identifies Jesus as having come from God (v. 24b) but the further amazement of the congregation is not because of that, but because of the authority behind exorcism and teaching alike (v. 27). Some of these things seem remote from our concerns. Perhaps we have to think in terms of things which enslave and 'possess' people now; personal habits and lifestyles, but also racism, stereotyping, economic deprivation etc. How do the teaching and presence of Jesus make real God's reign in those situations?

SUNDAY BETWEEN 4 AND 10 FEBRUARY

Fifth Sunday in Ordinary Time (Proper 1)

Isaiah 40.21–31

Who has not sometimes felt overwhelmed by a sense of their own insignificance? If the world is as vast and intricate and populous as it is, how can one person matter, or do anything? For religious people this can take a particular form: 'If God is the great creator of all that there is, the heavens and the earth and everything in them, how can he possibly be concerned about me?' As the child perceptively asked her mother on leaving church: 'How can God hear my prayer when everyone else prays louder than me?' A dispirited people might feel much the same, that God has forgotten them, is too great to be bothered with them (v. 27). This magnificent passage stresses the incomparable majesty and glory of God who is, literally, beyond compare (v. 25). Surely this only exacerbates the problem? No, says Deutero-Isaiah, quite the contrary. Precisely because God is so great and wonderful, (a) nothing, however seemingly insignificant, escapes God's understanding (v. 28); (b) God's immense reservoir of power and strength is available to those who are weary and powerless (vv. 29–31). If this reassuring message is to be proclaimed we must explore what it means to 'wait' on God (v. 31a). We might also note that, even then, not everyone will fly: some will only run and some will merely walk (v. 31). Even the walking is a gift of God.

1 Corinthians 9.16–23

Paul deals here with two issues. First, some in the Corinthian church have accused him of not being a 'proper' apostle because, if he had been, he would have exercised the 'rights' of an apostle as others did and, in particular, the entitlement to be paid for his ministry. In vv. 15–18 he asserts that if a right may be exercised it may equally not be exercised, and his choice is to preach the gospel 'free of charge' (v. 18). He adds his testimony that the preaching itself is not a 'right' he exercises, it is an obligation laid on him. This leads to the second issue. When we say someone is 'all things to all people' we do not mean it as a compliment; we mean that they have no principles. Perhaps some were saying this about Paul. If so, he glories in the claim (v. 22b). He spells out in what ways he has lived like that (vv. 20–22a). An example of what he says in v. 22a can be found in last week's Epistle! But it is not because he is inconsistent or has no principles. It is in obedience to a higher principle, that of winning all sorts and conditions of people for Christ – the phrase 'that I might win . . .' occurs five times in four verses – that he is prepared to be adaptable. Paul believes in getting alongside people and understanding where they are coming from. In what ways does the contemporary Church have to get alongside people in very varied circumstances, in order to win them for Christ – e.g. a ministry alongside the poor and a ministry to the rich?

Mark 1.29–39

The exorcism Jesus performed in the synagogue is followed by the simple healing of Simon's mother-in-law from a fever (vv. 29–30). News of this brings the crowds to the door seeking the help they, or others, need (vv. 32–34). They receive it of course. This demanding ministry required spiritual support, and Mark reports that Jesus got up 'while it was still very dark', without telling the disciples where he was going, in order to pray (vv. 35–36). He is then ready to move on elsewhere, for like Paul in today's Epistle, his mission of preaching God's reign in human life is not an optional extra but the whole purpose of his coming (v. 38b). Verse 39 is Mark's summary of the preaching tour through Galilee which follows. We might note v. 34b, where the demons are not allowed to speak because they know who Jesus really is. So, of course, does the reader of the Gospel! But those involved in the story, disciples included, usually do not, at least until after Easter when it is made plain. How do we help those around us to know who Jesus really is, the living Lord, as opposed to who they think he is, a figure from the past?

SUNDAY BETWEEN 11 AND 17 FEBRUARY

Sixth Sunday in Ordinary Time (Proper 2)

2 Kings 5.1–14

This little masterpiece of the storyteller's art has many vivid details to hold our attention. A 'great' man has his usefulness threatened by leprosy (v. 1); he is dependent for the thing he needs most on an insignificant and unnamed female slave (vv. 2–3); there is a diplomatic misunderstanding which nearly results in tragedy (vv. 6–7); the great man's pride is affronted and he cannot believe that God only requires something simple from him (vv. 11–12), and a lesson in humility, again dependent on a servant, needs to be learned (v. 13). All these make for good storytelling and preaching. Yet they are ultimately incidentals. It is the climax of the story which matters: only when Naaman acts 'according to the word of the man of God' (v. 14a) is he healed of his leprosy and becomes 'clean'. But there is more. By finishing at v. 14, the Lectionary deprives us of the crucial link between v. 8b and v. 15a. It might be better to read the passage as far as v. 15a. When Naaman is cured of his leprosy and made whole, a crucial part of that wholeness consists in learning about the source of such healing, the one true God whose servant is Elisha. The link with the leper in today's Gospel reading is clear enough.

1 Corinthians 9.24–27

'Brother ass' is how St Francis of Assisi is alleged to have referred to his physical body. There is a Christian ascetic tradition of punishing the body; the mortification of the flesh. It has sometimes been taken to unhealthy lengths and the body regarded as intrinsically evil. Self-hatred and prudery are among the results. It is hard to see how a Christian faith which is committed to the reality of the incarnation can rest content with such a position. However, Paul does not go so far here. The reason for bringing his body under discipline (v. 27) is that it might serve, not distract him, in the living of the Christian life, which he compares to competing in athletics (Corinth hosted the Isthmian Games so his readers would have found the comparison an apt one). Our own culture has a curiously dualistic attitude to these things. Although many in the medical world are concerned about the future health of today's children, criticizing them for being 'couch potatoes', health clubs and gyms have proliferated in recent years and are very popular, and joggers are a common sight. It seems that many people do want to keep their bodies 'in shape' for the sake of a long and healthy life, and are prepared for the hard work involved. Yet many of us want our spirituality without such effort. The hard discipline of learning to pray, persevering in reading the scriptures and getting out of bed to go to church, has been replaced by playing a CD of plainsong in the car on the way home from work, and burning an aromatherapy candle when we arrive. It could be profitable to explore in what ways we need to discipline ourselves (v. 27) and exercise self-control (v. 25) in order to grow in the Christian life. Has the contemporary slogan 'No pain, no gain' some validity in the sphere of spirituality as well?

Mark 1.40–45

Elisha sent a messenger out to Naaman. Jesus responds to the leper's request with a touch of his hand (v. 41), a gesture which signals his compassion for and identification with those outcast and marginalized. A sermon on the way in which the Church must continue this aspect of his mission today would be appropriate. However, we note that in v. 41a there is a variant reading about which emotion moved Jesus. If it was anger (see NRSV footnote), what might Jesus have been angry about? The fact that a child of God could be in such need, or at the powers of evil which enslave people? What might Jesus be angry about today, and how does the Church reflect that anger? Also important is the leper's plea (v. 40). It may not be faith in the fullest sense of that word, but it is a request he can make with confidence, as can we, whatever its particular meaning would be for us in our situation.

SUNDAY BETWEEN 18 AND 24 FEBRUARY

Seventh Sunday in Ordinary Time (Proper 3)

Isaiah 43.18–25

This is part of a longer passage celebrating the prospect of the fall of Babylon and a 'new Exodus' for Israel. Verse 18 is an impossible starting place; we need to begin two verses earlier. Verses 16–17 are a clear reference to part of the Exodus story (Exodus 14.21–29), remembered yearly at Passover time. Verse 18 is incredibly revolutionary because it calls on the people not to hark back to those great events of Israel's past but to open their eyes to the new thing God is about to do (v. 19). The prophet is not really telling them to stop observing the Passover (see Exodus 12.25–27). He deliberately uses bold language and the message must have shocked his hearers. Remembering those past events defined their identity; they were the people God delivered out of Egypt. Now God is about to cause a new Exodus (vv. 19b–21) and it will include the forgiveness of their sins, which they do not deserve (vv. 22–25). Our identity as a Christian community is also defined by the mighty acts of God for us in the past, especially in Jesus. We read them in scripture and rehearse and celebrate them in our worship. So we must, but we must also discern what God is doing, and calling us to share, in today's world. How we do that, and how we respond through new ways of being church, may be the difficult question Isaiah challenges us to confront.

2 Corinthians 1.18–22

The reading begins oddly, but it is difficult to see where else to enter into Paul's argument. He has been using the 'Yes/No' contrast to defend himself against charges that he changed his travel plans to suit himself (vv. 15–17). He then says that he has not been insincere (v. 18), for Christians must regulate their lives in accordance with the faithfulness of God (v. 19). This leads him (vv. 19b–22) into a kind of hymn celebrating God's faithfulness. The thought is that Jesus was the fulfilment of God's promises and Christian people are those who say 'Amen' to that. All this is God's work (v. 21) and they know it to be so because they have received the Spirit (v. 22). The idea of the Spirit as 'a first instalment' repays exploration (compare Ephesians

1.14). In a world of mortgages and extended credit we are familiar enough with the idea. What might it mean to see God's gift of the Spirit as a 'first instalment', and what is there still to look forward to?

Mark 2.1–12

This healing story brings the first mention in Mark of the forgiveness of sins (v. 5). Previous stories have shown God's reign in human life through exorcism and healing; here it is shown also through the forgiveness which forms part of the healing. Indeed, Jesus' first word to the paralysed man is of forgiveness (v. 5) and when he realizes that this has raised a question in the minds of the scribes (vv. 6–7) he directly and explicitly raises both the question of the relationship between the two and his own authority in the matter (vv. 8–10). Mark intends the story to reveal to the reader a further dimension of who Jesus really is. When the scribes say, quite correctly, that only God can forgive sins (v. 7b) it leads them to one conclusion (that Jesus is blaspheming), but the reader to a quite different one (that Jesus is the one through whom God is acting). Although there are sub-themes in this passage we can hardly avoid dealing with it in the context of the Christian understanding of healing. Jesus here explicitly links forgiveness and healing (and thus sin and sickness), but he does not normally do so and there is no basis for believing that all sickness is caused by sin. That it may be the case in some instances seems undeniable, and an unspecified paralysis is a credible example since it might be what we broadly term psychosomatic. The phrase 'paralysed by fear' – or guilt – is a vivid metaphor but may also be a physical reality. A proper Christian understanding of healing and wholeness includes a declaration of God's loving care for the sick. That may in some cases be heard, or even spelled out, as a declaration of God's forgiveness.

SUNDAY BETWEEN 25 AND 29 FEBRUARY

Eighth Sunday in Ordinary Time (Second Sunday before Lent)

Hosea 2.14–20

Although it is difficult to be sure how much autobiographical information about Hosea there is in chs 1–3, this much can be safely said: Hosea portrays Israel as 'married' to God as a wife is married to her husband. But Israel has committed adultery with other gods (Baals), and the prophecy is concerned with how God responds to this. The earlier part of ch. 2 dwelt on punishment, this part deals with restoration. In vv. 14–15 there is a picture of Israel being brought into the wilderness (the place of trial) where God will restore her, with Achor (a place which symbolized a terrible defeat, see Joshua 7) now a 'door of hope' (v. 15). In vv. 16–20 God promises purification for Israel, and will 'wipe from her lips'' (v. 17, NEB) even the names of other gods. This will be a time of peace when war is finally abolished (v. 18) and Israel will be God's wife in justice, steadfast love, mercy and faithfulness (vv. 19–20). A sermon might reflect on each of those qualities, seen as gifts from God to his people, as a result of which they will 'know the Lord' (v. 20). Consideration of Harry Mowvley's wise comment might also be profitable: 'God is the righteous one who judges sinners and also the loving one who rescues his people. Both views are found throughout scripture and must always be held in tension.'

2 Corinthians 3.1–6

Paul here continues his struggle with difficult factions in the Corinthian church. But he never aims to commend himself, except as Christ's servant. In this case he thinks the task ought not to be difficult, because their Christian existence is itself testimony to the missionary work he and his colleagues have done with them. The Corinthians are like letters of recommendation which Paul and others have already written by the Spirit of God (vv. 2–3). He goes on to disclaim any of this as his own doing (v. 5) – rather it is God who has given the competence for it (v. 6). The passage ends with a definition of the 'new covenant' within which Christian people stand, a covenant of the Spirit, contrasted with the 'old covenant' written on tablets of stone which could not, Paul thought, bring life. It is difficult to see how this passage can speak directly to a congregation today, though it does have some important insights into the character and purpose of ministry within the Church. Those in ministry are not church managers, but ministers of the covenant of grace, who write the Christian good news on people's hearts.

Mark 2.13–22

This is a tightly packed passage with many themes, only a few of which can be mentioned here. In vv. 13–14 Jesus calls Levi, who worked for the hated occupying Romans. He would not have been poor, but he would certainly have been marginalized: an outcast from the synagogue and respectable Jewish society. Jesus is not going to play for safety. In vv. 15–17 the religiously respectable express their disquiet. It is said that people are known by the company they keep, so why is Jesus sharing a meal in such company? Should he not rather be denouncing their sins and calling them to repentance? Jesus' reply (v. 17) is a gentle but decisive rebuke. He has come to 'call' sinners (as in Levi's case). The implication is that his friendship will transform them. In vv. 18–20 the disciples' feasting is contrasted with the engagement of John the Baptist and the Pharisees in the twice-weekly fasts, part of the purpose of which was to mourn the fact that the salvation of Israel had not yet appeared. Jesus' reply identifies himself as the bridegroom, and indicates that, though his questioners do not know it, the salvation of Israel has in fact appeared. Verses 21–22 involve two comparisons, in both of which the 'new' possesses dynamic life. When the new is fully revealed, many of the old practices will come to an end. Perhaps the greatest challenge in this passage is about whether Christians have become respectable in the wrong sense: too careful about the company they keep, too keen to judge, too quick to condemn and much too easily identified in the public mind as a moralistic pressure group. If so, what should we do about it?

SUNDAY BEFORE LENT

2 Kings 2.1–12

The threefold repetition of Elijah's request and Elisha's response, coupled in the first two instances with the predictions made by a 'company of prophets' (vv. 2–3, 4–5, 6), is probably intended to emphasize the solemnity and importance of what is about to happen. Elijah is to pass from earth to heaven without passing through death. When Elisha asks for 'a double share' of Elijah's spirit he is not asking to be twice as good a prophet as Elijah had been, but rather that he might be seen as a true spiritual son of Elijah by receiving the eldest son's inheritance (Deuteronomy 21.17) and thus continue Elijah's work. Elijah's reply (v. 10) indicates that it is not in his power to grant the request. Whether Elisha will truly be his successor 'depends on his ability to see and comprehend the spiritual world' (Gwilym H. Jones). The conclusion of the passage indicates that the request has indeed been granted. There is a deep mystery about the life of faith. As Elizabeth Barrett Browning, drawing on another biblical story, put it:

> Earth's crammed with heaven,
> And every common bush afire with God;
> But only he who sees, takes off his shoes,
> The rest sit round it and pluck blackberries.
> (*Aurora Leigh*)

Why do some people see spiritual realities, while others do not? How can people hear the story of God's love in Christ and be unmoved? In today's Epistle Paul attempts an answer.

2 Corinthians 4.3–6

The accusation had evidently been made against Paul that his message was 'veiled' or obscure. He agrees that in one sense it is, but only for those who are 'perishing' because they have been blinded to the truth by Satan 'the god of this world' (vv. 3–4). Unbelievers are those who have been prevented from seeing the light of Christ's glory dawning upon them. Paul contrasts this with the privilege of believers, for whom the God who created light in the first place (v. 6, see Genesis 1.2–4) has, in F. F. Bruce's fine paraphrase, 'shone in our hearts to illuminate them with the knowledge of His glory reflected in the face of Christ'. This is Paul's answer here to the mystery of unbelief, and it makes us uncomfortable. It suggests a clear, fixed and readily defined distinction between believers and unbelievers which does not readily correspond with contemporary experiences of discipleship, either our own or that of others; there is an incipient sectarianism about it. It also strongly suggests that if people are blinded by Satan there is nothing which can be done about it. Elsewhere, Paul wrestles with the themes of election/predestination and human free will in a more balanced way (Romans 9.6–10.21). We do well to handle such mysteries with humility, but to fail to handle them at all is to duck our responsibilities.

Mark 9.2–9

The transfiguration story is about seeing into the heart of God's reality. Jesus deliberately takes Peter, James and John with him to 'a high mountain', the traditional place for a theophany, where they see him in a new light, clothed in divine glory (compare Daniel 7.9). Moses and Elijah (the 'mighty ones of old', as Samuel Greg wrote) represent the Law and the prophets, the best of Israel's past. They stand with Jesus for encouragement as Calvary draws closer. Here indeed is the prophet who was expected (Deuteronomy 18.15, directly quoted in v. 7. See also the comments on the Old Testament reading on p. 30). The voice from the cloud echoes the voice at his baptism (Mark 1.11). Peter's nervous reaction to what is happening (v. 5) is seen as born of holy fear (v. 6). As the story ends we can see that these disciples have been fully initiated into the mystery of who Jesus is, though a secret it must at present remain (v. 9). We do not need to have a mystical disposition to experience 'disclosure situations' where God enables us to see more deeply into the heart of reality and faith is strengthened – 'mountaintop experiences', as they are sometimes called. Like Peter, we sometimes want to capture them and stay with them, but that is not possible. What matters is that as we come down from the mountain (v. 9) we are better prepared for the unknown which will come our way in the journey ahead.

ASH WEDNESDAY

Joel 2.1–2, 12–17

The entire message of Joel's prophecy is about judgment and salvation. Today's reading begins with a warning of coming disaster (vv. 1–2) and finishes with a call to repentance (vv. 12–17). The verses which are omitted here amplify the warning of disaster with a more detailed description of it and need to be read as part of sermon preparation, if not in the service. In the first chapter there is a moving lament for a land which has been devastated by a plague of locusts. There is some disagreement among scholars as to whether the disaster predicted in ch. 2 is also caused by an army of locusts, or whether a human army is in mind. The latter seems more probable, but either way it is an army of an apocalyptic character, unimaginably great (v. 2). The judgment which is coming upon the city is referred to as 'the Day of the Lord' (v. 1). This term was sometimes used to denote the day when God would vindicate his people; Amos, for example, had to warn people that their expectations of it would turn out to be wrong (Amos 5.18–20). Perhaps some imagined, as Jeremiah accused them of doing, that devastation could not happen to God's holy city Jerusalem, the place where the temple stood (Jeremiah 7.1–4). Unusually, we are not told what dreadful sins have called forth such calamity. That sin is the cause is evident when we come to v. 12 and the invitation to repentance. It is striking that in this verse it is God himself who invites repentance and promises mercy. God's nature is love and mercy; indeed, the whole biblical story shows how frequently God found new ways of communicating that love to sinful people, a story which will reach its climax in the coming of Jesus. We note that the repentance God invites must be genuine. Rending clothing concerns outward show; to rend the heart makes sincerity plain. In v. 13 the prophet adds his own call to repentance. In vv. 15–16 the population are urged to come together in a great assembly. It is not just individual sin that is involved, but the sin of a whole community. In that assembly there must be both genuine sorrow and prayer for deliverance (v. 17a). Often when we pray for forgiveness or to be spared disaster, it is because we are ashamed of having been found out in some way and want to be spared humiliation. But forgiveness is not about sparing our feelings, it is about our wholeness as God's children. It is also about our ability, as those who bear God's name, to be a witness to others about God's love. One of the most distressing things about our falls from grace is that they cause others to impugn the reality of that grace.

Isaiah 58.1–12

One of the most subtle temptations that can beset religious people is to think that worship and conduct have no essential relationship to each other. So it is in this passage. Here are people who read their sacred books and engage in prayer, since by these means they can seek God and draw near to him (v. 2). They even make sure that they observe the fasting regulations and are puzzled that God does not seem to notice this (v. 3a). So God commands that this people should be faced with what they are doing, that it is nothing less than rebellion and sin (v. 1). God's direct speech begins in v. 3b: 'Look, you serve your own interest . . .', though this, and the accusation in v. 4a, sound slightly odd to us. They probably mean that people are fasting only because it makes them look good in eyes of others, but since they lack inward motivation it only makes them angry and quarrelsome. In vv. 4b–5 God asks, somewhat ironically, what kind of a fast they imagine they are offering. Then follows a detailed description of true 'fasting' which is probably also a detailed indictment of what is *not* taking place. There are no difficulties in understanding either what is required of us (vv. 6–7, 9b–10), or the moving description of the blessings which follow from God's approval (vv. 8–9a, 11–12). A congregation gathered for a liturgical act on Ash Wednesday can hardly escape the uncomfortable implications of all this. Perhaps Ash Wednesday is one of the rare occasions when, in preaching, the demand of the Gospel takes precedence over its offer.

2 Corinthians 5.20b–6.10

Paul has been writing about the ministry of himself and his colleagues, and sums it up by saying they are 'ambassadors for Christ' (5.20a). But he does not write in restrained diplomatic language, this is a passionate outpouring: 'We entreat you on behalf of Christ, be reconciled to God.' To whom is he writing? There is no equivalent to the NRSV 'you' in the Greek of this verse, but there has to be an object and nothing else would fit. Some commentators find it hard to accept that Paul is addressing Christian people: surely the fact that they are Christians shows that they have already been reconciled to God? Perhaps, but he is certainly addressing the Corinthian church in 6.1, and there is no good reason to suppose he is not doing so here.

Even a superficial reading of the letters to Corinth makes it plain that there were factions in the congregation. They were not living at peace with one another and they were certainly not living at peace with Paul. This may well be what is meant by the possibility of accepting the grace of God 'in vain' (6.1): their conduct nullified its effects. An appeal, 'Let us be reconciled to each other', would not have been enough. Only when people are genuinely reconciled to God can true reconciliation with one another take place. Does this point us to the need for repentance and reconciliation with God, in order that divisions and disputes may be healed within the congregation to which we preach on Ash Wednesday? Paul points to the urgency of responding to the call for repentance (6.2) and then, in a moving testimony, sets out some of the undeserved suffering he has experienced (6.3–10). Undeserved suffering often turns us away from God, but not Paul. Why is this? Because he knows that Jesus also suffered unjustly, but he was suffering for us, to bring us incalculable blessings (5.21). Paul hopes that whatever he has to go through, and the way he responds to it, will bring blessing to others.

Matthew 6.1–6, 16–21

Jesus told his followers that their righteousness 'must exceed' that of the scribes and Pharisees (Matthew 5.20); here this is spelled out in relation to religious practices. Verse 1 sets out the general principle. It also introduces the notion of earthly and heavenly rewards, which will recur throughout the passage. You can have an earthly reward or a heavenly one, but not both. The first section, vv. 2–4, concerns charitable giving. This was well organized in the Judaism of Jesus' day. Kindness to the poor formed part of a well-ordered society (see Isaiah 58.6–8 from one of today's Old Testament readings). Jesus contrasts true almsgiving, which is done secretly with no thought of earthly reward, with that done by the 'hypocrites' who do it only to be praised by others. The second section, vv. 5–6, takes up the same principle in relation to prayer. In contrast with those who make a public show of their prayers, disciples are to pray in their room (literally, 'storeroom', an inner room). Following the 'Lord's Prayer' (an insertion in this context), the third section repeats the teaching, this time in relation to fasting (vv. 16–17). Public fasts were relatively rare, though called in time of national disaster (see the reading from Joel for today). Private fasts were considered virtuous. When the disciples fast they are not to look as though they are doing so. The earthly reward the hypocrite receives is clear enough: applause from other people. But what are the 'heavenly' rewards Jesus here offers? Joachim Jeremias points to Matthew 25.37–40, where those acquitted are completely surprised: they had forgotten all about the acts of love through which the acquittal comes. In the end, this is the radical abolition of the idea of 'reward' in religious practice. The heavenly reward consists in finding that the giving, the prayer, the fasting, all bring us closer to God and lead to fresh experiences of God's grace. What springs out of that is joy in the forgiveness and love we receive and the desire to give, pray and fast (in the proper senses) more than we do now. So what lies behind our own Lenten discipline?

FIRST SUNDAY IN LENT

Genesis 9.8–17

This reading is traditionally linked to today's Epistle because of what the author of 1 Peter makes of Noah and his family being saved through water (1 Peter 3.20). Few of us today find that kind of exegesis convincing, but this passage offers significant preaching opportunities in its own right. Following the universal flood, God establishes a covenant, first with the entire human race (v. 9) and then with 'every living creature' (v. 10). Covenants always involve two parties and one may be superior to the other. Here there is no requirement laid on the other party ('if you do this' or 'if you do that'): this covenant is God's gracious initiative. As a universal sign of it God will set his bow (literally 'war bow', v. 13) in the clouds – the war bow has become a rainbow! The natural order, saved through Noah, is under the care and protection of God. In Gerhard von Rad's words: 'The *natural* orders, fixed by God's word, mysteriously guarantee a world in which in his own time God's *historical* saving activity will begin.' Genesis says nothing here about human responsibility, but in today's world we can hardly avoid taking up ecological questions, care for this natural order, issues of global warming, our relationship with the animal creation and so forth. If global warming causes disastrous flooding in Bangladesh (and inconvenient flooding in Britain), what does it mean to say that God has guaranteed the natural order, and what is our responsibility for working with God?

1 Peter 3.18–22

This is the most difficult passage in 1 Peter. There are many disputed details of interpretation, and the passage probably incorporates credal statements well known at the time of writing. What matters most is the overall thrust of the argument: Christ suffered and was vindicated, and this gives us grounds for hope. In v. 18 there is a fine statement of what Christ has done for us. With regard to v. 19 we must make an effort to put aside the statement 'he descended into hell' which first appeared in AD 359 at Sirmium and is not what 1 Peter has in mind. Recent commentators suggest this is not a preaching of *salvation* to those in hell, it is an announcement of the *victory* of the risen Christ to the cosmic powers of evil, a thought which reaches its climax in v. 22. The mention of Noah (and thus, implicitly, the flood) causes the author to draw the analogy with Christian baptism which 'saves' in the sense that faith saves, by demonstrating a living relationship to God. Any preaching on this passage might be along the lines that our lives are not at the mercy of hostile forces: Christ has entered our human experience and triumphed over them. We participate in this triumph through our baptism.

Mark 1.9–15

For vv. 9–11 see the comments on the Gospel on p. 25. Mark then goes straight into the temptation story, though there is a link (there is no point in Satan tempting one whose status as God's Son has not been confirmed). Mark says the Spirit 'drove' Jesus into the wilderness (Matthew and Luke both have 'led'), which suggests the character of the ordeal. Nevertheless it is the Spirit's doing, something which God intends his Son to pass through before his public ministry. Mark's account of the temptations takes just one verse (v. 13). When we preach on the accounts in Matthew or Luke we may be tempted to enter into Jesus' psychological consciousness. We cannot do that here; the bare fact that the temptations took place in the wilderness must suffice. Like Matthew, Mark stresses the angelic ministry to Jesus. We often call those times in our own lives when we feel adrift from God a 'wilderness experience', and we are not wrong to do so. It is not necessarily an experience of temptation (and, in our case, perhaps fall) which causes this, though it may be. There can be many different reasons why we struggle with our faith, why God seems far off and why we may even be tempted to abandon the whole thing. The beginning of Lent is a good time to reflect on this, and remember Jesus' time of testing. If so, we shall remember that angelic ministry as a symbol of the fact that God is never as far away as we imagine.

SECOND SUNDAY IN LENT

Genesis 17.1–7, 15–16

This reading concerns God's covenant through Abram, where God promises a people through whom his will could be made known in history. In 15.1–6, Abram is assured that God knows about his childlessness. After the ambiguous episode with Hagar in ch. 16, Abram is no longer childless, but still has no heir by his wife, Sarai. Chapter 17 tells of the covenant which will change this. As in Noah's case, it is entirely God's initiative: Abram can only respond. The words 'walk before me and be blameless' are a statement of how things will be, not a condition that Abram must fulfil. Throughout, the emphasis is on the multitude of Abram's descendants (vv. 2b, 4b, 5b, 6, 10b) and the blessing will also be Sarai's (v. 16). The changing of their names to Abraham and Sarah does not mean what the storyteller want us to think it does, but that hardly matters: a new future is marked by new names. We need not take Abraham and Sarah's stated ages literally, but that they were past normal childbearing age is an important part of the story: this is not something that in the usual course of events they can achieve for themselves. It is a pity the reading does not go as far as v. 22, since it becomes increasingly clear that Abraham is not very happy. Here are an elderly couple who could do without such excitement, which is how we sometimes feel when God takes hold of our lives.

Romans 4.13–25

This is Paul's classic account of the grounds of the Christian's relationship with God. It has often been misread. To regard the Judaism of Jesus and Paul's day as a religion which attempted to earn salvation by good works, and to contrast this with Christianity which offers salvation by grace through faith, is a major distortion. Judaism at its best was always concerned with living in response to a gracious God who delights to save. But the Law (Torah) through which God saves those who live faithfully within it would not, Paul was clear, do for Gentiles. All that was needed for salvation now was faith in the one who raised Jesus from the dead, for Jesus died and was raised to put us right with God (vv. 24–25). And since that is all that is necessary, other things (such as circumcision or keeping the Law) cannot now be necessary. To establish that argument he considers the covenant with Abraham (though the key quotation in v. 22 comes from Genesis 15.6). All who have faith like that of Abraham are truly his children, whether Jews or Gentiles (vv. 16–17). The issue of whether Christians need to be circumcised or keep Torah no longer bothers us. But every generation creates its own version of what C. S. Lewis once called 'Christianity and . . .' in which the 'and', whatever it might be, is considered essential to being a 'true' Christian. What are the 'ands' in today's Church?

Mark 8.31–38

Verse 31 contains the first of three predictions of Jesus' suffering, death and resurrection. What does 'must' mean? It is often interpreted as pointing to the fulfilment of a plan which God has already decreed, but that raises huge problems. May it not reflect Jesus' awareness both of his enemies' plans and God's faithfulness and, in that light, his determination to be true to his mission? Peter's reaction is a contrast with his previous insight (8.29). Jesus deals with him harshly (vv. 32–33) because Peter's attitude, just as much as the actions of his enemies, could frustrate his mission. In vv. 34–38 Jesus addresses the crowd as well as his disciples about the cost involved in following him. The command to shoulder the cross (v. 34) was no metaphor: his hearers would be used to the sight of condemned criminals actually carrying the cross on which they would die (see John 19.17; compare Matthew 27.32/Luke 23.26). To follow Jesus might indeed involve being crucified, but those who become martyrs for his sake will gain the only life worth having (v. 35). We say, 'It's the cross I have to bear' very much too lightly. Lent is an appropriate time for considering the real cost of discipleship – martyrdom for many in our time, though not yet in our country. Following Jesus must never be our Sunday hobby.

THIRD SUNDAY IN LENT

Exodus 20.1–17

The Ten Commandments, or Decalogue, were probably originally recited in public worship when the covenant made on Sinai was recalled. Thus their liturgical use in Christian worship continues an ancient tradition. For many reasons they have entered deeply into public consciousness. Even in today's secularized Britain people with no personal Christian faith will ask that the Ten Commandments be taught to their children as a way of inculcating moral standards. At the same time, they are often criticized as representing a narrow 'thou shalt not' kind of religion, which people do not find appealing. What they appear to lack from the Christian perspective is the New Testament stress that 'ethics is gratitude'. They don't, of course, but we usually hear them divorced from their context, which is the celebration of the Sinai covenant and thanksgiving for the deliverance from Egypt. They are not really laws (there are no penalties laid down for breaking them), and R. E. Clements' description is helpful: 'They set out the way of life that was demanded from those who belonged to God's covenant people.' If their intention is indeed to help us to relate the basic requirements of moral life in society to God's will, we must find appropriate ways of relating them to the moral life of our own society without turning them into laws to be rigidly obeyed.

1 Corinthians 1.18–25

Paul reminds us that through the cross God has turned all our human values inside out. The world at large (represented here by the world of Greek philosophy) cannot come to know God by thinking and speculating. God is only made known by a self-disclosure which took place in certain historical events, the climax of which was the cross on which Christ died (v. 23). Yet this is quite extraordinary, 'folly' indeed, for who would look for the supreme revelation of the nature of God in the crucifixion of a Galilean preacher? As F. F. Bruce puts it, 'how could anyone accept as lord and deliverer a man who had not sufficient wit to save himself from so ghastly a death?' Nor would those who seek 'signs' of a powerful God (v. 22a) first look in this direction. Commentators remind us of the Roman graffito depicting a slave bowing down to a crucified figure with the head of an ass, with the slogan: 'Alexamenos worships his God.' It seemed like that then, and has done ever since. But Paul insists that the crucified Christ is both the power and wisdom of God (v. 24b). Indeed so, for here alone is shown the unconquerability of divine love which we could have known in no other way. The cross is the 'weakness' of God, yet stronger than human wisdom, for it can save as nothing else can. This message produces division, and always will. The contemporary Church, longing to be friends with all, sometimes finds that difficult. See further the comments on the Epistle on p. 68.

John 2.13–22

Whereas the synoptic gospels place the story of Jesus cleansing the temple near the beginning of his final entry into Jerusalem, John puts it at an earlier Passover festival. This alerts us to the fact that in John the story serves a somewhat different purpose. In the synoptics the centre of concern is that the temple should be a 'house of prayer for all nations' (Isaiah 56.7). This issue is not absent from John: v. 16, where Jesus refers to God as 'my Father' for the first time in this Gospel, takes the place of the Isaiah reference in the synoptics. But in John it goes deeper, provoking the exchange about Jesus' authority for what he has done (vv. 18–20), involving what C. K. Barrett calls 'a dark saying which the Jews misunderstood and the disciples understood only after the resurrection, to which event, in covert fashion, it referred'. John's placing of the incident immediately after his first sign, the story of the wedding at Cana (2.1–11), gives us a further clue how to interpret it. The true glory of Jesus has already been revealed. John now tells us that the body of Jesus is the dwelling-place of God and, crucified and risen, will become the true temple for the whole of humankind. This temple, no longer physically located, will be truly available as a house of prayer for all nations, as it is for us today.

FOURTH SUNDAY IN LENT

Numbers 21.4–9

On its own this is a rather problematic story. Even given that the Israelites were grumbling unreasonably (v. 5), we are not easily reconciled to a God who sends poisonous serpents to bite people as a punishment (v. 6). Perhaps we need to recall that ancient Israel thought of God as the only direct cause of every event. We do not share that perception and the story is certainly easier without it. Thankfully, the emphasis is not so much on the punishment as on the remedy God provides. The command to make a bronze (or copper) serpent, and set it on a pole so that it was publicly visible and thus universally available, introduces an image of forgiveness which will be picked up in today's Gospel reading. The whole community was complicit in the rebellion against God and Moses (v. 5), but relief from the effects of the serpent's bite does not come simply from being a member of that community. An act of human response is required: those who are bitten have to look at the serpent before they can know its healing power (v. 8b). At the same time, just looking is sufficient to bring the healing (v. 9b). God's salvation requires only a simple and basic response.

Ephesians 2.1–10

The other two readings point us to salvation which is God's gift, to which we are called to respond. Here Paul spells out what that means for Christian readers. Almost immediately he introduces a digression on the way of life which once characterized his readers (vv. 2–4, clearer in the AV, which borrows the verb 'quicken' from v. 5 and inserts it in v. 1, than it is from modern versions). That was due to following Satan, with predictable results – though we must be careful not to take 'passions of our flesh' to mean only sexual sins – this describes unregenerate human nature as a whole (v. 3). In v. 5, we reach the contrast and in v. 6 the astonishing statement that believers are already 'seated in the heavenly places'. This vision of God's intention is so sure of fulfilment that Paul can speak of it as if it has already happened. Verse 8 is one of the great summaries of the heart of the Christian good news. We sometimes talk loosely of being saved by faith. That is wrong: salvation, as the great Reformation phrase has it, is 'by grace alone, through faith alone, to God be the glory'. We must not miss v. 10, where 'we are God's work of art' is JB's lovely rendition. God's work of art – *us*? What a thought!

John 3.14–21

The reading begins part-way through the instruction which Jesus offers to Nicodemus. It is not clear whether the evangelist intends us to understand vv. 16–21 as the words of Jesus or as his own reflection. We take it to be the latter, but it makes little difference to the interpretation. In vv. 14–15 Jesus makes the direct comparison between his own 'lifting up' on the cross, and Moses lifting up the serpent (today's Old Testament lection). Both have the same purpose: the salvation of those who respond appropriately. There follows what is probably the best-known verse in the New Testament, summarizing the heart of the Christian good news. God wills salvation for everyone without exception (the object of God's love is, we note, 'the world' rather than some closed community), and in giving his only Son has provided the means by which that can come about (v. 16). Verses 17–21 work this out in more detail, expanding an image which we have already encountered (1.9). All that is required to receive salvation from the uplifted Son of Man is to 'believe' (vv. 15, 16b, 18). That is a simple act of response, such as anyone can make. Some commentators have noted that this passage, vv. 14–15 especially, sets out a simple understanding of the cross. No developed theology of the atonement is offered; rather it suggests that believing may come about by seeing the Son of Man 'lifted up'. There is a long Christian tradition of using a cross (and, from the twelfth century onwards, a crucifix) as a focus for devotion. In Lent this Gospel reading may help us to appropriate this tradition so that we too may truly believe and have eternal life (v. 15).

MOTHERING SUNDAY

Exodus 2.1–10

The most important thing about this ancient story is that it points us
to the overall providence of God and the crucial part which some
ordinary women play in that. We are to picture a people living under
tyranny, with a paranoid Pharaoh oppressing the ethnic Hebrew
minority in his country. He has ordered that every Hebrew male child
shall be thrown into the Nile (1.22). Jochebed (her name is not given
until 6.20 – perhaps omitting it here emphasizes her obscurity) trusts
her son not to the Nile but to God the Nile's creator, in the little
basket she has made (v. 3). Sister Miriam observes what happens. We
do not miss the irony in v. 9 where the Egyptian court ends up paying
a woman to nurse her own child who will one day, under God, set his
people free. On one side of the equation is a despotic king. On the
other side is an oppressed woman, her daughter and God (for who
else moved Pharaoh's daughter to have pity on a Hebrew baby boy?).
Without Jochebed's actions there would have been no Moses and no
deliverance from Egypt.

1 Samuel 1.20–28

One difficulty in preaching from this reading is that it requires
prefacing with some of the information in ch. 1 concerning the
circumstances surrounding Samuel's birth. We must be careful not to
give the impression that childlessness is a disaster or a punishment
from which a woman needs to be delivered. It was indeed so regarded
within the social structure of ancient Israel but this forms no part of
Christian thinking. Our preaching must be sensitive to pastoral
issues. Some people are unable to have children and it is a source of
great sadness; others deliberately choose to be childless and it is a
valid Christian choice. But perhaps that is a problem with Mothering
Sunday itself, not just this lection. At any rate, we need not hold
Hannah up as a model of submissive motherhood. Elkanah was not
consulted when Hannah made her vow (1.11) nor when she named
her child (v. 20). He was informed, rather than asked, when the time
came for the vow to be fulfilled (v. 22), and vv. 24–28 suggest that
Hannah alone took Samuel to Shiloh (though see 2.11). It seems to us
to be an extraordinary sacrifice on her part. So it was, but there is
more to it than the commonplace (though true) observation that the

ultimate parental duty is to provide for children and then let them go. Samuel would never cease to be Hannah's child but it was her free choice to lend (v. 28) him to God for the service of others. Does this lection really belong to Vocations Sunday?

2 Corinthians 1.3–7

Many of the conversations which take place over coffee after worship, and on other occasions when Christians gather to talk, are about children and grandchildren. Often it is about their success stories: how well they are doing at school or university or in their chosen professions. Others are excluded from such conversations for they have no such stories to tell. The woman whose daughter died of a drugs overdose at seventeen cannot share in that conversation, nor can the man whose son has not worked since he left school, nor the couple whose grandchild was born with cerebral palsy. So this reading, which at first sight seems as strange a choice as could possibly be made for Mothering Sunday, might enable us to deal with how Christians are supported and support one another. Granted that Paul is probably writing primarily about the sufferings that come as a result of being a Christian, what he says is more widely applicable to 'all' our afflictions (v. 4). God is the 'God of all consolation' (v. 3) or, in the fine REB rendering, 'the God whose consolation never fails us!' We, in turn, are enabled to support others in their need (v. 4). Verses 5–7 show how strong was Paul's understanding of the Church as a body whose members belong to each other and truly share each other's pains and sorrows. In order for that to happen there has to be an openness about the pain. Some of those who tell of their children and grandchildren's successes will sometimes add, 'But I'm afraid they don't go to church any more.' There is pain there too, for they may be counting themselves failures as Christian parents.

Colossians 3.12–17

Although this passage has primary reference to relationships within the Church (the 'one body' of v. 15), it has found widespread favour in recent years as a reading for the marriage service. The virtues it commends are clearly applicable within home and family as well as within the wider community. It uses 'putting on' and 'taking off' imagery which had wide currency at the time to denote initiation into a religion, but which in the Pauline tradition 'indicates the change of lordship that has taken place through baptism' (Roy Yates). The moral qualities of v. 12 might profitably be spelled out. 'Compassion' means literally 'a heart of pity', and encourages us to reach out to those around us who are in need. 'Kindness' is an attitude which reflects the attitude of God towards human beings (see Luke 6.35). 'Humility' is as misunderstood today as it was in the ancient world, where it was not counted a virtue at all. Matthew has Jesus describe himself in this way (Matthew 11.29). It is essentially about an appropriate attitude towards oneself (see Romans 12.3). 'Meekness' is also often misunderstood: it has nothing to do with being a doormat for others to walk on, but everything to do with what has been described as 'restrained strength'. 'Patience' is about a willingness to endure wrong without the anger and resentment which eat into the character. Verse 13 urges mutual forgiveness in language reminiscent of the Lord's Prayer, and v. 14 tells us that 'above all' we must be clothed in love, which holds all the other virtues together and without which they are worth nothing (1 Corinthians 13). God in Christ is like this, and God's people are called to be like it too, in home, in church and in wider society.

Luke 2.33–35

The context for this reading is explored in the comments on the Gospel on p. 17. The present lection begins abruptly and requires some prior introduction. Verse 33 strikes a very human note. Parents often *are* amazed at what is said about their children, which might suggest a way of entering into the reading. Despite Mary having already been told of the significance of their child (1.31–33) with a matching announcement to Joseph in Matthew's story (Matthew 1.20–21), Simeon's song of thanksgiving reawakens their sense of wonder. Yet Simeon's prophecy (vv. 34–35) introduces the idea that this child will be a source of division and that his mission will be opposed as much, or more, than it will be welcomed. It also makes plain that pain will come to Mary personally (v. 35b). The alternative Gospel reading for today tells us of the final fulfilment of that prophecy, but Luke's Gospel does not have that story. However, we can begin to understand what Simeon means when we read the story in Luke 8.19–21 where (despite Luke having toned down the incident as it appears in Mark 3.31–35), there is still a strong hint that Jesus' mission is taking him away from his natural family and into a new set of relationships. If there is joy in being a parent, there is also often pain. When children go their own way and that way is radically different from that of their parents, there can be a sense of rejection and loss. Today's preaching might explore this.

John 19.25–27

Mary's inclusion in the group near the cross primarily indicates her faithfulness to Jesus right to the bitter end. This, rather than the fact of being his mother, is why she is always found with those who 'believe'. This scene refers us back to Luke 2.35, though the Fourth Gospel does not know that story. In vv. 26–27 Jesus tenderly arranges for Mary to be looked after, but more is implied. In the words of Barnabas Lindars, 'What is actually said is that they should be in a new relationship. His mother loses her Son, but she gains a new son, one who most fully knows the mind of the Son she has lost.' Christian devotion has often made much of Mary at the cross, not least in the *Stabat Mater*, a thirteenth-century poem which has received many musical settings. Two lines from that may suggest a way of preaching on this lection:

> Jesus, may her deep devotion
> Stir in me the same emotion.

FIFTH SUNDAY IN LENT

First Sunday of the Passion

Jeremiah 31.31–34

The covenant Jeremiah has in mind in v. 32 is the one made at Sinai. That only applied so long as the Israelites faithfully kept their side of it. They did not; they 'broke' it and it had therefore lapsed. What was to replace it? Jeremiah promises a new covenant initiated by God (v. 31). There was no point in reinstating the old covenant, which Israel had shown herself incapable of keeping, nor in initiating a new covenant on the same terms as the old. Something revolutionary was required and v. 33b points to what this is: in the new covenant God will write his law on people's *hearts*. This means that God will act to make possible a change in people's nature – compare this with 17.9! God will bring about a new community where obedience will be second nature. This is not about 'inward' as opposed to 'outward' religion: Jeremiah is still concerned about an obedient community. The aim is 'to re-programme the will' (Henry McKeating) and this will be God's gracious work. In Pascal's phrase, 'grace gives what it demands.' Jesus is reported at the Last Supper as having inaugurated a covenant/new covenant in his blood and the Letter to the Hebrews sees Jesus as the mediator of a new covenant. Perhaps the real question preaching must address is why, if Christians are the people of the 'new covenant', the heartfelt obedience which Jeremiah envisaged being at its core is not more evident among us.

Hebrews 5.5–10

This passage is about Christ as our high priest. Earlier, the writer has argued that a priest requires (a) sensitivity to those he represents and (b) calling from God (vv. 1–4). Now he picks up the second of those and argues that Jesus was appointed by God as 'high priest' (vv. 5–6, 10). Those who have accepted Jesus as God's Son must also accept him as God's high priest. Verses 7–8 refer back to the first qualification a priest requires and argues that Jesus fulfilled this as well. Many have found these verses difficult. But if Jesus was truly human, even if without sin, he had to experience what it is like to be a sinful human being with all the shame and guilt that involves. And if we are to believe that he can help us now, we have to know that he experienced it. Most commentators point to Jesus' time in

Gethsemane, where the response of obedience came only as part of a prolonged personal struggle (Mark 14.32–36). There is a strong hint of this in today's Gospel too. It is in this sense that Jesus had to learn obedience through what he suffered (v. 8b). If as is likely, some of the readers of this letter were tempted to renounce their faith in order to escape suffering, even martyrdom, then knowing that Jesus had been there before them and won through would be very important. So it is for us when we are tested and prayer seems unanswered.

John 12.20–33

The opening verses show the Gentile world seeking Jesus as the hour of his passion approaches – they are included in the 'much fruit' of v. 24. 'The hour has come . . .' in v. 23 is very significant. Humanly speaking the die has been cast (John 11.53, 57). Whereas in the synoptic gospels suffering and glory are different things, for John the suffering of Jesus *is* his glorification; this is why he has come, that the world might be saved through him. Yet it is still real suffering, involving humiliation and an appalling death. Verse 27 is John's equivalent of Gethsemane, briefly voiced but agonizingly felt. NRSV very unhelpfully obscures this by putting the question mark after '. . . save me from this hour', as if Jesus was wondering whether this was an appropriate thing to say. The question mark belongs after 'should I say?' because it involves a real wrestling with his destiny. Jesus is able to understand the voice from heaven (v. 28) whereas the crowd hear only the sound. Some still recognize that it is a divine communication, but Jesus does not need it – he has come through, learned obedience, and understands the Father's will in what will happen. We too would see Jesus, the Jesus who faces all this for us. See further the comments on the Gospel on p. 69.

SIXTH SUNDAY IN LENT

Second Sunday of the Passion or Palm Sunday

Entry into Jerusalem

Mark 11.1–11

There are two related difficulties in preaching on Mark's account of this event. The first lies in keeping the other accounts out of our minds. The second is that if the worship has been arranged to celebrate a 'triumphal procession', perhaps including a donkey and palm-waving, it will be at odds with the tone and purpose of Mark's writing. The preparations are described in unusual detail (vv. 1–6). It is probably pointless to speculate about whether prior arrangements were made or whether Jesus is shown here as having supernatural knowledge, though Mark's language rather suggests the latter. In view of the reticence in this Gospel about who Jesus really is, what is striking is that he now takes the initiative for something which can be interpreted as a 'messianic event', however low-key. The final part of a pilgrimage to Jerusalem was normally undertaken on foot. By riding in, Jesus certainly makes a public statement about his messiahship, but a somewhat enigmatic one. Did the crowd think they were hailing a Messiah, or an honoured prophet and teacher? We cannot know, though the cloaks and branches have been compared to coronation customs (2 Kings 9.13), and to the triumphal entry of Simon Maccabeus and his followers into Jerusalem (1 Maccabees 13.51). The crowd shouts 'Hosanna!' which means 'save, now', but which by this time had become just a jubilant cry and is meant as such here. The rest of the citation from Psalm 118.25–26 suggests that the one who comes is also the one who brings the 'coming kingdom' with him. Jesus makes no acknowledgment of the greetings and is silent throughout. He is indeed entering Jerusalem as the coming Messiah, but this is not evident except to those who (like Mark's readers) have the faith to see it. There is no response either from the religious authorities or the Roman garrison. Commentators usually say that the story just fizzles out, but that is wrong: v. 11 is crucial. In Mark this is an entry not just into the city, but into the temple. Jesus looks round, not like a tourist, but as the one who has come to inspect what is rightfully his (Malachi 3.1), the religious significance of which will be changed beyond imagining by the events of the next few days.

John 12.12–16

In John the crowds, not Jesus, take the initiative (vv. 12–13) and they are responding to the raising of Lazarus (12.10–11). Only John specifies 'palm' branches. This may be because they were a symbol of national independence (see 1 Maccabees 13.51; 2 Maccabees 10.7). Here, Jesus himself finds the 'young donkey' and sits on it. No 'entry' into Jerusalem is described. The incident is focused on the action of Jesus in sitting on the animal. Despite what is often said, the point is not that his choice of a donkey over a horse symbolizes humility. In the Near East donkeys were regularly ridden by royalty, horses being reserved for battles. That seems to be precisely the point. The choice of a donkey symbolizes not humility, but peace. Zechariah 9.9, also quoted by Matthew and Luke, has in the same context the promise, 'He will cut off . . . the warhorse from Jerusalem', and continues, 'and he shall command peace to the nations' (Zechariah 9.10). Jesus demonstrates that he comes not as a nationalist Messiah, but as Prince of Peace. What is that going to be, we might ask, to set beside the might of Rome? But God's reign in human hearts has nothing to do with coercion or force. A church which has known power and privilege often finds it difficult to come to terms with loss of these things. This story helps us explore the paradox that humility is true greatness and peaceableness is true victory. Have we understood these things and taken them to heart (v. 16)?

SIXTH SUNDAY IN LENT

Second Sunday of the Passion or Palm Sunday

The Passion

Isaiah 50.4–9a

This servant song expresses the prophet's feelings as he reflects on his mission which originates in God's empowering (vv. 4a, 5a). NRSV indicates that in v. 4, 'tongue of a teacher' is a conjectural reading and that the Hebrew has 'tongue of those who are taught'. But the Hebrew makes good sense as it stands and the conjecture is unnecessary. JB's 'a disciple's tongue' captures the meaning well: what the prophet has to share is wise and informed because it expresses what has been learned from God. Indeed, God is then pictured awakening his hearing each morning so that he, as God's prophet, may understand what his message is to be. But delivering that message has brought its share of suffering at the hands of an ungrateful people (v. 6). Despite that, he has persevered ('set my face like flint', v. 7b) and is confident that God will defend and vindicate him before his enemies (vv. 8–9a). All this expresses a recurring biblical theme in the stories of the prophets and religious leaders. We are not therefore surprised when we also find it in the life and ministry of Jesus. He came announcing that the reign of God had 'come near' with him (Mark 1.15), and as the story unfolds we increasingly realize that it has come near *in* him. However, his mission provokes growing opposition and rejection. As the cross draws nearer it becomes clear that it is not a bolt from the blue but the inevitable consequence of how the story has unfolded. Jesus does not shrink from this, but on the contrary, sets his face like a flint to meet it (see Luke 9.51). When the vindication comes it is in the way he appears to have expected, but could not have guaranteed (Mark 8.31). In that sense this servant song truly points forward to the Christ event.

Philippians 2.5–11

Scholars are agreed that this is a very early Christian hymn, which Paul has adapted. Its precise form and shape need not concern us here, but that fact is a reminder that this is essentially the language of poetry rather than of theological argument. In the way in which Paul presents it, it is a celebration of all that God has done in Christ. If we preach on this lection we need to expound the entire passage because it takes in the entire sweep of divine grace. Verses 6–7a celebrate Christ's existence with God before the incarnation, a conviction which is found elsewhere in the New Testament in different words (John 1.1–3; Hebrews 1.2; 1 Corinthians 8.6), and which stems from identifying Christ with the divine Wisdom of the Old Testament (Proverbs 3.19 and elsewhere). But he did not then regard this relationship with God as something for himself alone. He 'emptied himself' (which probably means that he became weak and powerless, rather than that he divested himself of all divine attributes), and took the form of a servant. In Kenneth Grayston's fine phrase, 'He was not simply the servant of the Lord, but the Lord as a servant.' Verses 7b–8 celebrate his earthly life, born in the way all human beings are born (see Galatians 4.4), but then living a life of obedience, not centred on himself but devoted to the needs of others. His life of obedience to his Father's will leads inexorably to a criminal's death on the cross, described by the Roman Cicero as 'the most cruel and abominable form of punishment'. Verse 9 celebrates the reversal of all this. God has 'exalted' him (through the resurrection and ascension) and bestowed on him the name that is above every name. This 'name' is almost certainly not 'Jesus', it is 'Lord', as v. 11 shows. 'Jesus is Lord' was the earliest Christian confession of faith. If it is true, then it has implications not just for Christians but for the whole created order. We could easily miss the depths of what is said in vv. 10–11. This passage is derived from Isaiah ch. 45, in which God repeatedly emphasizes that he alone is the Lord. Here in v. 11, words which are used in Isaiah 45.23 of God alone, are used of Jesus Christ. This, Paul says, will one day be acknowledged by the entire created order ('in heaven, on earth and under the earth'). Does v. 11 contain a hint of universalism? Might it be that one day all will find salvation by acknowledging the Lordship of Christ, even if they do not do so now? It is just possible to read it in that way, but it is more likely that Paul is saying that everything will become subject to the Lordship of Christ. However that may be, we wonder at this profound conviction of Christ's universal reign, which seems to us so far from being achieved. Yet the logic of the sweep of divine grace as celebrated in this passage can lead nowhere else and it fits with Mark's account of the crucifixion as the final revelation of who Jesus really is. When this was written Christianity was a tiny religious movement in a pagan world. Humanly speaking it must have seemed even less likely to have such a fulfilment than it does today.

Mark 14.1–15.47 or Mark 15.1–39 (40–47)

It is an ancient tradition to read the whole of a passion narrative at the beginning of Holy Week. In this way we experience the wholeness and interconnections of the narrative and have it in our minds as we explore different parts of it during the week ahead. It is also a very sensible thing to do, because we know from experience that many worshippers will not attend all, or perhaps any, of the Holy Week services. They may therefore come on Easter Sunday to celebrate the resurrection without having either heard the passion story or reflected on it, which rather misses the point. However, a congregation needs to be prepared for such a long reading, which is very different from the short chunks in which the Lectionary normally presents the Bible. The interconnection of the themes means that the longer of the two options is preferable.

It is clearly not possible to offer detailed comments on this passage here. Instead, we reflect on a couple of the most prominent themes emphasized in Mark's presentation. Throughout this Gospel we have met the 'messianic secret', where those who know the real identity of Jesus are silenced, and Jesus never claims any title for himself. But at 14.61–62 this silence is broken dramatically and decisively. It is a moment of revelation which is picked up again in 15.30–32 where Mark (who often employs irony) offers us the supreme irony that Jesus' enemies, in complete ignorance, tell the truth – that he is both Messiah and King of Israel. What is happening here, then, is no ordinary death; these things interpret the crucifixion itself, which Mark tells briefly and with no comment (15.25–27). We now know who is on trial and as we see him undergoing suffering and death in fulfilment of his own intention (10.45) we realize Mark is pointing to Jesus on his cross and saying to us, 'This is what God is like.' Ironically again, the final (correct) judgment is given by the Roman centurion (15.39), but what has happened has redefined what it means to be God/God's Son. We now know that it means to share every aspect of human mortality, in order to redeem. Another important theme is that of discipleship. The constant interaction between Jesus and his disciples is crucial in Mark. They almost always fail him, and fail to understand. They include the traitor (14.18–21) and they fail in Gethsemane (14.37–42). The story of Peter's denials shows this supremely (14.66–72), following on his earlier protestations (14.29). And so there is not a single disciple at the cross. It is ironic, though appropriate, that only the women are there, even if in the distance (15.40–41). It was an unnamed woman who best demonstrated what discipleship is about, when, in Morna Hooker's words, she 'anointed him Messiah, proclaimed his death and resurrection and made an act of total commitment to him as Lord' (14.3–9). Our world finds it no easier than did the world of two thousand years ago to understand how we can best see the nature of the eternal God 'in a criminal crucified' (G. A. Studdert Kennedy). This is the 'scandal' of the cross and there is no evading it, either in our discipleship or in our preaching.

MONDAY IN HOLY WEEK

Isaiah 42.1–9

This servant song may have referred originally to Cyrus, King of the Persians who, in conquering Babylon, brought freedom to the Jewish exiles. Like other such passages it is not a prophecy waiting to be fulfilled but a statement of what God will do for his people through his servant. As God's purposes in salvation are eternal, the Christian Church has not been wrong to think that in the deepest sense such passages from the Hebrew scriptures come to rest in Jesus who both exemplifies and surpasses what is in them. This passage has a strong concern for justice (vv. 2b, 3b, 4a) and liberation for the oppressed (v. 7). Nothing is said about how the servant will achieve this, though the imagery of v. 3 suggests a special care for the weak and vulnerable. Above all, he will be a 'light to the nations' (v. 6b), thus carrying out the responsibility which had once been the very reason for Israel's election. He does this because he is God's 'chosen' (v. 1). Of course, we rightly think of a 'chosen one' (Mark 1.11) whose task is to be a light to the nations (Luke 2.32). This may prompt us to reflect on the way in which the ministry of Jesus made no use of those things which normally ensure power and influence, but spoke instead of the reverse of the world's values (e.g. Matthew 5.1–12).

Hebrews 9.11–15

The previous ten verses supply a background necessary to understand the point of this lection. The context is worship under the 'old covenant', familiar to the first readers, who were Jewish Christians. There are strong hints in the letter that some of them were tempted to revert to Judaism and the writer is concerned throughout to show the superiority of the 'new covenant' inaugurated in Christ. He writes about Jewish worship, only to say in v. 11 that it has been surpassed. The details of the argument (which are quite hard to grasp) need not greatly concern us once we realize that the writer is arguing that Christ entered into heaven (the meaning of 'the Holy Place' in v. 12 – see v. 24) bearing not the blood of sacrificed animals, but 'his own blood' (v. 12). His blood is not something separate from himself: it is his life, offered in sacrifice. And unlike the old sacrifices which needed to be repeated, this obtains 'eternal redemption' (v. 12). The effect is that we are purified in our conscience (v. 14), which means that we are cleansed of our guilt. We do not share the assumptions of the first readers of this letter about sacrifice. Language about being 'washed in the blood of the Lamb', so dear to a former generation, sounds quite repugnant to most people today. Nevertheless we need to hold on to, and find some way of re-expressing, the important truth that Christ's self-offering on Calvary is a once-for-all action of cosmic significance, the benefits of which are available afresh in each generation.

John 12.1–11

This passage is very difficult in several respects. It is impossible to suppose it narrates an anointing different from that recorded in Mark 14.3–9 (= Matthew 26.6–13) though it differs in significant details. Here it is Mary, rather than an unknown woman, who anoints Jesus' feet rather than his head (one of several details which better correspond to the different story in Luke 7.36–50). If we preach on this account, we might concentrate on the way in which Jesus sees this act of expensive devotion as prophetic of his death (v. 7), thus justifying the extravagance (v. 8 – see Mark 2.19–20). Jesus' statement in v. 8 is subject to much misunderstanding, and is sometimes quoted to justify lack of concern for the poor. It is quite the opposite; the quotation comes from Deuteronomy 15.11 where it is immediately followed by 'Open your hand to the poor and needy neighbour in your land.' This tension sometimes surfaces in church life when it is proposed to spend a considerable sum on something for the church – a new organ, perhaps. There will always be voices which insist that it is wrong to do this when there are people in dire need. Other voices will point to Jesus' rebuke, offered to Judas, not Mary! How does this story help us?

TUESDAY IN HOLY WEEK

Isaiah 49.1–7

This 'servant song' appears to be addressed to the whole nation (v. 3), but there are difficulties with this view and some scholars argue either for a 'remnant' within Israel or an individual. None of this greatly affects the interpretation. The servant was called before he was born (v. 1b), which mirrors the call of Jeremiah (Jeremiah 1.5). In v. 2 he says that God made him fit for his task and then hid him away until he was needed (compare Galatians 4.4). Verse 3 points to the way in which the servant fulfils God's purposes through his calling, and v. 4 to both the difficulty of prophetic faithfulness and to ultimate trust in God. The calling of the servant is laid out in v. 4: it is to bring Israel back to God. From Moses onwards this was almost always the purpose of the prophets' work. For Deutero-Isaiah it had meaning in the setting of God's people being called back to the promised land from their years of exile. Calling them back from sinful ways, to receive God's forgiveness and begin afresh, was bound up with that task. Now, however, there is a greater task: the servant's mission goes beyond the ancient covenant people of God. Verse 6b holds out the great vision that God's salvation will reach out to embrace the whole earth, as God had always intended. Christians will find no difficulty in claiming that in Christ this intention has been fulfilled (John 1.4b, 12.32).

1 Corinthians 1.18–31

For the first part of this lection see also the comments on the Epistle on p. 50. God has turned all our human values inside out, because it is through the cross, the last place anyone would have thought of looking for it, that the revelation of God's nature as suffering love is revealed. Human speculation about God has often concluded that God will remain forever hidden from us, shrouded in mystery far beyond our reach. By contrast Paul tells us that God is anything but unknowable. God has revealed himself, though in the last place human wisdom would have thought of looking. What God has revealed is that he is self-giving love to an extent we could never have imagined. Moreover, such reversal of the world's values and expectations is mirrored in those who have responded to the gospel and become members of the Church. 'Not many' (he does not say 'not any') of them were wise, powerful or socially significant in society (v. 26). It was the least and lowest who could perceive the paradoxical wisdom and strength of God where others were perhaps too proud or blind to look (v. 27). They know, none better, that they have nothing to boast of except what God has done for them in Christ (vv. 29, 31). Christ has become for them, the wisdom, righteousness, sanctification and redemption they could have had in no other way (v. 30). As we turn our eyes towards the cross, we need to see in what Christ did there the source of all our true knowledge of God and evaluate everything else we have and are in that perspective.

John 12.20–36

See the comments on the Gospel on p. 59. As the time of his death draws near, Jesus gives voice to a shout of agony, 'Father, save me from this hour', but much as he longs for such deliverance, he knows that if he is to be obedient to the Father's will it cannot come. Yet through his death the Father will be glorified (vv. 27–28). He does not need the reassurance of the voice from heaven (v. 30), but he does interpret what is to take place as a cosmic conflict in which the 'ruler of this world' will be defeated (v. 31). The defeat will be total, for when Jesus is 'lifted up from the earth' (a description both of the act of crucifixion and the 'exaltation' this will mean for him) he will draw 'all people' or 'all things' to himself (v. 32). Jesus will now be the ruler not only of this world but of all worlds (Philippians 2.9–11). As his 'public' ministry draws to an end his last word is about walking in the light (v. 35) and believing in the light (v. 36). In the Fourth Gospel the light is always Jesus himself.

WEDNESDAY IN HOLY WEEK

Isaiah 50.4–9a

For this reading see the comments on the Old Testament on p. 62.

Hebrews 12.1–3

It is always unsatisfactory to begin a reading with 'therefore'! In what precedes it the writer has been reflecting on some of the great men and women of faith in Israel's history and has indicated that, despite their great faith, they did not receive everything which was promised – there was something better to come. In v. 1 he pictures that great 'cloud of witnesses' who have their own testimony to bear to God's faithfulness, encouraging us by their presence in the 'race that is set before us' in which we need to be unencumbered by any handicap. But v. 1 is really a slight digression; the point is that we need to look to Jesus 'the pioneer and perfecter of our faith' (v. 2), who is, of course, the 'something better' that was to come. In what sense is Jesus a 'pioneer' of faith for those who lived before him? The writer is probably again thinking of the 'pre-existence' of Christ, a conviction already expressed at Hebrews 1.2, and elsewhere in the New Testament in different words (John 1.1–3; 1 Corinthians 8.6). If so, he thinks of Christ leading God's people along the path of faith even before becoming incarnate in Jesus of Nazareth (a similar thought is found in 1 Corinthians 10.4b). Now that he has appeared in the flesh, he is also the 'perfecter' of our faith, in that having 'endured the cross' he has now taken his rightful place (v. 2). Hebrews has already reminded us of the human struggle through which Jesus went in order to be obedient to God's will (see the comments on the Epistle on p. 58). If we ask what is this 'joy' which motivated Jesus to endure the cross (v. 2), an answer might be found in those Johannine passages where Jesus expresses a deep desire to share his joy with others (John 15.11; 17.13). Whether or not this is exactly what Hebrews has in mind, it is surely true that in opening a new and living way into God's presence for us he does indeed share his joy with us.

John 13.21–32

It is tempting to preach on the human motivation of Judas. The question is, after all, of considerable interest: why did Judas betray Jesus? Numerous answers have been attempted (including the one made popular by William Barclay, that Judas was hoping to provoke Jesus into leading an uprising, for which there is no evidence whatsoever). We indulge in such speculation because the question troubles us and we are reluctant to accept that none of the Gospels provide us with the material which could help us answer it. Even though John goes so far as to say that Judas was a thief (12.6) he does not make greed his motive. There is a lesson to be learned from what John does say. As Gerard Sloyan puts it, 'John situates the struggle on higher ground: the all-holy God challenged by the ruler of this world through a contemptible weakling.' This, unpalatable though it may be, is what is clearly meant at 13.2 and 13.27, and nothing is said about why Judas allowed himself to be thus persuaded. Verses 21–22 come into sharp focus: when Jesus makes his announcement each of the disciples wonders, 'Is he referring to me?'– a point made even more explicitly in the synoptics (Mark 14.19 = Matthew 26.22). We would be wise to ask ourselves the same question, to reflect as the hour of the passion approaches, on our own lesser, but very real, betrayals of Christ. When we give space in our hearts for the 'ruler of this world' to direct our values we are, however unwittingly, among the betrayers. When Judas had accepted the dipped bread (a final plea for loyalty?) he went out into a darkness which John surely intends us to understand was more than physical (v. 30). The final train of events had been set in motion and this leads into the passage which shows us more clearly than any other that for the Fourth Gospel the crucifixion of Jesus is his 'glorification', the time when he will do the will of God utterly and completely (vv. 31–32).

MAUNDY THURSDAY

Exodus 12.1–4 (5–10) 11–14

The conviction that God had delivered them out of slavery in Egypt by miraculous means was central to Israel's sense of calling as God's people. Death and destruction would 'pass through' the land of Egypt, but it would 'pass over' them (vv. 12–13). Exodus tells us how this was to be marked by a special meal, the 'Egyptian Passover' as it was called later. An essentially domestic occasion (v. 4) it nevertheless involved the entire community (v. 3). It celebrated the hour of the nation's birth and God's power in the defeat of the false Egyptian gods (v. 12b). They are commanded to continue to hold this meal as a 'perpetual ordinance' (v. 14) and to explain its significance afresh in every generation (12.26–27). If the Egyptian Passover became part of their religious identity, the continuing annual observance became both a celebration of what God had done in the past and a means of renewing that relationship. If we take this reading along with today's Epistle we may reflect on the way in which the Lord's Supper shapes and constitutes the identity of the Christian community. Part of its significance is the celebration of what God has done in human history for our salvation and deliverance. This too requires interpreting and reappropriating afresh in every generation.

1 Corinthians 11.23–26

Paul's account of the institution of the Eucharist is the earliest we possess. He handed on the tradition of observing the meal to his converts in Corinth having, as he says, received it from the Lord (v. 23), which probably means that he was taught it after his conversion by those who could be trusted, rather than that he had received it in a revelation. Paul's tradition represents Jesus as commanding his followers to 'do this in remembrance of me' (vv. 24–25), as if paralleling the command about the Passover (Exodus 12.14). The phrases 'this is my body' and 'this cup is the new covenant in my blood' are central to Paul as to the synoptics. Whether or not the Last Supper was a Passover meal, the association between the sayings over the bread and wine and the coming death of Jesus is unmistakable. All the accounts of the Last Supper were written after the resurrection but Paul's account shows the greatest awareness of this. His converts are not simply re-enacting the Last

...me the Lord's Supper where the risen Christ ... o do this 'in remembrance' of Jesus is our ... who once died for us is now present with us. ... feast' as Charles Wesley put it. As such the ... in hope, sustaining our faith and Christian ... nent (v. 26).

...ast Supper has no institution narrative, but ... washing the disciples' feet. Here we see the ... (Philippians 2.6–7). The passage offers two ... means. The first comes during the exchange ... embarrassed Peter (vv. 6–10); it is about ... sus, being cleansed and purified by him (a ... with the conversation in Mark 10.38–39). In ... on narrative this must mean receiving the cleansing benefits of his death. It is almost certainly wrong to look for a direct reference to baptism in this passage, though in view of the way the New Testament develops baptismal theology (e.g. Romans 6.3–11) the theme cannot be excluded in preaching. The second explanation comes in vv. 12ff where Jesus commends what he has done as an example of the unselfconscious service which must characterize his followers. The rather self-conscious reintroduction in recent years of a ceremony in which the worship leader washes people's feet during the Maundy Thursday liturgy must not become a substitute for what Jesus clearly intends as an entire way of life for them (v. 17). Verses 34–35 introduce the 'new commandment'. What is new here? Probably that the mutual love between believers has to be measured by the standard of Jesus' love for them (v. 1b). That will go far beyond 'footwashing', though including it; 1 John 3.16 is probably the best commentary on these verses.

GOOD FRIDAY

Isaiah 52.13–53.12

It is unclear to what extent the servant who is the subject of this poem was thought of as a Messiah figure before the time of Jesus. The earlier New Testament documents reach their conclusions about the vicarious suffering and death of Jesus with virtually no reference to it. But once the early Christians realized its significance it became a very important passage. After many centuries of such Christian use we find it almost impossible to read it in any way other than as a reflection on the story of Jesus. There is no problem with this: the prophet has seen deep into the heart of vicarious suffering as a way in which God is revealed. This insight will indeed reach its fullest expression in the death of Christ. In 52.13–15 God introduces his servant by contrasting his true greatness (vv. 13, 15) with his disfigured appearance (v. 14). Isaiah 53.1–6 seem to be spoken by observers making a report, deeply involved in what they describe. At first (vv. 2–3) they describe the servant's suffering, which is both physical and mental, so extreme that people ostracize him. This might be thought to invite (say) pity, but no! In vv. 4–6 they (perhaps the entire community) recognize that through the suffering one they are healed and forgiven. Isaiah 53.7–12 begins with reflections from the prophet but from v. 11b onwards God offers direct comment. In vv. 7–9 the servant's unmerited suffering, and death as a common criminal, are the topics. Verse 9 makes it plain that he really died and v. 10 interprets that death. This is 'an offering for sin'; somehow, through this death, God has done something for his people that they were unable to do for themselves. Some have pointed to the way Moses was subject to the anger of God because of what others had done (Deuteronomy 3.26) or to the function of the scapegoat (Leviticus 16.22), but these hardly meet the case. This passage goes far beyond anything else we find in the Old Testament in working through how God can use unmerited suffering and death for redemptive purposes. Sometimes, Christians have been very sure that they knew precisely how this works, but there is a reticence in this passage which is important. The Church has wisely never insisted on any particular understanding of the atonement as orthodoxy. What matters is that like the community of 53.1–6, we experience ourselves as healed and forgiven.

Hebrews 10.16–25

That Jesus is our high priest whose death on the cross constitutes such a perfect offering that it has for ever done away with the old sacrifices and the old priesthood, is an argument that runs throughout the first ten chapters of this letter. It reaches a conclusion in vv. 16–18 where, after quoting from Jeremiah's promise of a new covenant, the author asserts that where there is forgiveness for sins (as there is now through Jesus), there is no longer any need to make an offering for sin. What difference might this make to us? Simply that we can have 'confidence' (v.19) to enter 'the sanctuary' (which means the presence of God). Those who are deeply conscious of personal sin or unworthiness, and wonder about their acceptability to God, certainly need to hear this message. By and large however, we live in a society where, for all sorts of reasons, most people don't find this a problem. The three exhortations which follow may still be thought helpful. The first is to 'approach . . . in full assurance of faith'. As we come to God we can be sure of being provided with spiritual resources to sustain our Christian journey. This is shown by our baptism, which is both a washing of the body with water and a cleansing of our hearts (v. 22). The second is to 'hold fast to the confession of our hope' (v. 23). Some of the readers were in danger of not holding fast, but of sliding away from their Christian faith. This is sadly true of some contemporary congregations, especially among our young people. If Hebrews is right, what is at stake is not just a change of lifestyle choice but the prospective loss of that relationship with God which alone brings proper hope for the future. The third exhortation is that we should 'consider how to provoke one another to love and good deeds' (v. 24). Love and good deeds should be the consequences of Christian profession (James 2.14–16) and our author suggests that we serve one another well when we 'provoke' (the word is a strong one) each other about such matters. In order for this to happen, of course, it is necessary that people should meet regularly together for worship and fellowship and not imagine that they can be Christians all on their own (v. 25).

Hebrews 4.14–16; 5.7–9

The risen and ascended Jesus, God's Son, is our 'high priest' who intercedes with God on our behalf. He understands what we go through in the way of trials, temptations and weaknesses, since he has been through all this as well. This gives us confidence to approach

God, from whom we find not judgment and punishment but mercy and grace when we most need it (4.16). 'There is a human being in heaven,' cried Martin Luther, and this is one of the foundations of our Christian hope. Hebrews 5.7–9 stress the humanity of Jesus. Jesus goes through all that we face, is in agony about it, and obedience is a struggle. This directly addresses our human condition in which suffering is often totally unsought, very real and tests us up to or, as we most fear, even beyond the limit to which faith can go. God has been there too, Hebrews tells us. For further remarks on 5.7–9 see the comments on the Epistle on p. 58.

John 18.1–19.42

Comparison with any of the other Gospels quickly reveals how different is John's account of the passion of Christ. It is not just that there are many differences of detail and emphasis (most notably the separate appearances before Annas and Caiaphas) but, what is equally important, the whole tone of John's account is different. This Gospel has already prepared us to see the crucifixion as the time when Jesus will make an act of perfect obedience to the Father, who will be glorified through it (see John 12.27–33 and the comments on the Gospels on pp. 59 and 69). The way in which John now narrates the story itself brings out that particular understanding. The humiliation and the horror are not of course denied (how could they be?), but in a very important sense Jesus is seen as still being in charge. He knows what is going to happen to him (18.4), he firmly resists Peter's futile attempt to stop it happening (18.11), and he says that Pilate only has authority over him because it has been given him 'from above' (19.11). Gethsemane is not a place of agony, but of calm and dignified confrontation with those who have come to arrest him, in which Jesus himself takes the initiative (18.4). Jesus has an innate dignity and authority which communicates itself right from the beginning (18.6). His defence before Annas has the same sense of unassailable dignity and authority (18.20–23), and the defence before Pilate rehearses, in good Johannine terminology, the purpose of the incarnation (18.36–37). John is at pains to stress that Jesus carried his cross 'by himself' (19.17; compare Mark 15.21). Even while nailed to the cross Jesus calmly makes arrangements for Mary to be cared for (19.25–27). He knows when everything necessary has been done (19.28) and in this Gospel there is no cry of dereliction (Mark 15.34 = Matthew 27.46). 'It is finished' is not a cry of despair but a declaration that his self-offering has been made, his full obedience to the Father's purpose in sending him into the world has been accomplished in the way he himself said it would be (John 10.18). So Jesus dies not with a 'loud cry' (Mark 15.37 = Matthew 27.50), but with quiet dignity (19.30). In preaching on almost any aspect of the Johannine passion narrative we are dealing with the portrayal of a pure act of love for a needy world. John stresses the perfect self-giving obedience of the Divine Son. The Son was under no compulsion to become incarnate but, as in R. S. Thomas's poem 'The Coming', looked at the world of human misery and said, 'Let me go there.' On Good Friday we are reminded supremely that the world is embraced by a love which knows no limits and at which we can only wonder and then respond.

HOLY SATURDAY

Job 14.1–14

We must be careful not to tame this passage, tone it down, or read it too readily through the lens of Easter Day. This is part of Job's dispute with God about the sheer injustice of the treatment he has received at God's hand. In cold anger he asks God why, since human life is so short and miserable, God harasses people instead of leaving them alone (vv. 1–3). So far as Job is concerned this life is all that we have. Even trees sprout again after being cut down or after a drought (vv. 7–9), but human beings die and that is the end of them (v. 10). When mortals lie down they do not rise again 'until the heavens are no more' – a condition which, of course, will never be met (v. 12). Even if Job can faintly wish for some kind of life after death (v. 13b) he is not expecting it; the best he can hope for is that he might be hidden in Sheol as a kind of temporary refuge while God's anger lasts (v. 13a). This bleak passage offers several possibilities for preaching. We might enter into the experience of the followers of Jesus who saw him killed and truly believed it was the end of all their hopes (Luke 24.20–21). How could God be so unjust? We might reflect on the way in which belief in any kind of life after death is at a low ebb in our society even, if several surveys are to be trusted, among church-goers. Does Christian faith without that element leave us with something as bleak and despairing as we find here in Job? We might also reflect that for huge numbers of people in our world today human life is still, as Thomas Hobbes described it in 1651, 'solitary, poor, nasty, brutish, and short'. And should not there be anger about that?

Lamentations 3.1–9, 19–24

The Book of Lamentations consists of poems mourning the destruction of Jerusalem in 587 BC. The city is personified, her sufferings described as if they were the sufferings of a single individual left behind in the devastated city after the fit and able had been deported to Babylon. Even though the poet knows that Jerusalem has brought it all on herself through her sin (1.5), this does not lessen the horrible reality of the sufferings she now endures. They are seen as the result of God's wrath, repeatedly expressed (vv. 1–3). Even prayer is impossible in such a situation (v. 8). The poet is brought to the edge of total despair (vv. 19–20). Yet even in the midst of such affliction

78

the last word has not been spoken. What can and must be called to mind (v. 21) is that 'the steadfast love of the Lord never ceases' (v. 22). In other words, the poet recalls the character of God as God's people have always known it to be. Whatever the present appearances, God is really steadfast love, mercy and faithfulness. If that is so, is it not still so, and might it be seen to be so again in the future? Robert Davidson points to the way in which in vv. 23b–24, the poet 'suddenly turns to grasp what is still there, and new day by day'. Therefore, hope for the future must be available even when we cannot see it (v. 24). Dare we say that this is the kind of faith with which Jesus went to the cross? And must we not also say that this is the only kind of faith which is of any use when the afflictions of life (however caused and whatever form they take) overwhelm us? If so, we will remember that it is faith we are talking about, not knowledge. It is about things hoped for, but unseen (Hebrews 11.1), and it is based solely on God's love, mercy and faithfulness, as revealed to us in the life and death of Jesus Christ.

1 Peter 4.1–8

Verses 1–6 are about how Christians should live when their environment is sinful and hostile. The 'therefore' in v.1 refers back to 3.18, but the verse is very difficult. Wayne Grudem suggests that the phrase bracketed in NRSV means 'whoever has suffered for doing right, and has still gone on obeying God in spite of the suffering it involved, has made a clean break with sin.' Verses 3–4 describe how the believers behaved in the past, before they became Christians, and the hostility of their former companions towards their new way of life. But these former companions will also be judged (v. 5). Verse 6 is very obscure. Some scholars think it refers to 3.19 (which may be why this lection is chosen for today), but that interpretation is unlikely (see the comments on the Epistle on p. 46). It probably refers to Christians who died before this letter was written; either way it remains obscure. Verses 7–8 concern life within the Christian community. There is to be a seriousness and discipline about the way life is ordered (v. 7) and the maintaining of 'constant love for one another' is commended 'above all'. That is an issue of perpetual importance to any congregation. An amazing number of problems can be coped with and imaginative ventures in mission can be undertaken when people genuinely love one another. But there seems no obvious reason for preaching on that topic on Holy Saturday.

Matthew 27.57–66

The first five verses of this passage record the burial of Jesus, a story which appears in all four Gospels, which agree on the essential details. In Matthew (as in Mark) there is no anointing of the body – that has been done already (Matthew 26.12) – but there is an emphasis on the part played by the two Marys. Whereas Mark simply says that they saw where the body of Jesus was laid (15.47), Matthew stresses their presence (v. 61) and thus their devotion. It is they who keep Jesus company to the end. There is also no possibility on Easter morning, however dark it was, that they could have mistaken the tomb. Verses 62–66 are a different matter, and occur only in Matthew. The consensus of scholarly opinion is that they are Matthew's invention, designed to ensure that the story related in 28.11–15 is seen to be false right from the start. We have no means of knowing whether or not this is so, but it is interesting that some of the apocryphal writings (the *Gospel of Peter* in particular) have very elaborate versions of this incident in a growing attempt to 'prove' to non-believers that the resurrection was a real historical event. The difficulty with this is, as Eduard Schweizer says, 'Faith dies from proofs, just as true love perishes when it demands proof of another's love.' The risen Jesus will not appear in triumph to his enemies. The only 'proof' of the resurrection will be the redeemed community's experience of his risen life. But for the moment, Jesus has most certainly died and most certainly been safely disposed of. Friend and foe alike are agreed on that, and all are wrong.

John 19.38–42

John's account of the burial of Jesus has several additions to the synoptic record. Only John says that Joseph was a 'secret' disciple (v. 38), and Nicodemus is not involved in the story the synoptics relate. He, of course, only appears in the Fourth Gospel, and the other references are entirely consonant with this one. Following his conversation with Jesus in ch. 3 we find him defending Jesus against unjust accusations from his fellow Pharisees (7.50–51). We are obviously expected to note the huge quantity of spices which he brought (v. 39). This is many times more than would be needed for the burial of one person, however extravagantly they were used. John clearly intends some significance, and the most likely suggestion is that he wants us to think of the burial of Jesus as being like the burial of a king, as indeed it was. In the passion narrative John gives a special solemnity to the trilingual inscription which Pilate had fixed on the cross (compare John 19.19–22 with Matthew 27.37/Luke 23.38). For John, what Pilate had written was, in the deepest sense, the truth. So the corpse of Jesus is not tossed into the common grave reserved for criminals, or left on the cross for the vultures as the Romans often did, but buried in a garden (v. 41) with proper Jewish burial rites, as was only fitting. But however fitting it was, it was still a burial. For everyone involved, the story of Jesus has come to an end.

EASTER DAY

Acts 10.34–43

This passage is the most complete compact summary of the Christian 'good news' in the New Testament. This sermon from Peter makes it quite clear that without the resurrection there would be no good news to proclaim. Also, this sermon is delivered to Cornelius and his household, the first systematic unfolding of the gospel to Gentiles, and is thus a reminder that its truth is universal. These things are highly relevant to Easter Day. Peter tells the story of Jesus, setting it out as a story of salvation, which demands a response. What he says about the resurrection (vv. 40–41) is crucial. Neither then, nor subsequently, did the risen Jesus appear before the Sanhedrin, Pilate, or any of his enemies, as if to say, 'I told you so'. Here, 'not to all the people' is stressed, and the Gospel accounts of the appearances make it plain that they did not *compel* faith (Matthew 28.17). All depends on the credibility of those 'chosen by God as witnesses'. God will not make us believe in the resurrection. But when we find their witness credible (as it surely is), we discover in our own experience that Christ is risen and also learn for ourselves the truth of what Peter told Cornelius: 'everyone who believes in him receives forgiveness of sins through his name' (v. 43). That is the Easter good news.

Isaiah 25.6–9

In this passage Isaiah depicts a banquet which God will give on Mount Zion (v. 1 picks up where 24.23 left off), the holy city of God. But, and this is important, it is not just for God's chosen people the Jews, it is for 'all people' (v. 6a). This universalism is stressed twice in v. 7, where the prophet promises that God will remove the signs of mourning, and twice in v. 8 with the promise that tears and disgrace will be wiped away. Not just mourning but death itself will come to an end (v. 8a). This belief is rare, and late, in the Old Testament, but is clearly stated here, and it makes this passage especially suitable for Easter Day. In 1 Corinthians 15.54 Paul specifically says that the promise Isaiah holds out will be fulfilled when we are raised in the age to come. Verse 9 expresses general rejoicing in God who saves us. This is what the world has been waiting for, even though it may not yet know it.

1 Corinthians 15.1–11

Later in this chapter Paul will deal with people who deny the possibility of resurrection, so he begins by setting out the essential content of Christian faith, from which it is clear that the resurrection is at its heart. There is a tone of reproof in v. 1, which 'remind you' does not quite catch. James Moffatt's 'I would have you know' is better. Nevertheless, what he writes is a reminder of what the Corinthians heard Paul preach when they first believed. If they are still holding firmly to it they will be saved (v. 2). The core of the proclamation is given in vv. 3–4: Christ died for our sins, was buried and was raised, and this is in accordance with the scriptures (which probably means in accordance with the long-term plan of God as the whole of scripture presents it). That the resurrection is an essential part of this is shown by the list of appearances in vv. 5–7. This is not a complete list, and there are some puzzles. Why, for instance, does Paul not mention the women, who were the first to see the risen Lord? Possibly because their testimony was not formally admissible as legal evidence. And we have no canonical record of the appearance to James. The list is given because, although nobody actually saw the resurrection itself, those who testified to the appearances are trustworthy – the implication in v. 6 is that many of them could be questioned about it should the Corinthians so choose. The resurrection is real because the risen Lord appeared again and again. We ought to note how v. 4 says that Christ 'was raised', i.e., by God. That is the way the New Testament writings always put it, though some of our Easter hymns unfortunately give the impression that the resurrection was something Christ did for himself ('Up from the grave he arose'). The resurrection is God's action, God's 'yes' to all that Jesus was, the final vindication of the incarnate and obedient Son. When Paul has added his personal testimony (vv. 8–10), he concludes with the reminder that he and all the other apostles proclaim the same fundamental message, at the heart of which, as he has shown, is the resurrection. Without it there is no living Lord, no good news to be believed. It really is that crucial.

John 20.1–18

When Mary arrives at the tomb she finds it empty. She reports this to Peter and the beloved disciple. The inference is that the body of Jesus has been stolen (v. 2b). The orderly scene they discover when they return (vv. 6–7) makes that very unlikely. The beloved disciple begins to understand what has happened, and so is described as the first believer (v. 8). And yet, both of them return to their homes (v. 10)! It is to Mary that the first resurrection appearance will take place. C. H. Dodd's observation that this passage 'has something indefinably first-hand about it' finds an answering echo from many readers. The description of Mary's distress (vv. 11–13), her initial failure to recognize Jesus (v. 14) or his voice (v. 15), her extravagant offer to take the heavy body away herself (v. 15), all point to the kind of experience people recount of themselves. So does the moment when Jesus speaks her name (v. 16a). Of this moment Lesslie Newbigin says: 'the good shepherd calls his own by name, for he knows them and they know him (10.3, 14).' It is evident that in response Mary took hold of Jesus, as if determined not to let him go again: 'Let go of me', or the NRSV's 'Do not hold on to me', are what Jesus' words in v. 17 mean. Why so? Because Mary (like others, and indeed like us ourselves, as this Gospel will show) must learn that those who 'believe' have a real relationship with Jesus, but it is now different. Empty tomb and appearances alike are signs to lead people into the experience of full communion with Jesus, which will be through the agency of the Spirit. Jesus goes to the Father who, because of what Jesus has accomplished, is 'my Father and your Father/my God and your God'. This message which Mary has to take to the others (v. 17b) puts in a nutshell the difference which Jesus, crucified and risen, has made to the relationship between God and all who 'believe'.

Mark 16.1–8

The two Marys and Salome go to the tomb to anoint the body of Jesus, for which there had been no previous opportunity (v. 1). They are clear that he is dead. They are too late because the body is no longer there. At this point we see the story Mark tells at 14.3–9 in a new light. In Morna Hooker's phrase, 'the women fail to do belatedly what was in fact done by another woman prematurely.' The women were anxious about the 'very large' stone (Mark's emphasis, v. 4), but what happens catches them unprepared. The stone has been rolled back, there is a stranger in the tomb with a message for them. These women are aware that they are in the presence of the transcendent and the divine. They are given a message for the disciples (and Peter, who has denied that he is a disciple – Mark 14.66–72), and it is the beginning of a new call and commission from the risen Lord. Ironically, they are so terrified that they flee and say nothing (v. 8).

Mark stresses the unexpectedness of what happened and the impossibility of accounting for it in human categories. Jesus has been raised by the power of God. The women receive this as a revelation from God, not as something they have worked out, and they are, literally, dumbfounded by it. Who would have thought of this? Human desire for a neatly rational or entirely comprehensible religion, shorn of mystery, will always stub its mental toe on this story. Here, says the young man in white, is what God has done: Jesus the crucified One is alive. You may either accept it or not, but without it what follows does not make sense. The risen Lord will re-assemble and re-call his followers. The existence of the Church was then, and is now, the only 'proof' we can have of the truth of the resurrection. It is all we need.

SECOND SUNDAY OF EASTER

Acts 4.32–35

In today's Gospel we see Jesus re-forming his disciples as a community, by his Spirit. This reading is a preview of how that begins to work out as the post-Pentecost community seeks to live out the 'new commandment' (John 13.34–35). We also see that the preaching of the resurrection remained central to the Christian mission (v. 33). The description of the community's life (vv. 32, 34–35) has sometimes been used to suggest that the first Christians were 'Christian socialists'; that is anachronistic. They were not motivated by theories of economic justice, but concerned to work out the implications of what it meant to be 'new people'. What lesson are we to draw from this? Some have held up this picture (even if Luke draws it idealistically) as a model of how things should be, seeing the Church's subsequent abandonment of it as a sad decline from ideals. Others have pointed out that it failed in practice. It was capable of abuse (Acts 5.1–5), and within a few years Paul had to organize a collection among his Gentile converts to assist the impoverished Jerusalem church. We may conclude they were mistaken to think that the gospel required them to live in this way. But often it is better to have tried and failed than never to have tried. What implications does our fellowship as believers have for the way we relate to one another in practical matters?

1 John 1.1–2.2

The writer insists that he teaches that which is 'from the beginning' – which means 'from the beginning of the good news', revealed in the ministry of Jesus. The writer claims to have witnessed these saving events (1.2–3) – 'Trust me, I was there.' He wants his readers to have 'fellowship' with him, as he has fellowship with God in Christ (1.3). For this to be possible, they must know the nature of the God who invites them into such a relationship; that nature is *light*. This is not a startling statement; it would be at home in most of the world's religions. But John contrasts light and *darkness* (compare John 1.5, 9–10; 8.12). God is the source of holiness, goodness and truth. Those who claim fellowship with God must show those qualities in their own lives (1.6). As Marianne Meye Thompson puts it: 'We cannot see the light, but by and in the light we see everything else.' It seems that some of those in (or formerly in) the community to which John writes, claim that they have no sin (a kind of spurious 'advanced' spirituality?). They deceive themselves (1.8 – see John 8.44) and make God a liar (1.10) since God has provided Jesus as a remedy for sin. True Christian experience, now as then, is found in 1.9, along with 2.1–2. F. F. Bruce writes: 'I know of no commentary on 1 John 2.2 so apposite as Charles Wesley's hymn, "Arise, my soul, arise"' (*Hymns and Psalms* 217).

John 20.19–31

The disciples are met in fear (v. 19), so the risen Jesus comes with a repeated greeting (vv. 19, 21) showing them the marks of his death (v. 20), as if to stress that this is no hallucination or vision. The one they see has a continuity of identity with their Master who was crucified. After a word of commissioning (v. 21b) he breathes on them saying, 'Receive the Holy Spirit . . .' (vv. 22–23). Suggesting that the most helpful background to this is Ezekiel 37.9–14, Lionel Swain comments: '. . . here the risen, glorified Jesus is making his disciples into one reality, recreating them as the new people of God, alive with his Spirit.' Like Mary (20.17), the disciples enter into a new relationship with Jesus. Thomas, however, has not shared in all this and does not believe the testimony of the others (v. 25). Despite this, he is not excluded from the community of faith (nor excludes himself, v. 26) and is present when Jesus appears again. Thomas is invited to do as he has asked, but there is now no need. Meeting with Jesus elicits the most profound confession of faith in the New Testament (v. 28). Now Thomas also enters into a new relationship with his Lord. Verses 29–31 indicate that the purpose of writing the Gospel is that others should come to this same relationship and have this same life-giving faith.

THIRD SUNDAY OF EASTER

Acts 3.12–19

The healing of the lame man (3.1–10) produces an astonished response among the populace. Peter seizes the opportunity to say something about Jesus. Addressing them as 'Israelites' (v. 12), he speaks as if they were the people who demanded the death of Jesus (Luke 23.18). Some of them could well have been, though Luke also records a very different crowd reaction (Luke 23.48). It is very important to recall the specific context of Peter's speech here: it is a Jewish man addressing a Jewish crowd about a Jewish Messiah. If we take the language of vv. 13–15 out of this context it will contribute to the appalling way in which the Church has treated Jewish people down the centuries. Such is not Peter's purpose and, in any case, he allows that they acted in ignorance (v. 17). Now there can be no excuse for ignorance: the healing came not from the apostles, but through faith in Jesus (v. 16), and Peter's proclamation of Jesus as the crucified and risen Servant gives the opportunity for repentance and forgiveness (v. 19). This passage has such a specific context that it is difficult to see what immediate relevance it has to a contemporary British Christian congregation, except possibly to remind us that if forgiveness can be extended even to those accused of being directly responsible for the crucifixion nobody is beyond its reach.

1 John 3.1–7

Our faith may be so familiar that we take it for granted. It is good to be caught up in the wonder of it, as John is here. It is astonishing that we should be called God's children, especially since that is not a token 'naming' but the actual conferring of the status of children (v. 1 – compare John 1.12). But that is not all: there is more to come, a future transformation (v. 2)! John is reticent about its nature: it is enough for us to know that we shall one day be like 'him' (v. 2b). Is the 'him' here God, or Christ? We cannot be sure, but we cannot go far wrong if we think of 'God as made known to us in Christ'. If we are children of God and will one day become like God, what about the family likeness now? This is the concern of vv. 4–7, and their general thrust is clear enough. Verse 6, however, presents a diffi-culty. As we saw in last week's Epistle, the writer, while hoping that Christians will not sin, knows that they will, and writes eloquently of the remedy God has provided (1.8–2.2). Verse 6b must therefore mean something like: no one who deliberately persists in sin really knows God. The family likeness involves abiding in God (v. 6a) and also some human effort (v. 3). Our motive for so living must surely be gratitude for the love the Father has given us (v. 1).

Luke 24.36b–48

Luke places this story on the evening of resurrection day, by which time the disciples had received the testimony of the women (24.8–11) and of the two on their way to Emmaus (24.33, 35), and know of an appearance to Peter (24.12, 34). Yet when Jesus appears among them they think he is a ghost (v. 37) and have to be convinced otherwise. Merely hearing the testimony is not enough to produce 'belief'. Even when Jesus has shown them his hands and feet and has eaten, showing that he is no ghost or vision and that there is a continuity with his earthly body (vv. 39–42), it is not enough, despite their emotional response of joy (v. 41). For belief to happen, Jesus must interpret the scriptures to them (vv. 44–47) just as he had done in the previous story (24.32). For Luke the bare fact of the resurrection is not the most important thing: what matters is what it means. Until Jesus has interpreted the meaning to the disciples they neither understand nor fully believe. However, once they have understood it they are commissioned to be witnesses both to the fact and to its meaning (v. 48). If we gather for worship with attentive and open hearts and minds, listening for what the risen Christ says to us through scripture and our table fellowship with him, we too may discern his presence and become witnesses to these things in our day and generation.

FOURTH SUNDAY OF EASTER

Acts 4.5–12

This week we have Peter's address to the Sanhedrin, before whom he and John were on trial. The enquiry in v. 7b gives him his opportunity (compare 3.16). As before, Peter ascribes the healing to 'the name of Jesus Christ of Nazareth' (an especially solemn version), not themselves. Again, the crucifixion and the resurrection form the heart of the message (v. 10b). When Peter says, 'whom you crucified', he does not have to speak as if they had been personally involved (as in 3.14–15). Some of those involved in handing Jesus over to Pilate were present (v. 6). This is why, in his quotation from Psalm 118.22, he can identify the builders with his hearers (v. 11). Verse 12 is an implicit appeal to them to believe the good news which has just been preached to them. It has been interpreted in ways which are not always helpful. James Dunn says of it: 'Its character as an expression of enthusiastic hyperbole (whether Peter's or Luke's) should be noted.' At one level it is a logical outcome of all that the first Christians believed about the exaltation of the risen Lord to the right hand of God. That position could hardly be shared! It is proper for Christians to say: 'In confessing Jesus as my Lord I believe him to be God's final and most complete way of salvation.' It is not proper to go on to assert that the other great world religions are therefore valueless deceptions and their adherents destined for hell. We may know the first, but we do not know the second. In a multi-faith society especially, this verse must not be made to say more than it will bear.

1 John 3.16–24

The old wayside pulpit notice read: 'If you were arrested for being a Christian, would there be enough evidence to convict you?' If we ask what kind of evidence we would look for John's answer is unequivocal: loving actions. In v. 16 we are told that we know that God loves us because of what God has done for us. John then says that if we truly love then we must be prepared to do the same, if not by making the supreme sacrifice, at least by more ordinary loving deeds (v. 17; compare James 2.14–16). If we do love 'in truth and action' we can be assured of the reality of our faith. But some people have over-tender consciences, are unnecessarily burdened by guilt and worry that they have never done enough. For such people there is a reassurance that God knows us better than we know ourselves (vv. 19–20). As William Loader puts it: 'Faith means trusting in God's love and making ourselves available for its action despite what we may feel.' In the last three verses there is quite a bit about obeying God's 'commandments'. No list of commandments is in mind; the author is not trying to turn the teaching of Jesus into a new Law of Moses. Rather, this is about attitudes and relationships being patterned after those of Jesus, just as he 'commanded' his followers (John 15.12–17).

John 10.11–18

This passage picks up themes from Ezekiel 34, where God promises to rescue the flock from the rapacious shepherds. The flock need protection from wolves, but who is to do it? Hired hands may only be counted on until the danger comes, when the protection is most needed (vv. 12–13). The good shepherd, by contrast, knows the sheep, even to the extent of surrendering his life in their defence (vv. 11, 14–15; compare v. 1 in today's Epistle). There can be times when even those closest to us may fail to care for us as we really need. But God's tender loving care for us never fails and we never reach the end of it. With v. 16 the thought changes slightly; there are 'other sheep'. Jesus' mission is not just to Israel (see 11.52). The 'one flock' has traditionally been used as a phrase about the unity of Christ's Church. We are reminded here that it is to be sought as a sign and foretaste of the unity God wills for all humankind. The world is the focus of God's love, not the Church (see 3.16), and it is the whole world for which Jesus will lay down his life (v. 17; see 12.32).

FIFTH SUNDAY OF EASTER

Acts 8.26–40

If a sermon on this lection began by reading Deuteronomy 23.1, followed by vv. 27b–28, a good deal of the point would be made! This highly placed Ethiopian eunuch could not become a convert to Judaism, nor worship in the temple, because of his physical condition. He was a 'godfearer', a Gentile who loved the Jewish faith and worshipped the God of Israel. He was returning from worshipping in Jerusalem with a scroll of Isaiah in Greek – an expensive item. Philip heard him reading aloud (which was then the custom). The eunuch asked him a question about the original meaning of the text (v. 34). Philip may not have known the answer, any more than we do, but he did know that its fulfilment had come in Jesus. Accordingly, he taught him the good news. The eunuch requested baptism (presumably Philip's instruction had included something about this). The question in v. 36b is significant: there was a hindrance to his worshipping in the Jerusalem temple, but there was no such hindrance to his becoming a Christian: Isaiah 56.3–5 is being fulfilled. God's complete acceptance of all sorts and conditions of people is shown in Christ, and Luke stresses three times that this mission is undertaken at the direct command of God (vv. 26, 29, 39). So an influential convert is able to take the gospel to a distant part of the world (v. 39b). The story asks questions about the inclusiveness, or otherwise, of today's Church.

1 John 4.7–21

We are learning that damaged and abused children often grow up to become abusive and violent adults. Those who receive genuine and unconditional love in their early years often grow up to be affirming and life-giving adults. This is not always true, but this admittedly imperfect analogy may help us see what John means here. 'God is love' (vv. 8b, 16b) is one of the most precious statements in the New Testament: precious, but not vague or sentimental. John writes of what it cost God to reveal this to us (vv. 9–10). He also tells us (another precious verse), about the priority of God's love. We love in response to the love we receive, and it, in turn, enables us to become more loving (v. 19). An important goal of our pilgrimage as Christians is that we learn to love God rather than obeying him out of fear or duty (v. 18). But John will not allow us to take refuge in the fiction that loving God is a vague 'spiritual' thing, or that we can ever claim to love God unless we love others (vv. 11–12, 20–21). John thus sees a loving life both as grounded in a grateful response to unconditional love already received from God, and (consequently), as expressed in the quality of our relationships. This is a direct challenge to the way our worship and conduct relate to each other.

John 15.1–8

In March each year, Alf pruned the roses in front of the church so hard that you could scarcely see the stems over the top of the soil. 'You have overdone it this time', the congregation would say, but he just smiled knowingly. Sure enough, within a few short weeks there would be vigorous bushes, every stem heavy with roses. The analogy of vv. 1–3 is not difficult to understand at that level, but it is extremely uncomfortable. Who are those who bear no fruit? If this came from James or 1 John or even Paul, we might think of those with no good deeds to show they have faith. But for John there seem to be only alive or dead branches, and the aliveness or deadness is determined by 'abiding' in Jesus as he does in us – or not (v. 4). As Raymond Brown puts it, 'The total dependence of the Christian upon Jesus, which is a leitmotif of Johannine thought, is expounded nowhere more eloquently than here.' So there is warning here: we must remain in Jesus if we are to bear fruit (v. 6). Perhaps, in a world (and a church?) where we are casual about commitment this is a word we need to hear. Verses 7–8 develop the positive side: those whose minds are in harmony with Jesus will receive what they request – not status or possessions of course, but increased fruitfulness to the glory of God.

SIXTH SUNDAY OF EASTER

Acts 10.44–48

Last week's reading from Acts concerned the conversion and sub-sequent baptism of an Ethiopian godfearer. In this passage the Christian mission moves decisively beyond Judaism as Luke records the results of Peter's preaching to the Roman centurion Cornelius and his household. The Holy Spirit descends (presumably both visibly and audibly) upon a group of Gentiles – the 'Gentile Pentecost', as it has been called. The Jewish Christians who accompany Peter (believers from Joppa, see 10.23b) could not deny what had happened. Peter's question in v. 47 mirrors that asked of Philip by the Ethiopian (Acts 8.36) and the answer is the same and self-evident: where God is clearly at work it is our task to recognize this and act appropriately. We often make the mistake of thinking that we set the agenda, in mission as in other aspects of church life. But Christian mission is about recognizing where God is already at work in the world and co-operating with God in that task. Opening our eyes to our prejudices, as Peter had to have his eyes opened (v. 34 – see also vv. 9–15), and recognizing that God has already been at work preparing the way where we might never have expected it (see 10.1–4), are among the requirements for engaging in mission, today as then.

1 John 5.1–6

Here John continues the intertwined themes of love (from God and towards God and others) and right belief, already encountered in previous readings from this letter. Verse 2 says precisely the opposite of what was said at 4.20 (see the comments on last week's Epistle)! But in reality these are two sides of the same coin, for to 'love God' is to 'obey his commandments' (v. 3) and those commandments include loving others (4.21). Those who love God, therefore, do what is pleasing to God. Our relationship with God is personal, but not private. It has consequences for our relationships. Yet John does not see the commandments of God as 'burdensome' (v. 3b; for the mean-ing of 'commandments' in this letter see the comments on the Epistle on p. 90. The faith which 'conquers the world' (i.e., overcomes worldly forces and values systems) itself confers the power to obey the commandments, and obedience follows naturally from who we are as children of God. But what is this faith? John is clear that it is faith in Jesus as the Christ (v. 1), the Son of God (v. 5), who came 'by water and blood' (v. 6 – this last phrase probably refers to the baptism and death of Jesus as summing up his incarnate life). It is not enough to believe that Jesus was a good man or an inspired prophet. Only faith in Jesus as God's Son can conquer the world. Any list of core Christian beliefs must, then, include this one. Since many people stop at believing Jesus to be a supremely good man, preaching on this theme would be worthwhile.

John 15.9–17

This passage continues and develops the thought of last week's Gospel concerning abiding in God's love and keeping God's commandments. Here, though, there is less warning and more encouragement. There are plenty of people around who suffer from what we call 'low self-esteem'; they believe themselves to be unworthy of being loved when that is not the case. There are also plenty of people around who are extremely difficult to love and they do not always know it. As the Gospels tell the story, the disciples often come into this latter category. They are frequently quarrelsome, competitive, disloyal and rather stupid. To them Jesus says, 'I do not call you servants any longer . . . but I have called you friends' (v. 15). The initiative lies with Jesus (v. 16). So (because of who he is) we discover that this is how God acts towards us. The heart of the gospel is, in the words of Samuel Crossman's great hymn, 'Love to the love-less shown/That they might lovely be'. What Jesus shares with his friends is the sheer goodness of God, God's forgiveness, acceptance and love, which makes the unlovely lovable and, in turn, loving to others (vv. 15b, 17). Leslie Weatherhead discerningly called one of his books about discipleship *The Transforming Friendship*. It well describes the kind of relationship with God-in-Christ which Christian people need to cultivate, for it does not leave us where it finds us.

ASCENSION DAY

Acts 1.1–11

The ascension story probably causes real difficulties for people, even if within the Church they are not always readily admitted. The problem lies in its spatial reference. In one way or another, vv. 9–11 refer to heaven as being 'up there' no fewer than three times. The first Soviet cosmonaut famously said that he did not see God while he was in space. Of course not; with our knowledge of astronomy we know that heaven cannot be, in any physical sense, beyond the clouds. It is probably necessary to address this potential stumbling block fairly directly. The fact is that we do not possess the language to adequately describe heaven and the divine. It is a dimension of reality which completely transcends the one in which we live. The biblical writers understood this perfectly well. As James Dunn helpfully puts it, 'In trying to speak of heaven they, like us, spoke of what was beyond every day experience. With their more limited perspective on the cosmos, it was sufficient to express that "beyond" in terms of beyond what eye can see.' We may be more sophisticated, but it is doubtful whether we can do any better than this picture language. So, in our preaching on the ascension we need to acknowledge the limitations of our thought and speech and concentrate on its meaning. Luke tells us that Jesus first prepared his disciples (now apostles, v. 2) for the coming of the Holy Spirit (v. 5). Then he warned them against useless speculation (vv. 6–7) and finally charged them with a missionary task (v. 8). The earthly ministry of Jesus is over. From now on his ministry will be through the Spirit, no longer limited to particular localities. It will now be the task of a Spirit-filled Church to make him known.

Ephesians 1.15–23

Paul gives thanks for the faith of the Ephesian Christians (vv. 15–16). Then he prays that they will (1) grow in their faith and come to a full knowledge of God (v. 17); (2) grasp the immensity of the heritage of faith which is theirs (vv. 18–19); and (3) acknowledge with amazement the authority of the risen Christ, head of the Church (v. 20). All this is a reminder that however long we have been believers there is still more about the faith for us to discover and delight in. Verses 20–23 spell out the theological significance of the ascension, which is not so much an event in itself as a conclusion, in earthly terms, of the resurrection ('raised' and 'seated' in v. 20 form one continuous movement). We cannot miss the tone of wonder in this writing. From Galilean carpenter to the One under whose feet all things have been put: that is what resurrection and ascension mean here. The Church does not exist for its own sake, but in order to witness to the character of our Christlike God (Acts 1.8). We may need to examine the day-by-day life of our own Christian community to see in what ways it remains faithful to that calling.

Luke 24.44–53

By presenting the ascension as the final event of resurrection day itself (rather than after the forty days of appearances of Acts), Luke makes the point that the ascension is not an event separate from the resurrection. Even so, it must be preceded by instruction (vv. 45–47). The apostles are to be witnesses 'of these things' (v. 48; Acts 1.8), and in order to be that they must understand what the resurrection means and be clear about the content of the good news which is to be proclaimed. The instruction is an exposition of scripture (see Luke 24.32b and the comments on the Gospel on p. 89). No specific texts are mentioned, but the Old Testament is seen as reaching its climax and fulfilment in the passion and resurrection. However, the apostles require not only instruction but also power. Without this they will have nothing to say which is worth hearing, but they must wait for it (v. 49). It would be wrong to say that we too must wait for the Spirit before we witness to our Lord, for as Luke will show, the Spirit was given to the Church on the day of Pentecost. But we certainly need to claim the promised presence of the Holy Spirit in all our Christian work and witness.

SEVENTH SUNDAY OF EASTER

Acts 1.15–17, 21–26

This seemingly straightforward story presents some major puzzles. Why did Judas need to be replaced? And why before Pentecost when afterwards, presumably, they could have received the guidance of the Spirit instead of casting lots? We never hear of either candidate again; is this of any significance? Some suggest that the apostles made a mistake and should instead have waited until after Pentecost, but Luke's account does not support that view. Others suggest that Paul should have been the twelfth apostle, but that is a misunderstanding: Paul lacked the essential qualifications (vv. 22–23). The key lies in the fact that Jesus deliberately called twelve disciples, symbolically representing the twelve tribes of Israel, thus constituting a new or restored people of God. Judas' betrayal was therefore more than an individual failure: the gap left by his departure fractured the symbolic integrity of the group. Judas had to be replaced before Pentecost because, as L. T. Johnson rightly says, '. . . once the Twelve had definitively been constituted at the heart of the people *and the Spirit bestowed*, the faithful Israel would have come into existence, and the promise of God would have reached fulfilment.' Once Pentecost had come, the death of an apostle would not necessitate a replacement (see Acts 12.2). It is hard to see the immediate relevance to a contemporary congregation. We may, though, note that the qualifications of an apostle (vv. 21–22) are about sharing in the tradition in order to hand it on. The Church is not free to reinvent its message in each generation, though it must necessarily reinterpret it.

1 John 5.9–13

For John it is crucial that we believe in Jesus as the Son of God (5.5). God has given testimony to this, not least through the Spirit (v. 6b). Now he challenges his readers: if they are prepared to accept the testimony people offer in everyday life they certainly ought to be prepared to accept this testimony which God has provided (v. 9). To believe is to have accepted it in our hearts (v. 10a). Conversely, to refuse to believe that Jesus is the Son of God is tantamount to making God into a liar (v. 10b). It is not clear whether John here has in mind unbelievers in general or, as is more likely, a heretical group which had defected from the church to which he wrote. Here is the assurance that believers have been given eternal life, not just as a future promise, but as a present possession (v. 11; compare John 10.10). In v. 13 'these things' almost certainly refers to the whole letter, not just this passage (compare John 20.31). Some Christians are wary of saying that they 'know' they are saved, while others claim it gladly. A sermon which explored the proper grounds on which this claim might be made could strengthen and encourage faith.

John 17.6–19

The Fourth Gospel depicts Jesus looking forward to the time after his glorification (John's way of referring to the crucifixion). This passage continues the theme of last Sunday's Gospel (what Jesus shares with his friends) and is a meditation on the spiritual relationship between Jesus and his disciples in the light of the task the Father has given him to perform. Jesus has revealed God's 'name' (v. 6) to them. Those who have heard his teaching, seen his actions, and come to realize that they have thereby seen God at work, now need to be kept true to that faith (v. 11). Jesus has kept faith with the Father's purposes for him. Now those who will be left on earth after his departure need in turn to keep faith with what they have experienced (v. 9). This will bring persecution to them (as it has to him), and so they need God's protection (vv. 14–16). In this passage we are reminded that what people experienced in the presence of Jesus was an awareness of his extraordinary intimacy with the God he called 'Father', and the spiritual authority which accompanied this. He did not keep this relationship to himself but shared it freely with them. After his death and resurrection they would experience his presence in a new way. In John V. Taylor's words, 'He who had shown God to them now showed himself to them, and from that time they would never think of God without thinking of him.'

PENTECOST

Acts 2.1–21

Luke begins with the statement that the believers were all together in obedience to the Lord's command to wait in Jerusalem (Luke 24.49; Acts 1.4). They experienced the sound of a strong wind and also tongues of flame, and began to speak in different languages (vv. 2–4). The account continues with the effect of these phenomena: the astonishment of the hearers and, in some cases, their abrupt dismissal of them (vv. 5–11). Luke does not encourage the reader to dwell on the supernatural aspects; he is more concerned with the effects. Whether this was a miracle of speaking or of hearing (or both) cannot now be determined, but the hearing aspect emerges as more important (vv. 7–10). The ascension proclaimed the universality of the rule of Christ; Pentecost enabled Christ's Lordship to be universally understood. And the immediate effect of the Spirit's coming is that Peter gives voice boldly to the faith (vv. 14ff). There are good grounds for seeing the events of the first Christian Pentecost as a reversal of the effects of the tower of Babel (Genesis 11.1–9). The linguistic list in vv. 9–11 is impressive. It indicates that what Christ has done is for all, no matter who they are or where they come from. This poses a tough question to the contemporary Church. We have striven to make the gospel available to all nations. The missionary enterprise has gone alongside translating the scriptures into many languages. But have we spoken in the language of others, the young, the poor, the marginalized? Or have we expected them to learn our language in order to hear what we are saying? How do we make contact with those whose culture is very different from that of a middle-class church? The account in Acts insists on the importance of it, for what we have to share is nothing less than the 'marvels of God' (v. 11) which will save those who respond (v. 21). What different 'languages' does our church need to speak in order that those without saving knowledge of the marvels of God may hear?

Ezekiel 37.1–14

Ezekiel's famous vision of the valley of dry bones is so vivid that it makes its own effect in the telling and ought not to be explained in the kind of detail which can easily spoil that effect. It makes a superb Pentecost reading because it is about the bringing back to life of a community which is dead, by means of God's *ruach*. This Hebrew word can mean 'breath' or 'wind' or 'spirit', and the relationship between its meanings in this passage is important, if ambiguous. We do not need to know Hebrew to appreciate it: NRSV footnotes indicate where the word comes and we can trace it easily enough. The vision builds skilfully to its climax. From the utter hopelessness of 'very dry' bones (v. 2b), it moves to God's promise to put *ruach* in them (v. 6, twice), then describes how they become corpses (vv. 7–8). Ezekiel is then told to summon the *ruach* in the name of God (v. 9), and the corpses come alive (v. 10). Only God can bring life, by his *ruach*, to lifeless bones. Even so does God promise the Spirit to a lifeless and defeated people, that they may live (v. 14). No prophecy about Pentecost is either intended or found here. But what Ezekiel speaks of in one context is described by Luke as equally true in quite another context: only God can give life of any kind, and at Pentecost God does indeed do just this. The anxious and uncertain disciples suddenly become fearless witnesses for what God has done in Christ. As W. E. Sangster once put it, Pentecost is the day 'when rabbits became ferrets'.

Romans 8.22–27

A famous philosopher once said that if Christianity were really true the world would look more redeemed than it does. The force of this observation was felt long before he articulated it, even in the first flush of enthusiasm as the Christian mission got under way. Despite all that Christians believe God has done through the death and resurrection of Christ, all is not well with the world. The created order is not yet set free from its travails and agonies (vv. 22–23). We too feel the force of this as we watch our televisions and see the effects of earthquakes, floods and other things we call 'natural disasters'. It is a strange thing to call them: deep down we want to protest that they are *un*natural, that this is not how things ought to be in a properly ordered and functioning world. It isn't that we believe that God sends such things (or, if we do, we ought not to), but rather that God might have made the world in such a way that these disasters do not occur. This is an agonizing dilemma for the spiritually sensitive, and we are quite incapable of solving it. Paul could not solve it either, but he acknowledges that not everything has yet been sorted out and believers must live with the tension (vv. 23–24). When the burden of all this seems too great to bear and we cannot even find words for it, God's Holy Spirit does the praying for us and within us (vv. 26–27). There are deep mysteries here (and some exegetical problems which there is not space to discuss). Paul is writing of what John Ziesler calls 'the frail attempts of Christians to reach out in their prayers to what lies ahead and beyond'. It also seems clear that Paul's writing communicates a strong note of authentic personal experience. All this challenges, at a very deep level, our frequent domestication of prayer. Too often, both in our personal devotions and our congregational worship, prayer is confined to our immediate and personal concerns. W. H. Auden termed the twentieth century 'the age of anxiety', and it seems also to be true of the opening of the twenty-first. We are often anxious about cosmic-sized problems that we scarcely understand, such as the problem of global warming and the future of our planet. Paul here encourages us to see that prayer is not a retreat from such things but an immersion in them with the Spirit's help.

John 15.26–27; 16.4b–15

The Advocate (Counsellor, Helper or Paraclete) has been previously referred to at 14.15–17, 25–26). In 15.26 as in 14.17 he is referred to as 'spirit of truth'. In 16.4b–7 Jesus introduces the idea of his own departure. When this has been mentioned on previous occasions the disciples have questioned him about it (13.36; 14.5), but the repetition of the theme here makes them so sorrowful that none of them says anything (16.5–6). They need to learn that it will actually be to their advantage that Jesus should depart because, unless he does, the Advocate cannot come to them (v. 7). Two distinct short passages concerning this Advocate then follow. The first, vv. 8–11, is very difficult; even some early church writers complained of the problems in understanding it. The NEB rendering of v. 8 is helpful: 'When he comes, he will confute the world, and show them where wrong and right and judgement lie.' Verses 9–11 expand this thought, though the details are rather obscure. The general thought is of a trial where the verdict which will be given at the trial of Jesus will be overturned and shown to be wrong. In this sense we may say that the continued existence of the Church and its continuing proclamation of the good news, through the power of the Spirit, is in itself a demonstration of the truth of Jesus' claims. The second short passage is vv. 12–15. Here the function of the Advocate is to be a teacher, in the sense of guiding the believers into all truth (v. 13). John sees the Advocate as continuing and prolonging the ministry of Jesus by enabling believers to understand the truth, and thus bear witness to it, just as

Jesus did in his incarnate life. No doubt as John wrote his Gospel, conscious that in doing so he was reflecting on the traditions he knew, he believed that the very process of gospel-writing was one of the ways in which the Spirit was guiding the Church into all the truth (v. 13). That process has continued down the centuries as Christians have reflected on what the Good News means for their own day and generation and have sought to express that by, among other things, preaching, teaching, writing and broadcasting. It is a process which demands humility: Christians are to be open to being guided 'into' the truth. We do not 'know it all' – we are on a journey.

TRINITY SUNDAY

Isaiah 6.1–8

'The King is dead or dying, but there is a King who never dies – the Living God,' wrote J. Yeoman Muckle about v. 1. It is of the living God that Isaiah receives a 'seeing', not physical but of the imagination and understanding and none the less real for that. God is not described; it is enough to note that merely the hem of God's robe filled the temple to know how great he is. The seraphs wait on God in worship and their 'Holy, holy, holy' (v. 3a) is a superlative, meaning 'most holy'. At one time holiness was thought of as primarily cere-monial purity. Isaiah was to become one of those largely responsible for redefining holiness as involving moral and ethical purity. So it was that, in the midst of this shattering vision (v. 4), the prophet is struck first and foremost by his own sinfulness and the moral uncleanness of the people as a whole (v. 5a). All this adds up to a deep unworthiness to have seen such a vision of a God who is hymned as 'holy' by the heavenly hosts (v. 5b). His cry of despair is met by a ritual not recorded anywhere else in the Old Testament (v. 7a), accompanied by the assurance that he is cleansed from his sin and guilt (v. 7b). As always in scripture, God takes the initiative in forgiveness and new life, and Isaiah is transformed from observer to prophet.

Romans 8.12–17

Belonging to a family will mean different things to different people, and for some brings real pain. But at its best it is about knowing relationships of commitment and care and, above all, a sense of 'belonging' which is not easily found elsewhere. The heart of Paul's argument in this passage is that through the Spirit we have been adopted as God's children (v. 15b). Although there is only one Son of God ('begotten, not made', as the Nicene Creed puts it), by the Spirit we are 'made' children of God. More, we can know that this is so. Evidence of that fact is that in worship and prayer, Christians address God as Jesus did (v. 15b; compare Mark 14.36 – *Abba* is the Aramaic word a Jewish child would use to the father within the household, implying both intimacy and trust). To call God 'Father', as in the Lord's Prayer, is a sign of our belonging. Paul can call Jesus our 'firstborn brother' (v. 29) and says that we are 'joint heirs' with him

(v. 17). All this is set in the context of transformation from a previous life of rebellion against God (vv. 12–13). Preaching about this undeserved privilege which is ours must avoid presumption. But we cannot avoid it, since it is how God regards us unless, of course, we throw it away (v. 13).

John 3.1–17

We sometimes think that all Pharisees opposed Jesus. But here is a Pharisee, evidently impressed by what he has heard of Jesus, coming to him for a serious conversation about theology. His opening remarks are courteous (v. 2) and establish the topic he wishes to discuss. Jesus abruptly changes the topic. In order to really see the kingdom of God it is necessary to be born 'from above' (v. 3). Nicodemus expresses puzzlement, as well he might: being born a second time is a physical impossibility (v. 4). In response, Jesus reiterates what he has already said, though extending it. Now 'from above' becomes 'of water and Spirit' (v. 5). Some later Christian thought understood 'water' here as a reference to baptism, and argued that baptism is therefore essential to salvation, but this is unlikely. Both water and Spirit refer back to John the Baptist (John 1.26–34), so 'water' here probably means 'repentance'. Verses 6–8 revolve around the Greek word *pneuma*, which has a similar wind/spirit ambiguity to the Hebrew *ruach* (see the comments on the Old Testament on p. 101). Ultimately, what Nicodemus must learn (as must we) is that a total transformation by the Spirit is needed if we are to enter a new relationship with God. It is, as always, God's initiative. For further comments on this passage see those on the Gospel on p. 53.

For the Lectionary for the Sunday between 24 and 28 May (Eighth Sunday in Ordinary Time) see the material for the Sunday between 25 and 29 February on pp. 38–39.

SUNDAY BETWEEN 29 MAY AND 4 JUNE

Ninth Sunday in Ordinary Time (Proper 4)

1 Samuel 3.1–10 (11–20) Continuous

For this reading see the comments on the Old Testament on p. 26.

Deuteronomy 5.12–15 Related

The Old Testament offers two reasons for keeping the Sabbath day holy, one deriving from the theology of creation, the other from the theology of salvation. Exodus 20.11 offers the creation theology: God rested from creating on the seventh day and so commands us to do likewise. Here, v. 15 offers the salvation theology: the nation was once delivered from slavery in Egypt, where they had no day of rest, and the Sabbath is seen as a day to remember that deliverance and to celebrate it. Both reasons have their validity, but the Deuteronomic command, though possibly less familiar to most worshippers, has the greater resonance for us. Early on, Christians began to observe a first day of the week 'Lord's Day' (Revelation 1.10) instead of the seventh-day Jewish Sabbath. It is the weekly celebration of the resurrection of Jesus, through which we have been delivered from sin and death (Ephesians 2.4–6). If observance of the Sabbath could degenerate into legalism, as today's Gospel suggests, Christian observance of the Lord's Day has often done the same. In twenty-first-century secular Britain, Sunday is very different from even fifty years ago. We need to reflect on how we respond to that and still make it the day when we celebrate our salvation.

2 Corinthians 4.5–12

We are easily seduced by powerful and successful people, even within the Church. So were the Corinthians, who admired and followed some 'super apostles' (2 Corinthians 11.5; 12.11). These were outwardly impressive people, possessing some of the showier spiritual gifts. By comparison Paul appeared unimpressive – and often in trouble – which they saw as demonstrating his inferiority. Paul's defence of his ministry tells us something crucial about the nature of Christian life and community. He and his colleagues do not promote themselves (as the 'super apostles' did), but Christ alone (vv. 5–6). The apostles themselves were expendable, like cheap clay containers from the Corinthian market (v. 7). Yes, they were often in all sorts of trouble (v. 8), but such things are the genuine marks of an apostle who is willing to suffer persecution for the sake of Jesus (v. 10). The paradox is that those who are so clearly powerless and unimpressive are the bearers of a message of extraordinary power which enables them to live daily through their hardships (v. 7b). The proper response to suffering (of any kind) is not a stiff upper lip, but reliance on the grace of God to bring us through, if not always out of it. This brings blessing to the lives of others, an interchange of spiritual benefit. As Ernest Best says: 'Every Christian by faithfully enduring affliction builds up other Christians in life and joy.'

Mark 2.23–3.6

These two stories centre on Sabbath observance. In 2.23–28, the disciples contravene scribal interpretation of the Law rather than the Law itself, by 'reaping'. When challenged, Jesus refers to the incident recorded in 1 Samuel 21.1–6, which is not about Sabbath observance. But in a case of necessity David did something prohibited. How much more, then, must human regulations – in this case about the Sabbath – be set aside when one greater than David is here with his companions? The principle is set out in v. 27, but does not mean that the Sabbath may simply be disregarded whenever people please. It is the 'Son of man' (Jesus himself) who is Lord of the Sabbath (v. 28). When Jews and Gentiles in the early church needed to resolve the issue of Sabbath/Lord's Day they could remind themselves that they were now companions of Jesus. In 3.1–6 the point is that the man's life was not in danger and, therefore, according to scribal teaching, the healing could have waited. In v. 4 Jesus points to the purpose of the Law, which is to enhance life. That is his purpose too, in the fullest sense. The story is not about what is permitted on the Sabbath, but about the rightness of doing good at all times and in all circumstances. This helps us to work out how we treat the Lord's Day in contemporary Britain.

SUNDAY BETWEEN 5 AND 11 JUNE

Tenth Sunday in Ordinary Time (Proper 5)

1 Samuel 8.4–11 (12–15) 16–20 (11.14–15) Continuous

It does not make much sense to read the verses from ch. 11, since they describe the final stage of Saul's ascent of the throne of Israel, and the rest of the lection does not mention him. However, since next week's Old Testament reading begins, oddly, with God repenting of having made Saul king, there needs to be some mention of how it happened. Perhaps 9.15b–17 could be substituted. Today's reading suggests that there was more than one attitude to the monarchy. The elders of the people approach Samuel to complain about his sons (v. 5b), just as Samuel had once replaced Eli because of the behaviour of *his* sons (1 Samuel 3.13). Their reasons for requesting a monarchy seem to have been pragmatic, but are seen at a deeper level as a rejection of God's rule over them (vv. 7–8). Samuel does God's bidding, warning that monarchs do not come cheaply (vv. 11–18). However, the request is renewed (from 'the people' now, not just the elders, v. 19). This is more than a remote piece of Israelite history. The issue focuses in the twice-repeated insistence that they want a king in order to be 'like other nations' (vv. 5b, 20a). The whole point is that they were not supposed to be like other nations. They were God's chosen people, intended to look to God and those, like Samuel, whom God appointed. This is why the writer sees the demand for a monarch as a rejection of God. There is, at the least, a reminder here that when we reorganize our church structures – including at the most local level – the object is not to be as much like other organizations as possible, but to enable us to respond to God's mission.

Genesis 3.8–15 Related

This passage does not so much provide us with an explanation of human sin as confront us with the reality of it. The man is anxious not to appear before God naked, which would be disrespectful (v. 10), but he thereby gives the game away. How does he know that he is naked? Because he has eaten the forbidden fruit. When God challenges him on this point (v. 11) he immediately passes the responsibility to the woman, though there may be a hint that he thinks

God is also partly to blame since he describes the woman as 'whom you gave to be with me' (v. 12). When the woman is challenged in turn (v. 13a), she immediately passes the responsibility on to the serpent (v. 13b). In this account the buck stops with the serpent (v. 14) and God passes judgment on all three. The effect of the fall is to drive a wedge between the man and the woman and another wedge between them both and God. It is a pity that the Lectionary reading does not include vv. 21–24 since it completes this part of the story: God is angry about what has happened, but takes measures to limit the damage. The couple are driven from the garden, but God has first made them substantial clothes. Even in their exile they will know God's care, and so there is the hint that God will not allow everything to be lost. Paul traces the outcome of this when he writes: 'as all die in Adam, so all will be made alive in Christ' (1 Corinthians 15.22). If we ask why this passage is provided as a 'related' reading for today's Gospel, the answer is that in later Jewish thought the serpent came to be identified with the devil (Wisdom 2.24 says: 'through the devil's envy death entered the world'), which provides a link with the 'Satan' passage in today's Gospel. However, it is a very weak link and we are better staying with the plain sense of the story.

2 Corinthians 4.13–5.1

Paul stresses that he has confidence in the gospel; he preaches it because he believes it to be true (v. 13). The outcome of this gospel is that in raising Jesus God will also raise us with him (v. 14a). If we are inclined to think of the resurrection of Jesus as a 'one off', here is a corrective. It is the start of God's renewal of everything. The Corinthians will be included (v. 14b) even if some denied the possibility (1 Corinthians 15.12). In this sense, the resurrection was for their sake (v. 15a). More and more people will join the Church (this is how NRSV takes the Greek of v. 15b, which is difficult and could also mean that present believers will grow in grace). The result, in either case, is that there will be greater praise to God for the salvation which is experienced. All this is a solid reason not to lose heart. Our 'outer nature' (by which Paul means our nature as it experiences persecution and affliction) may be wasting away, but our 'inner nature' (by which he means our nature as centred on God) is being renewed daily (v. 16). This daily renewal is like a foretaste of resurrection (v. 17), and so we do not give much thought to what 'can be seen' (the afflictions and hardships) but concentrate instead on 'what cannot be seen' (God's future intentions for us). What are those future intentions? That when our 'earthly tent', our physical body, is destroyed in death, we have a 'building from God' which will be eternal (5.1). Paul is saying that God will give us new spiritual bodies after death. He can write that 'we have' this (present tense) not because it will happen immediately at death (1 Corinthians 15.23 gives the proper order), but because he is utterly confident of it happening. Surveys regularly show that even among Christians there is much uncertainty about life after death. There are many good reasons for believing in it. The major one provided in the New Testament is not about survival, but about resurrection. Just as God has raised Christ from the dead, so God will raise us too (v.14). If God has 'made us for himself', as Augustine put it, that purpose cannot be fulfilled in this life alone.

Mark 3.20–35

The crowd's enthusiasm for Jesus (v. 20) is in intentional contrast with the opposition of two groups of people, the scribes and Jesus' family. Mark has inserted one story into the other. The scribes are emissaries sent by the Sanhedrin in Jerusalem to make a formal investigation into what is happening in Capernaum. Their problem is that on the one hand they cannot deny that Jesus is able to work miracles, while on the other hand they cannot believe he is from God, since in their view he teaches and acts in ways contrary to the Law (see last Sunday's Gospel). They are fixed in this belief, unwilling to allow the evidence to change their minds. So the only logical conclusion they can reach is that Jesus casts out demons by the 'ruler of the demons', i.e., Satan (v. 22b). In vv. 23b–26 Jesus offers a logical refutation of this. But v. 27 introduces a different note: indeed Satan's 'end has come', not because he is fighting himself, but because Jesus is in the act of 'tying up' the strong man Satan, and plundering his house. Satan's power is crumbling around him even as Jesus expels demons by the power of the Spirit. Verses 28–29 are introduced by 'Amen', which injects a special note of authority. There follows the saying about blasphemy against the Holy Spirit, which has been variously interpreted. Some ultra-sensitive Christian souls have been known to fear they have committed it. However, v. 30 tells us plainly what it is. It is committed by those who see the Holy Spirit at work in the ministry of Jesus but, because of their own prejudice, ascribe that work to Satan. Clearly such an attitude forms a permanent obstacle to a relationship with God and, equally clearly, anyone sufficiently spiritually sensitive to think they might have committed it has, by definition, not done so. But these scribes were on the verge of it. Then in v. 31 Mark returns to the story which started at v. 21. Jesus' own family become the second group with whom he is in conflict. Mark is not telling a story about Jesus' attitude to them, but about their attitude to him. Whatever the grounds for their concern, they have evidently not understood the urgency of his mission. To do the will of God comes first and last for him, and those whom he regards as truly his family share that with him. Both stories challenge us to be alert to where and how, through his Spirit, Jesus is at work in today's world, bringing healing, wholeness and new life – and to be part of the enterprise ourselves.

SUNDAY BETWEEN 12 AND 18 JUNE

Eleventh Sunday in Ordinary Time (Proper 6)

1 Samuel 15.34–16.13 Continuous

This reading begins rather strangely; 15.34 records the parting of Saul and Samuel and adds the comment that God regretted having made Saul king in the first place. Many worshippers may find this puzzling; the story recorded in the earlier part of ch. 15 provides the reason, but has not been read. Preachers may be grateful that the Lectionary omits that story but, in its absence, it may be better to begin the reading at 16.1. Whatever the reason for the rejection of Saul, the important thing is the choice of David. In last week's Old Testament reading God is represented as only very reluctantly instructing Samuel to anoint a monarch, but there are no hints of reservation here. David is clearly God's choice for the people, even though the choosing and anointing must be done in secret, for Saul is still alive, and king. The narrative is quite straightforward, and it is structured to emphasize that David, though as the youngest brother the least likely choice in human terms, is marked out by God. We might infer from v. 12 that David's handsome appearance was regarded as the reason why he was chosen, but vv. 6–7a suggest that Eliab was also good-looking and he was not chosen. Indeed, v. 7b explicitly states that God's choice depends not on outward appearance but on what is in the heart. David will become the greatest of Israel's monarchs, and the covenant God will make with him is ultimately fulfilled in Christ (see the comments on the Old Testament and Gospel on pp. 8–9). We must therefore be careful not to trivialize the present story. Nevertheless, v. 7b does give rise to the reflection that contemporary British society seems far more concerned with people's 'image' than with what they are really like. What does it matter if a political leader is bald, overweight, or even downright ugly? Young women (and increasingly young men) are victims of media-promoted stereotypes concerning physical appearance, and spend a great deal of time and money trying to fit in with them, sometimes becoming ill in the process. It is not a trivial matter to insist that character matters far more. Some of our young people could find this a liberating message.

Ezekiel 17.22–24 Related

This passage was no doubt chosen as a related lection because v. 23b is picked up by the second parable in today's Gospel. It comes from the time when Israel was a vassal state of Babylon, with many of her people in exile. In its original context it refers to God taking action to establish the future of the nation after human attempts to do so have failed (see the earlier part of the chapter). The 'sprig from the lofty top of a cedar' (v. 22a) is to be understood as part of the dynasty of King David. The 'I myself will plant it' of v. 22b is very emphatic and means that the kingship of David's line will be established by God's direct action. It will, in due time, have a widespread dominion, providing shelter and protection (v. 23b). This passage is therefore an expression of hope, even messianic hope. Ezekiel has no idea how, humanly speaking, all this is to be accomplished. But hope has its origins not in what human beings can observe or foresee but in the character of God. What God has promised will surely come to pass. It is difficult for us, both as individuals and Christian communities, to see how, humanly speaking, some of God's promises in scripture can ever be fulfilled (e.g. Philippians 2.10–11). Those are the times when we must simply trust in the character of the God who has been made known to us in Christ.

2 Corinthians 5.6–10 (11–13) 14–17

It is generally agreed that 2 Corinthians 5.1–10 is the most difficult passage in Paul's letters. The Lectionary partly avoids the problem by treating v. 1 as the conclusion to last week's Epistle and omitting vv. 2–5. Stepping out boldly where experts fear to tread, we may say that vv. 6–9 tell us that after death we shall be 'at home with the Lord', with whom we will then enjoy unimpeded communion. However, since even now we travel by faith, we are not deprived of his company in this life and the aim of our living is to please him. Paul then stresses that there will be judgment for all, a judgment from which neither Christians in general, nor apostles in particular, are exempt (v. 10). If we read this alongside 1 Corinthians 3.10–15, we see that, although we will ultimately be saved by faith (or rather by God's grace), the true value of the work we have done for God in this life will be disclosed and on that we will be judged. However, nothing is said about the nature of possible rewards or punishments. With v. 11 Paul resumes the defence of his ministry as an apostle. He has tried to be open before God and if his Corinthian converts had really understood what his ministry was about, particularly that his sufferings are the marks of a true follower of the Crucified, they would be proud of him too and would say so to those who criticize him (vv. 11b–12). Yes, he is passionate for God, but it is for their sakes (v. 13). The controlling passion of Paul's life is the love of the Christ who has died for all in order that they may die to self and live in him (vv. 14–15). In v. 16 Paul contrasts the way he saw Christ before his conversion and after it. Prior to his conversion he regarded Christ 'from a human point of view', as NRSV translates two Greek words which literally mean 'according to the flesh'. NIV's 'from a worldly point of view', and the NEB/REB rendering 'by worldly standards' both catch the meaning rather better. Only after his conversion was he able to see Christ through new eyes and thus realize who he really is. Finally, in v. 17 we find one of Paul's favourite phrases, 'in Christ', by which he means those who are united with Christ by faith. Such people are a 'new creation', which took place at the death and resurrection of Jesus. This is not about having undergone a particular kind of conversion experience, it is about the way God looks at those who are 'in Christ'. God can, and does, re-make human nature. In some circles great value is placed on the 'testimonies' of those who have been converted from a spectacularly sinful way of life. There is nothing wrong with this unless it is used to imply that others with different experiences are second-class Christians. All who believe are a 'new creation' and should look for evidence of God's renewing work in their own lives.

Mark 4.26–34

The first of these two parables (vv. 26–29) is only found in Mark. It makes a strong contrast between the initial activity of the sower (v. 26b) and the complete inactivity which follows (v. 27). Once the sowing has been done, nothing more needs doing until the harvest (v. 29) because, in the meantime, the ground in which it is sown does all that needs to be done (v. 28). The second parable (vv. 30–32) picks up the imagery from today's Old Testament (related) lection. In this case the contrast is between the size of what is sown, the smallest of all seeds (v. 31b), and the eventual largeness of the resulting shrub (v. 32). Two closely related questions are being addressed. First, why is this mission to bring in the reign of God, in which Jesus is engaged, not producing quicker or more obvious results? Thus far in his writing Mark has depicted Jesus as preaching, teaching and healing, yet although there is support, there is also growing opposition (see last week's Gospel). Should something more be done? No, Jesus is saying: the seed is being sown and it is God's work to bring it to harvest. This was a lesson that Paul learned well (1 Corinthians 3.6). Second, is it really credible that a wandering Galilean preacher with just a few followers is going to bring in the reign of God for the whole world? Yes, Jesus is saying: the seed is being sown and God will bring it to the splendid plant it is intended to be. God's work is ultimately God's business. We are invited – expected indeed – to be co-workers with God, but it does not depend on us. We are not, therefore, to be overanxious, or discouraged about our part in it, even in times like the present which are difficult for the Western Church.

SUNDAY BETWEEN 19 AND 25 JUNE

Twelfth Sunday in Ordinary Time (Proper 7)

1 Samuel 17.(1a, 4–11, 19–23) 32–49 Continuous

It is probably no longer safe to assume that this story will be known by everyone in the congregation. The longer version is therefore the better choice. David is the unknown warrior who comes into a dire situation and, against all the odds, achieves victory. The idea of a 'fight of the champions' seems strange to us, but it was evidently a real option. A great deal depended on the outcome (v. 9). Verses 4–8 emphasize how awesome a figure Goliath was. The failure to find anyone to take on his challenge would have been a real disgrace. David is a very unlikely choice and Saul's misgivings (v. 33) are perfectly reasonable. The amusing little incident recorded in vv. 38–39 may be intended to emphasize that David will owe nothing to Saul as he progresses towards the throne. At another level it makes a deliberate contrast with Goliath's heavy and ultimately useless armour. When the combat takes place David has no physical protection but he does have the protection of God. This motif is woven into the story, not extraneous to it. Goliath's challenge is heard as coming from the 'uncircumcised' to the 'armies of the living God' (vv. 26, 36), and his insults to David are offered 'by his gods' (v. 43). David's reply to the Philistine is equally specific about his dependence on the only true God (vv. 45–47). That the living God cannot be attacked with impunity is certainly a lesson here, but it needs sensitive exploration from those who believe that the living God is best revealed through the weakness of the cross.

1 Samuel 17.57–18.5, 10–16 Continuous alternative

The chapters which relate the relationship of Saul and David have been compiled from a number of sources, embodying variant traditions. In 16.19–23, Saul takes the initiative in making David his armour-bearer well before the conflict with Goliath. In 17.58 he has to ask David who he is, and 18.2 narrates a different tradition of how David came to be in Saul's service. There is no way of deciding how things actually happened, but it is not very important. The fundamental issue is that God has decided David is to replace Saul as king (see the Old Testament reading for last Sunday). Saul's mental instability and aggressive acts against David (18.10–11, compare 19.9–10) are seen as the direct result of the spirit of God having been withdrawn from him (18.12, see 16.14), not just as the reactions of a leader who fears he is losing out in the popularity stakes. At the same time David, God's choice, is building up his popularity in some unexpected quarters (18.5) as well as among the populace in general (18.16). The friendship between David and Saul's son Jonathan is a marked feature of the narrative. It was not a strategic friendship designed to serve the political interests of one or both of them but a personal relationship both deep and genuine (18.1, 3). A cynical world would have us believe that there is always an ulterior motive in friendship but this story suggests otherwise.

Job 38.1–11 Related

The sonorous poetry of this passage creates a powerful impression when it is read well, and we may take away a generalized impression of the power and majesty of our creator God. There is rather more to the reading than that. Throughout the book Job has responded to his misfortunes by protesting that he does not deserve them and by calling on God to admit that he is innocent and to put things right for him. Until now God has, as it were, been silent. But here God answers Job 'out of the whirlwind' (v. 1). At one level it is a devastating answer, which puts Job firmly in his place. How dare he, a mere mortal, question the decisions of Almighty God? What can Job possibly understand of the great scheme of things? So God says to Job. Many have found this is a deeply unsatisfactory answer at some levels, but for the present purposes that may not matter too much. The point is that God's 'answer' describes the things that, so far as Job was concerned, only God can to do. One of these is to control the activities of the sea (vv. 8–11). The reason for this being chosen as an Old Testament lection related to today's Gospel now becomes clear. However, a further reflection is necessary, though it takes us beyond today's reading in more than one sense. Many of the things which between 38.1 and the end of the book are claimed as being solely God's prerogative are so no longer. Scientific research (not least astronomy) has uncovered what in Job's day were secrets indeed. We can now control the physical world in increasingly astonishing ways. If we are not careful with this reading we can create a 'god of the gaps' with fewer gaps than there used to be. Christians will want to say that God works through science as through other things, and if we now know some of the secrets of the universe which were hidden from Job, that is because through the work of scientists God is sharing them with us. Properly understood this makes God more wonderful, not less.

2 Corinthians 6.1–13

When we defend ourselves against criticism, we may be acting out of injured pride or personal vanity. Paul's defence of his ministry which has run right through the lections from 2 Corinthians, is for a different reason. It reaches a climax here and shows us why he is so deeply concerned about it. The Corinthian Christians were his converts, his spiritual children (v. 13). In being led astray by the 'super apostles' (see the comments on the Epistle on p. 106), they were in danger of nullifying the value of their conversion (v. 1). The point of being a Christian is not to gain worldly success or prosperity, whatever some would have us believe. Those who think it is have not understood what the life and death of Jesus was all about. The very things for which the 'super apostles' criticized Paul are the very things which ought to commend him to them as God's servant (v. 4). Verses 4–5 describe Paul's sufferings and verses 6–7 the way in which, as a servant of Christ, he has endeavoured to respond to them and the resources on which he has drawn. In vv. 8–10 he offers two assessments of his ministry: one is the superficial appearance of things, the other is what it has really been about for those who have the spiritual discernment to recognize it. Above all, Paul does not just want to win the argument, he wants to re-establish a relationship of genuine warmth, affection and openness with his Corinthian converts (vv. 11–13). Perhaps congregations have always been prone to look for success from their ministers when they ought to have looked for faithfulness. Certainly, unless there is a mutual relationship of warmth, affection and openness between minister and congregation, no progress will be made.

Mark 4.35–41

The otherwise irrelevant details concerning the other boats (v. 36b) and the cushion (v. 38a) suggest an incident recalled with great immediacy. We are left in no doubt that the storm was a real threat; their lives were in imminent peril (v. 37). In this context, that Jesus continues to sleep, and has to be woken (v. 38a), is a clear sign of his security and sovereignty. The disciples wake him with an angry expression of despair (v. 38b) significantly toned down by the other synoptics (Matthew 8.25; Luke 8.24). In response Jesus does two things: he rebukes the wind and he silences the sea. Mark's phrase about there being a 'dead calm' emphasizes the effectiveness of what Jesus did (v. 39). His questions to the disciples (v. 40) and their awestruck comments (v. 41) remind us that, though the disciples understand some things, at this stage only God and the demons know the full truth about Jesus. As already noted, control of the sea is the prerogative of God alone (see today's reading from Job, and Psalm 107 which accompanies it). The disciples will not fully understand until after his crucifixion and resurrection, though the reader can, of course, see what was hidden from the disciples. Mark's first readers probably also saw in this story the assurance that when they (as individuals or a Christian community) were menaced by dangers which threatened to overwhelm them, they had, in the presence of their Lord, a Saviour whose power was a never-failing source of help. Providing we do not turn it into an allegory, we too can treat the story in this way without trivializing it.

SUNDAY BETWEEN 26 JUNE AND 2 JULY

Thirteenth Sunday in Ordinary Time (Proper 8)

2 Samuel 1.1, 17–27 Continuous

We react to the death of public figures by publishing obituaries in the quality newspapers, followed by magazine articles and television documentaries incorporating tributes from those closest to them. These will be fair, maybe even fulsome, about the person's life and achievements. But we will not have to wait long before investigative journalists suggest that the deceased had feet of clay. It is just the same here. David can have had little love for Saul who had tried to kill him many times (1 Samuel 18.10–11, 17b, 20–29; 19.1, 8–17 etc.), and his lament suggests no personal loss. Yet there is still something to be properly remembered. David had spared Saul's life at least twice (1 Samuel 24.1ff; 26.6–12), giving as his reason that Saul was 'the Lord's anointed', which was the heart of the matter. Saul may have been his bitter enemy, even insane, but he was still the Lord's anointed. It is on the achievements of Saul as the Lord's anointed that David's lament concentrates. Only when the books of Samuel are written will it be said that he had feet of clay. But when David comes to lament Jonathan, who had so often saved him from Saul's vengeance, a note of real personal grief intrudes (vv. 25b–26). Only a prurient and suspicious world (and church) would interpret this as suggesting a sexual relationship between the two men. It is very sad if we cannot recognize and celebrate friendship as one of God's gifts to us.

Wisdom of Solomon 1.13–15; 2.23–24 Related

It used to be argued that a clear distinction must be made between Hebrew and Greek ideas concerning life after death. Hebrew thought (rather late Hebrew thought at least), looked for the resurrection of the body, whereas Greek thought looked to the immortality of the soul. We are now realizing that such a sharp divide does not fit the facts, not least because leading Jewish teachers sought to express and interpret the Jewish faith, using Hellenistic (Greek) ideas and expressions in order to do so. The Wisdom of Solomon, though its date of composition is uncertain (it is not by Solomon), stands within this tradition. Wisdom 1.13 suggests that God did not create death and does not desire death for anyone (compare Ezekiel 33.11). Wisdom 1.14 suggests that God's purpose in creation was that humankind should share in God's own divine (and therefore immortal) nature. Verse 15 probably means that people who follow righteousness become immortal by virtue of doing so. A strong reiteration of the idea that God created human beings specifically to share in immortality is given in 2.23, and in 2.24 the very existence of death is ascribed to 'the devil's envy'. The stress throughout is on the idea that death is somehow unnatural, not part of God's intention. We find this a difficult idea because we regard biological death as natural and inevitable (except when it takes place prematurely, which may give a link with today's Gospel). But if we are intended to have eternal fellowship with God a death which would snuff us out like candles *is* unnatural, and may properly be called 'the last enemy' (1 Corinthians 15.26). Biological death may be inevitable, but that it should be the end of us, is not.

Lamentations 3.23–33 Related alternative

We need to begin at v. 22. Out of an experience of bleak despair (see the comments on the alternative Old Testament reading on p. 78), the writer has a surge of hope. We may not be able to see it, but the character of our God, whose faithfulness is great (v. 23), establishes the existence of such hope for the future (v. 24). Nevertheless, hope and trust in God do not produce, and are not to be confused with, perpetual cheerfulness or ease of life. The poet has a realistic understanding of human existence. He knows the need to wait quietly to experience what salvation might mean for us (v. 26), that there are burdensome tasks to be done (v. 27), times when we have nothing to sing or speak about but can only be silent (v. 28), times to accept being humbled (v. 29), times of unjust suffering and humiliation (v. 30). Yes, there is much through which we feel rejected and afflicted (vv. 21–33) and, perhaps, days when we do not understand this at all. The hope we have in God can only be founded on God's character, and Christians must point to the man on the cross as the vital clue to that.

2 Corinthians 8.7–15

Paul is in the process of organizing a collection of money for the church in Jerusalem which has fallen on hard times. The Corinthians were the first to respond to this (v. 10), but their enthusiasm has flagged and Paul aims to revive it. He could have played on their emotions with graphic descriptions of the need, much as we often do in our charitable appeals, or even our fund-raising for the church roof! He does nothing of the kind, but instead appeals to basic principles of the Christian faith. The first derives from what God has done for them in Christ. If Jesus became 'poor' for their sakes (by laying aside his heavenly glory and giving himself to share our human life and death), they must recognize that to share their riches with the needy is an appropriate response to that fact (v. 9). This goes far beyond what we put in the collection, or give to charity. It is a fundamental and indispensable principle for all Christian giving and living. The second principle is that such giving is an opportunity to show that love is genuine (v. 8) – otherwise they would be convicted of hypocrisy (see James 2.14–17). The third principle concerns equality and fairness, which God demonstrated to be important when the Israelites were provided with manna in the desert (vv. 13–15). These principles do not exempt us from responding to the needs of those caught up in poverty and distress through famine, earthquake, tornado, war or other disasters, all of which have a proper emotional appeal. But they do insist that we go further, recognizing that issues of justice and fairness are raised by third-world debt and trade. We must work to solve these, not out of sentiment or pity but because, as Paul tells us, this is what God in Christ is like.

Mark 5.21–43

Two powerful interwoven stories in one reading! The woman with the haemorrhage (vv. 24b–34) was ceremonially unclean (Leviticus 15.25–30), and therefore forbidden to touch any holy thing. So, as Larry Hurtado comments, she is delivered 'precisely by touching Jesus, the Son of God!' Yet Mark wants to show that this is not mere magic. The physical contact is sufficient to ensure physical healing (vv. 27, 28, 30a), but Jesus responds by seeking personal contact (v. 30b). To make sense of the story we need to note v. 33b: the woman does more than admit to her action, she tells him her whole story. This means that her motives and intentions are voiced to Jesus alongside her desperate need. This is why he can speak of her faith (v. 34a): she has told him of it. She has taken a risk but departs cured, able to go on her way in peace (v. 34b). The story of Jairus's daughter (vv. 21–24a, 35–43) again involves touch, or at least the request for it (v. 23). Jesus has interrupted dealings with a synagogue ruler in order to deal with an 'unclean' woman! The delay this has caused makes it seem that he is too late to do anything: she who was 'near death' (v. 23a) has now died (v. 35b). But it is never too late for Jesus. He does not deny that she has died (v. 39b); he means that death is but a 'sleep', and she can be woken from it – at which the professional mourners, who have seen death many times but have never seen anyone brought back from it, laugh at him (v. 40a). The actual Aramaic words of Jesus are, unusually, preserved (v. 41). As in the case of the unclean woman (v. 34), not touch (v. 23) but faith (v. 36b) is what matters. Not illness alone, but death even, is subject to the authority of the Son of God. Jesus demonstrates what the Wisdom of Solomon can only voice as a hope: that God did not intend death to be the last word, and that it will not be. Jairus's daughter will one day die physically again. But because of the one who will rise from death never to die again, all who have faith can share that risen life.

SUNDAY BETWEEN 3 AND 9 JULY

Fourteenth Sunday in Ordinary Time (Proper 9)

2 Samuel 5.1–5, 9–10 Continuous

There was no question about who would succeed Saul as king. David had been chosen and anointed by Samuel long before (1 Samuel 16.13). In v. 2 there is a recognition that for considerable periods during Saul's reign David had been the de facto leader of the nation. Nevertheless, this is the real beginning of David's reign and a second anointing recognizes that he commands popular support (v. 3b). According to the account we have, his first major step was to secure Jerusalem as his capital, alluded to in v. 9. Apart from the Jebusites, who were the occupants of Jerusalem, all this would have passed without notice in the wider world, for Israel was of no political importance. Often we cannot foresee the long-term consequences of the actions we take, but the consequences of this action were far-reaching indeed. Jerusalem became not only the political capital of Israel but, with the temple at its heart, the religious capital as well (Zion). Many centuries later Jerusalem was the place where the promised Messiah was put to death and raised, and so it became important in the Christian story too. We do not forget that it is a holy city for Muslims as well. The tensions which are also involved in this frequently make the news headlines today. In making Jerusalem his capital, though he could not be aware of it, David did something which has resulted in both joy and pain through all the succeeding centuries.

Ezekiel 2.1–5 Related

The first chapter of Ezekiel records the prophet's detailed vision of the glory of God, and ends with him falling face downwards, awe-stricken in God's presence. Now God addresses him directly: 'O mortal' is the NRSV translation. As the NRSV footnote indicates, the Hebrew is literally 'son of man', familiar to us from older translations such as AV and RSV, and even some more recent ones such as NIV, JB and NJB. In later literature (Daniel 7.13–14, 8.14) the term may have acquired a more technical meaning, which is probably carried over into Jesus' use of it to refer to himself. Here in Ezekiel, where it is used over one hundred times, it certainly has the simple meaning which actually stresses that Ezekiel is a mere human being.

This is rendered variously as: 'Man' (NEB), 'O man' (REB) and 'Mortal man' (GNB). NRSV's 'O mortal' is excellent; we are not being deprived of anything of doctrinal significance by losing 'son of man' here. The prophet is immediately told to 'stand up' (v. 1) in order that God may speak with him, and with these words came a rush of spiritual energy which set him on his feet, ready to hear God's word (v. 2). But the expected message does not come immediately. Instead he is warned that the people of Israel, to whom he must speak, have a long history of rebellion against God (vv. 3–5). Despite the use of the formula which indicates a prophetic message (v. 4b), the clear implication is that they will not hear what God has to say through Ezekiel. However, and this is the point at issue, whether they hear or whether they do not hear, they will be in no doubt that there has been a prophet among them (v. 5). In other words, if they fail to hear they will be without excuse. Today's Gospel reading picks up this theme. What are the things which prevent people today from hearing God's word? Or, to bring the question nearer to home, what are the things which prevent *us* from hearing God's word spoken among us: habit, custom, familiarity? How can we ensure that we are alert and attentive to God's word today?

2 Corinthians 12.2–10

It seems that Paul's opponents in Corinth – those who followed the 'super apostles' – gave special honour to 'revelations' and ecstatic phenomena. They may have challenged Paul about whether he could match the 'super apostles' in such things. So, in the verse which precedes this reading (and which should ideally be included), Paul reluctantly concedes that he needs to show that he too has had such an experience, though he will assess it very differently. So reluctant is he to boast that he begins by referring to a 'person in Christ' (v. 2) as if this was someone other than himself, though by v. 7 it becomes evident that he is writing about himself. The description of the experience is extremely vague (vv. 2–5). Indeed, Paul says not only that it is impossible to describe what he heard, it would be forbidden even if it were possible (v. 4). What matters to Paul is not so much the content of the revelation as its effects. Nevertheless, he asks the Corinthians not to judge him by such visions but by their normal experience of him both in person and by letter (v. 6). It seems that he thought of the 'thorn' which he received (v. 7) as directly associated with the revelation, perhaps a way of bringing him down to earth. We do not know what this 'thorn' was though commentators are not short of suggestions. The most probable explanation is some kind of physical condition. While painful, it was not of a kind to prevent his travelling great distances in the cause of the Gospel; Galatians 4.13–14 may already have referred to it. Like most of us in such circumstances, he was clear what the Lord ought to do about it (v. 8) but received a different answer (v. 9a). We should note that the promise is that Christ's grace is sufficient for *him*, not just as a means of coping with his thorn. It therefore contains a future promise: the grace that is sufficient for Paul now will go on being sufficient, no matter what he encounters or endures. While he could not share the content of his previous personal revelation (v. 4), he can, and must, share this (v. 9b), for though it too springs out of a personal word from the Lord its truth is for all believers. A sermon on the value of religious experience could be preached from this reading. But it might be more helpful to concentrate on vv. 7–10, and reflect on the ways in which we can find Christ's grace to be sufficient for us in the difficulties and problems which come our way in life. We too have heard this word from the Lord because we have heard it through his servant Paul.

Mark 6.1–13

The reading falls into two sections. Verses 1–6a describe a visit to the synagogue at Nazareth. There are some oddities in Mark's phrasing which make it less easy to follow than it seems at first glance, but the general meaning is fairly clear. Jesus was able to perform a few (unspecified) healing miracles (v. 5b), which presumably gave rise to the population's sense of amazement (v. 2b), though Mark oddly suggests that these were not really 'deeds of power' (v. 5a), even though they are regarded as such elsewhere in the Gospel. The point is that not only his healings, but also his teaching, give rise to astonished exclamations (vv. 2b–3). What they do not give rise to is faith, and it was this fact which in turn amazed Jesus (v. 6a). Verse 3 tells us that the reason people could not look beyond the healings and teachings to see God at work was that they knew Jesus, his family and his occupation. The implication is that they would have accepted him if he had come as a stranger, an accredited and official rabbi, properly trained and identified with one of the rabbinic schools. But would they? Verses 6b–13 relate how the disciples were sent out on a mission. It is characterized by a sense of travelling light (vv. 8–9) and is of such urgency that only one real chance to respond is to be given (vv. 10–11). The essence of the mission is to spread more widely the message which Jesus himself proclaimed concerning the need to prepare for God's coming reign (v. 12; compare 1.14–15). It is not helpful to read this story as if it offers detailed instructions for the Church's mission in all times and all places (vv. 8–11 are particularly specific to their own time and place). However, two things remain true. First, mission is to be undertaken at Christ's behest and with his authority (v. 7). Second, mission is about proclaiming the reign of God in Christ and the need for a response to that (v. 12). It is not, as we sometimes appear to believe, about promoting St Peter's Parish Church, Pond Street Methodist Church (or their equivalents), as institutions deserving of support.

SUNDAY BETWEEN 10 AND 16 JULY

Fifteenth Sunday in Ordinary Time (Proper 10)

2 Samuel 6.1–5, 12b–19 Continuous

Last week's reading from 2 Samuel briefly mentioned how David captured Jerusalem with the intention of making it the political capital of Israel. Today's reading records the first step in making it the religious capital as well. The ark of the covenant was a box, intended as a repository for the stone tablets on which were recorded the commandments and laws which constituted God's covenant with Israel (Exodus 25.10–16). It was regarded as a sign of God's presence and, as such, required to be treated with great reverence. Human capacity for misusing religious symbols and sacred objects being what it is, we need not be surprised by the story of its being used as a talisman to ensure victory in war, with the result that it was captured by the Philistines (1 Samuel 4.3–11). This was regarded as a great disaster (1 Samuel 4.22). After various curious adventures (1 Samuel 5.1–6.21), it came to rest back among the Israelites at the house of Abinadab in Kiriath-jearim (1 Samuel 7.1–2). There ensued a long period of neglect, until David resolved to bring it to Jerusalem, as told in today's reading. The Lectionary's omission of vv. 6–12a is understandable enough. However, recommencing at v.12b, where the ark is collected from the house of Obed-edom, is decidedly strange, the reading having given no indication of how it got there. Its eventual arrival in Jerusalem involves appropriate religious ceremonies (v. 17), and great popular rejoicing and feasting (v. 19). We too have visible signs of God's presence, shaped according to the convictions of our tradition (e.g., an open Bible on the communion table; the consecrated host reserved in a tabernacle). Why do we need them? What use do we make of them? What dangers are inherent in them?

Amos 7.7–15 Related

It is good practice to have buildings, especially old ones, inspected regularly. One of the things to be checked is the straightness of the walls. If there has been significant movement and a wall is out of true, remedial action needs to be taken. On rare occasions, perhaps because a building has become dangerous to the public, demolition will be the only realistic course of action. In vv. 7–9 Amos sees God with a builder's implement in his hand. God is testing to see whether the wall (Israel) is straight and true. It is not, and the only answer is demolition. God will not 'pass them by', which means that their offences will no longer be ignored (see 2 Kings 21.13, Isaiah 28.17 and Lamentations 2.8 for similar imagery). The destruction to come involves the hill shrines, the sanctuaries of popular religion (vv. 8b–9a), and King Jeroboam (v. 9b). These threats enrage Amaziah, priest of Bethel, the ancient shrine where Amos has uttered this prophecy. Amos is a religious radical whose words threaten the establishment in both 'church and state' and the personal positions of Amaziah and Jeroboam. It is no surprise, therefore, that those who are so threatened join forces against him. In telling Amos to flee to Judah and earn his living there, Amaziah is suggesting that Amos is a professional prophet who has no right to exercise his calling at the shrine of Bethel (v. 17). In reply Amos stresses that this is untrue: he is not a professional prophet, he does not earn his living by exercising such a calling (v. 14). Rather, he has been specially called by God out of his ordinary occupation for the specific purpose of prophesying to Israel (v. 15). Where better to do this than Bethel, a 'temple of the kingdom' as Amaziah himself has described it (v. 13)? For Amaziah, one of God's priests, to suggest that a prophet should not say what God has given him to say may seem extraordinary to us. But, of course, the message of Amos threatened his place within the established order of things. We can all react defensively when this happens to us. Real prophets often do say things which are uncomfortable for us to hear and painful for us to act on. But if they are real prophets they carry God's authority and cannot be told to keep silent. This passage in Amos focuses the issue, which emerges from time to time in human history. The religious authorities in Jerusalem asked the same question of Jesus (Mark 11.28). The apostles experienced the same pressure (Acts 4.18). Today's Gospel reading tells of how John the Baptist spoke unpalatable truths and paid the price for it. This raises the issue not so much of how the Church *hears* God's uncomfortable prophetic word, as of how the Church *speaks* that word in today's society, and what reaction we may expect when we do.

Ephesians 1.3–14

For this reading see the comments on the Epistle on p. 19.

Mark 6.14–29

Verses 14–16 are directly paralleled by Mark 8.27–28 where the disciples report to Jesus about public discussion on who he was. Here Herod is credited with thinking that Jesus might be John the Baptist resurrected, and the story of John's death is then appended. It has often been noted that this is the only story in Mark which is not directly about Jesus. The care with which it is told, and the length and detail involved, all suggest that Mark attached considerable importance to it. Herod Antipas could only be called 'King', as Mark does in v. 14, as a popular or courtesy title (though his request to Rome for it to be officially accorded to him provided the opportunity for his enemies to get him banished in AD 39). John the Baptist was no respecter of persons, and what he preached to crowds publicly (Mark 1.4) he was evidently prepared to preach privately and specifically, even to those who had the power to harm him (v. 18). The historian Josephus tells us that the adultery of Herod and Herodias, prior to their respective divorces, caused grave public scandal. When they married it was in clear violation of the prohibition in Leviticus 18.16; 20.21, and John said as much. It was Herodias who bore the grudge (v. 19) and initiated the murder (v. 24). Josephus says that John was executed because he posed a political threat, but his criticism of the marriage could be enough to undermine Herod's credibility and that would be a political threat, so Mark and Josephus are probably describing two sides of the same coin. Herod himself is portrayed as having a rather mixed attitude to John (vv. 20, 26). But he is caught in a trap which he sets for himself. The rash promise to Herodias' daughter by her first marriage is made at what was clearly a drunken and dissolute occasion (Mark's phrase 'his daughter' in v. 22 may be a mistake, or it may mean 'step-daughter'; he certainly gets her name wrong – Josephus tells us it was Salome). Having made it Herod cannot lose face, and so John pays the penalty for speaking his unpalatable truths. Yet Mark may intend more by the story than that simple, if significant, fact. Some scholars have been struck by the similarities with the story of Ahab and Jezebel's opposition to Elijah (1 Kings 16.29–19.3), though Herodias was successful in her plotting whereas Jezebel was not. There is no doubt that Mark wants us to understand that John the Baptist was indeed the Elijah figure who was to come before the Messiah in fulfilment of Malachi 4.5 (see Mark 9.10–13) and his presentation may be influenced by that. There is an implication here: if John is the Messiah's forerunner then the identity of Jesus becomes clear for the reader, if not for the characters in the story. The death of John also prefigures that of Jesus. In Mark's account of Jesus before Pilate (15.1–15) there are some echoes of Herod's dilemma over John. The difference is, of course, that John's death really is the end of his story, but with Jesus that will not be so.

SUNDAY BETWEEN 17 AND 23 JULY

Sixteenth Sunday in Ordinary Time (Proper 11)

2 Samuel 7.1–14a Continuous

Although this reading is virtually the same as the Old Testament reading for the Fourth Sunday of Advent, the inclusion there of v. 16, and the choice of lections which accompany it, mean that the focus and intention is different in each case. In Advent we are encouraged to reflect on the Davidic covenant. Here, with this passage forming part of a semi-continuous reading of the books of Samuel, we see how the narrative fits into the developing story of Israel's golden age under David. With Jerusalem established as both the political and religious capital of the nation, and with their enemies the Philistines at least temporarily routed, David's mind turns to the possibility of building a 'house' (temple) for God. He shares the thought with Nathan, who agrees that it would be a good idea (vv. 2–3). But then God instructs Nathan to tell David that it is an idea whose time has not yet come. The anthropomorphism of vv. 6–7, with its suggestion that God has been perfectly happy living in tents, and would have asked someone for a wooden house had that been necessary, probably causes us to smile. Nevertheless, it makes a vivid point: David's building a temple for God is not the most important thing at this moment. It is much more important for God to build a 'house' (dynasty) for David (v. 11b) and, indeed, to ensure that the people are settled into a stable and prosperous way of life (vv. 10–11a). The temple can come later, and be built by another (v. 13a). Sometimes our priorities and plans, however well sorted and thought through they may be, are not those which God wants for us. And sometimes we can be so caught up in the things we believe we are doing for God, that we forget to leave space in our lives for God to do something important for and in us – which may be the real priority of a loving God.

Jeremiah 23.1–6 Related

When Jesus said that from those to whom much has been given, much will be required (Luke 12.48), he was stating a spiritual principle which is well illustrated in this passage and in similar passages elsewhere in the Old Testament (e.g. Ezekiel 34). Those who have been appointed as shepherds to God's flock have indeed been given great responsibilities. What is required of them is that they discharge those responsibilities faithfully and well. When those whose task is to safeguard the flock themselves become the predators it is a double disaster; then the flock has nobody at all to look after and care for it. In such a situation Jeremiah envisages God taking personal action. First, those who have neglected God's flock will quickly discover that God will not be so dilatory in attending to *them* (v. 2b)! Then, God will step into the situation to gather the scattered sheep back together (v. 3). Finally, God will 'raise up' new shepherds to take the place of the old and the new shepherds will care for the people in an exemplary way (v. 4). In the context of Jeremiah's prophecy the unworthy shepherds are probably the previous kings of Israel, who led the nation into such bad ways that they ended up scattered, most in exile in Babylon, some in Egypt and some in other lands. This passage therefore also contains an explicit promise of restoration. Verses 5–6 (which may be from a later hand) contain an even more explicit promise, of a 'righteous Branch' who will be a descendent of David – a messianic hope. As Christians we see the fulfilment of these things in Jesus, in whom we believe that God acted to look after the flock in ways that Jeremiah could not have dreamed of. If this passage is matched with today's Gospel there is some rich material on which to preach.

Ephesians 2.11–22

This reading contains many treasured verses that we are apt to take out of their context. We must not ignore vv. 11–12: Paul is writing to Gentile Christians, reminding them that 'at one time' (i.e., before the coming of Christ) they were outside the chosen people of God, 'strangers to the covenants of promise' which God had made with Abraham and his descendants. They had no hope and were without God. This strong statement is not too strong: they were 'outsiders'. In our century the theme of alienation has been powerfully explored in art, and when there are so many asylum-seekers and stateless people in the world, imagery of alienation still speaks directly to us. What has changed this, Paul asserts, is what Christ has done on the cross, not for God's ancient people the Jews alone, but for the whole world (vv. 13–18). Christ has brought the outsiders in (v. 13). His death has abolished those religious distinctions which once defined who was 'in' and who was 'out' (v. 15a), and the Christ who is our peace

(v. 14a) has proclaimed that peace to Gentiles (who were 'far off') and Jews (who were 'near') alike (v. 17). Paul hammers home the equality of spiritual benefit through the cross of Christ: (a) he makes both groups into one (v. 14); (b) he reconciles both groups to God (v. 16); (c) through Christ both groups have a continuing relationship to the Father in the Spirit (v. 18). The result is that alienation is finished (v. 19a) and all have an equal part in the Church (v. 19). The passage ends with a picture of the Church as built on the apostles and prophets – both in the historical sense and in the sense of being built on their teaching – held together by Christ, the cornerstone (vv. 20–21). In its original context this passage addressed the issue of how Jewish and Gentile Christians should regard each other and live together in the churches to which they both belonged. That issue does not concern Christians in twenty-first-century Britain, but issues of exclusion and alienation certainly do. Usually without intending to, we make our churches into exclusive clubs. We have so many black majority churches in Britain because when Afro-Caribbean Christians started coming to Britain in the 1950s they were treated as strangers and aliens by the local churches they tried to join. Despite the 'welcome' at the door we have subtle ways of making people feel they do not belong (such as seating baptismal parties at the front where they cannot follow the lead of others in standing up and sitting down during the worship). Either Christ has broken down the dividing wall, the hostility between us (v. 14b), or he has not. If he has, there are very real consequences for our life together.

Mark 6.30–34, 53–56

These two passages enclose Mark's account of the feeding of the five thousand (which is not included in the Lectionary). The Gospels do not spend much time on Jesus' feelings or emotions, but we may be grateful that Mark here records the compassion Jesus felt for the crowd 'because they were like sheep without a shepherd' (v. 34a). Verse 34b immediately tells us how Jesus responded. Mark does not tell us what he taught them; it is enough to know that Jesus acts here as the 'good shepherd', gathering the flock together to impart divine wisdom to them (so fulfilling the promise of Jeremiah 23.3). We have an advantage over Mark's first readers because unlike them we know the picture the Fourth Gospel gives of Jesus as the Good Shepherd (John 10.11ff). It is also impossible for us to forget that great parable – not in Mark – of the way the shepherd seeks out even one lost sheep (Matthew 18.12–14; Luke 15.3–7) which, in turn, seems like an expansion of the final phrase of Jeremiah 23.4. All of this is relevant, for when the reading from Mark resumes, we discover Jesus being besieged by every kind of need and demand and meeting them all with compassion (vv. 54–56). This is not to be confused with perpetual availability; in this same chapter Mark records Jesus and the disciples seeking rest and time away from the crowds (vv. 31–32), as well as Jesus' own need to cease his public ministry and be alone with the Father (vv. 45–46). There are important lessons here for those who are 'shepherds' to Christ's flock, as indeed for all who seek to serve others in Christ's name. Mark may also be reminding us that Christian service is offered in response to need and without strings, because there is no mention in vv. 53–56 that any of this results in the 'belief' which elsewhere in Mark is more important than the healings (Mark 6.6).

SUNDAY BETWEEN 24 AND 30 JULY

Seventeenth Sunday in Ordinary Time (Proper 12)

2 Samuel 11.1–15 Continuous

This reading describes some discreditable conduct on David's part. It is remarkable that it was ever recorded at all. When his adultery with Bathsheba resulted in her pregnancy (vv. 2–5), he attempted to wriggle out of his responsibilities by creating a situation whereby her husband Uriah might reasonably conclude that the expected child was his own (vv. 6–13). That stratagem failed because Uriah was a soldier on active service. He had a strong sense of patriotic duty and was unwilling to avail himself of privileges denied to his colleagues (v. 11). David then devised a plan which he knew would result in Uriah's death, as he intended it to, and callously sent Uriah back to battle carrying his own death warrant (vv. 14–15). At one level none of this ought to cause us much surprise. David was, after all, the king! The story comes from an era when monarchs had a great deal of power and, as we well know, those who have great power often misuse it for their own ends. This was how rulers were expected to behave and stories like this one could doubtless have been told about many of David's contemporaries: 'There is one law for the rich, and another for the poor', as the proverb expresses it. But is there? Today's reading ends with David ordering a murder in order to conceal his adultery, evidently feeling neither guilt nor remorse. We already know that he is not going to get away with it. If he had done, this story would never have been told. That it *is* told, and told about Israel's greatest king, is itself a reminder that nobody is above the law of God. God sees what has been carefully concealed from other people.

2 Kings 4.42–44 Related

This little story from the Elisha cycle is told very simply. It assumes the presence of a company of prophets (present in the previous story, v. 38), though 'a hundred' (v. 43a) may be a traditional way of referring to a company of prophets, rather than an exact number (see 1 Kings 18.4). The first fruits of the harvest were normally taken to the priests (Leviticus 23.10), but perhaps it became customary to include the prophets as a mark of respect. Elisha gives orders that the food be shared with the whole company but his servant – elsewhere called Gehazi – queries the order on the grounds that there is not enough for everyone. Presumably the loaves of v. 42 were each very small, otherwise Gehazi's question makes no sense. In any case the entire supply had been carried in a sack by one man. Elisha repeats his order but this time adds a word from the Lord about the food being sufficient (v. 43b). Elisha is not quoting a prophecy which is being fulfilled: the Lord has given him this word for this occasion. The story stands in the tradition where God directly feeds the people, the most famous example of which is the provision of manna in the wilderness (Exodus 16.4ff). The link with today's Gospel offers an opportunity to explore the theme of God's abundant provision for our deepest needs.

Ephesians 3.14–21

This prayer is offered to God the Father, 'from whom every family in heaven and on earth takes its name' (v. 15). The meaning of this is not immediately obvious. The Greek might be literally translated: '. . . the Father, after whom all fatherhood . . .'. The thought is that God is the archetypal Father. All other fatherhood in the world is derived from that of God. Jesus said that if even sinful human beings are capable of being good parents, how much more is God such a good parent to us (Matthew 7.11). There can be a difficulty with this language for those who have had unhappy experiences of their human fathers (though the 'how much more' comparison is important there too). We must also recognize the problem of using exclusively masculine terminology for God who is beyond gender. Nevertheless, the idea of God as the supremely good Father is an important part of the Christian understanding of who God is. We may supplement it with other images (e.g. Isaiah 42.14, 66.13; Matthew 23.37), but not replace it. To this supremely good Father, Paul now prays that the Ephesians will be strengthened in their 'inner being' (v. 16). This refers to who they really are as they experience daily renewal in Christ. He prays that Christ may 'dwell' in their hearts (v. 17), which reminds us of what he says elsewhere about Christ living in him if he has been crucified with Christ (Galatians 2.20). We are apt to privatize our faith, so it is important to note that the 'your' in v. 17 is plural: Paul is praying for the whole community here. If we are to grow in grace in the way that is described in this passage, it is best done 'with all the saints' (v. 18); Christians need one another for a deepening spirituality. Paul never sees the Church as a collection of private individuals. It is a community of faith, a Christian family, whose members are in relationship with one another as they are with God in Christ. He wants them to 'comprehend' the true greatness of God. Is that possible? When the question is asked elsewhere, the implication is that it is not (Job 11.7–9). But for Paul, Christ has made it possible and disclosed that greatness. So his prayer is for nothing less than an increasing realization of the 'fullness' of God in their own experience (v. 19, compare 4.13). Verses 19–21 are a doxology, a spontaneous outburst of praise. He even coins the word 'superabundantly' – 'abundantly far more' in NRSV's translation – to describe what God can do in us. Glory is ascribed to God in the Church (which displays this glory as a reconciled community seeking to further God's purposes), and in Christ (without whom none of this would be possible), for all generations. What is *our* prayer for one another?

John 6.1–21

Both the stories in today's Gospel are regarded as miracles by the evangelist. Attempts to explain them in other ways (by saying for instance that the feeding of the multitude was really a 'miracle of sharing', other people producing the food they had brought when they saw the boy do so) have no basis in the text and are unhelpful. Whether we can accept these incidents as miraculous must be a matter on which each preacher must make up his or her own mind. Even so, it is not the most important question: what matters is what the evangelist intends to tell us through the stories. The feeding of the multitude (vv. 5–14) is the only story about Jesus, prior to the passion narrative, to occur in all four Gospels. Its inner meaning is spelled out in vv. 25–59, which means that we will be able to explore it further over the next four Sundays, and can concentrate here on the story as John presents it. If we compare it with the synoptic accounts (Mark 6.35–44; Matthew 14.15–21; Luke 9.12–17) we see at once that in John's narrative Jesus takes a more direct initiative and is at the centre of the story. Verse 11 describes Jesus performing four actions. He *takes* the bread, he *gives thanks* and he *distributes* the bread, also *distributing* the fish (in the synoptics the disciples distribute). This is language familiar from the Church's eucharistic liturgy. It is also God feeding the people. Jesus is like Moses, through whom God provided manna (Exodus 16.4ff). The promise of a prophet to come, a second Moses (Deuteronomy 18.15–18) is seen by the crowd as fulfilled here (v. 14). The implication of v. 15 is that they thought, since Moses had led them out of slavery in Egypt, the new Moses would lead them against the Roman occupation. But Jesus was the new Moses in a different sense: he had come to give them new manna. The implications of this have yet to be spelled out. The story recorded in vv. 16–21 describes the darkness in which the disciples find themselves without Jesus (v. 17b). Their initial reaction on seeing him walking on the water is fear (v. 19b), but all changes when he says to them: 'It is I' (v. 20, NRSV's rendering of the Greek, which means, 'I am'). The reason for this becomes plain when we look at the phrase elsewhere in the Fourth Gospel. In 4.26, 8.24, 8.28, 13.19, 18.5 and 18.8 it describes Jesus as the one who reveals God – the 'I am' of Deuteronomy 32.39 (see Isaiah 43.10, 13). When 'I am' comes to his disciples fear vanishes, and the boat immediately reaches its destination (v. 21).

SUNDAY BETWEEN 31 JULY AND 6 AUGUST

Eighteenth Sunday in Ordinary Time (Proper 13)

2 Samuel 11.26–12.13a Continuous

After the appropriate period of mourning for Uriah, Bathsheba and David were married (11.26–27). But God knew what had happened; either he revealed it to Nathan (12.1) or rumours had begun to spread. Kings in ancient Israel were also judges (2 Samuel 8.15; compare 2 Samuel 15.2–6), and so Nathan tells a story which requires David to make a judgment (vv. 1b–4). David's instinctive reaction is to protest at the injustice he is hearing about (vv. 5b–6). By so doing, he condemns himself out of his own mouth, so that when Nathan says, 'You are the man!' (v. 7a), he knows it to be true. As the story is written David's repentance seems genuine, not just reaction to the harsh punishments announced in vv. 10–12. Nathan's words in v. 13b amount to a declaration of forgiveness. Though not included in the Lectionary passage, it would be right, for this reason, to read the whole of v. 13. The ascription of Psalm 51 to the penitent David is almost certainly not historical, but we can see why the tradition arose. What David has to learn is that sin is always against God even when it is also sin against other people (Psalm 51.4), and that only God can deal with our sin (Psalm 51.10). That is a lesson which has permanent validity.

Exodus 16.2–4, 9–15 Related

It is human nature to think that the past was better than the present and there is something of that in the present story. The people might have remembered their days in Egypt as a time of sitting by the flesh-pots and having their fill of bread (v. 3), but the reality seems to have been very different. Nevertheless, they have a point: in the wilderness food is indeed scarce. Death by starvation must have seemed a very real possibility. In this situation God provides food of a kind which they had never seen before (v. 15) but which is said to have sustained them during the whole of their forty years wandering (v. 35). There have been various attempts to offer naturalistic explanations for the 'manna', but they are all rather beside the point. So far as the Israelites are concerned, what has been provided is

God's direct gift, even to the point that double rations are provided on the sixth day but none on the Sabbath, so that the Sabbath day will not involve work (v. 5). The quails of v. 13a do not appear in the story again, and can be ignored (though they do appear in Numbers 11.31–33 as God's angry response to people's grumbles that they were fed up with manna). This miraculous provision is sustaining and life-giving, the work of a God who, having brought them out of slavery, wills to bring them to their final destination.

Ephesians 4.1–16

In Ephesians 1–3 Paul unfolds a vision of God's eternal purposes in Christ, in which the Church is seen as a 'new community' of Jews and Gentiles together. It is God's creation, intended by God to be the vehicle of reconciliation. The remaining chapters need to be read against that background. They describe what it means for this 'new community' to live in ways 'worthy of the calling' it has received (v. 1). Paul begins by urging the necessity for the unity of the Church; this is not of human manufacture, but 'of the Spirit' (v. 3; compare Philippians 2.2–5). Verses 4–6 introduce a series of key statements with a repeated 'one'. There is one 'body' (in God's sight there is only one Church, so why does our church life not reflect that?); one 'Spirit' (whose presence makes the Church what she is, and who is at work in diverse ways in all Christians); one 'hope' of our calling (all Christians are promised eternal life with Christ); one 'Lord' (this claim has taken many to martyrdom); one 'faith' (it is not something we invent for ourselves, but is the gift of God to the Christian community); one 'baptism' (we are baptized as Christians, not as Catholics, Anglicans or Methodists etc.); one 'God and Father' (the fount and origin of this unity, because 'above all and through all and in all'). Then Paul turns to the diversity. Christians are not clones, each of us has received a personal grace from the risen Lord and our gifts differ (v. 7). Verses 8–10 are rather difficult both to translate and to interpret, and break up the flow of the argument. Verse 11 begins emphatically: the giver of the gifts is almost certainly understood to be the risen Christ (compare this with 1 Corinthians 12.4–11). What Christ gives his Church is people; God communicates with human-kind through people and their gifts. God's greatest gift to the world was the person of Jesus, not a book of religious instructions. The five ministries mentioned in v. 11 are not intended to be exhaustive and we cannot be sure about the precise function of each. What matters is that all gifts of ministry in the Church (however they are expressed and whatever they are called) are intended to equip the Church for her total ministry in the world and to 'build up' the whole body (v. 12). Verses 13–16 stress, not for the first time, that Christ is both the goal and the means to the goal. Very simply: what difference would it make if we saw the unity of the Church in the way which is described here, and if we saw our fellow Christians as God's gifts?

John 6.24–35

Notes: (1) The Lectionary divides the synagogue sermon into four readings, each of which begins by repeating at least one verse from the previous week's reading in order to retain continuity. (2) Some scholars treat this as an extended reflection from the evangelist, others as an actual sermon which Jesus delivered. The weekly comments allow the preacher to take either view, and phrases such as 'Jesus says', are used for convenience. (3) Ever since the early church fathers, commentators have been sharply divided about whether this sermon is in some sense John's replacement for the story of the Last Supper and thus a 'eucharistic discourse'. The view taken here (which there is not space to defend) is that while John is not writing directly about the Eucharist, the truths this passage sets out are the same as those which the Eucharist embodies: the life of Christ, offered in sacrifice for the world, the benefits of which we receive by faith. The Fourth Gospel's language is, as always, multi-layered.

There is more than one kind of hunger. That which can be satisfied with bread and fish is one thing, and this is what the crowd are taken with (v. 26). But what of other sorts? There is a 'food that endures for eternal life', and it is the gift of the Son of Man (v. 27). The crowd are aware that work is necessary before physical food can be purchased, so ask what kind of work they would have to do for the food which imparts eternal life (v. 28). The reply of Jesus (v. 29) makes it plain that belief in him as the one whom God has sent is the key to spiritual understanding and new life. This is not quite enough for the crowd, who want another 'sign' (v. 30). If he is really the 'prophet like Moses', and Moses gave them manna in the desert, what is *he* going to do? After all, it was widely believed that when the Messiah came the miracle of the manna would be repeated (vv. 30–31). In reply, Jesus reminds them that it was not Moses but God who gave the manna, and says that this 'true bread' (new manna?) is something God is giving *now* (v. 32). The crowd then asks for this bread from heaven (v. 33; compare 4.15). It seems likely that what they expect to receive in response to this request is some teaching, some heavenly wisdom. This is why v. 35 is key: not teaching, but Jesus himself is the 'bread of life'. This is the first of the 'I am' sayings in John's Gospel, a moment of self-revelation on the part of Jesus and, therefore, of God's self-disclosure. If Jesus is the one who can take away hunger and thirst for ever, then those who 'come to' him have no need of any other spiritual nourishment. Many in our contemporary world are aware of spiritual hunger. They turn to New Age and other movements, not to the Church. Is this because we have given the impression that the Church is about no more than what comedian Mark Steel memorably described as 'bringing an unwanted tin of apricots to the Harvest Festival'?

SUNDAY BETWEEN 7 AND 13 AUGUST

Nineteenth Sunday in Ordinary Time (Proper 14)

2 Samuel 18.5–9, 15, 31–33 Continuous

The difficulty with this reading is that it lacks a context. That context is supplied by 15.1–18.4, which tells of a period of turmoil in the nation's life, caused by the action of David's son Absalom. He had himself declared king, and led an open rebellion against his father, causing David and those loyal to him to flee from Jerusalem. Today's reading begins as David's army sets out for what proves to be the final battle with Absalom and his followers, though David himself has been persuaded not to take part. Despite Absalom's disloyalty and rebellion, David had a deep love for him, so issued orders that he was not to be harmed (v. 5). However, David's commander Joab could be more objective; he realized that so long as Absalom remained alive there would be civil war. From the outset he was determined that Absalom should die in the battle (vv. 11, 14b, not included in the lection). When the news of Absalom's death was brought to David he was utterly distraught (v. 33). The Lectionary does not give us the conclusion of this story: Joab made David confront the political necessity of what had been done, and come to terms with it. In this he was successful (19.1–8a). The story is told in such a way that the reader feels involved, and unsure of what was right. On the one hand we see the depths of David's grief and we admire his love for his rebellious son. This, it seems to us, is the way a good parent should be. On the other hand, we remember that David is not a private individual; he is king, responsible for the welfare of a nation which is being torn apart, and so we can see why Joab takes the decision he does. What is the right thing when there is a conflict of interest between our natural feelings and the welfare of others? Sometimes, when the police are hunting a murderer or a rapist, they will say something like, 'Someone must be shielding this person, someone close to him must have their suspicions.' On what principles should Christians act in that kind of situation?

1 Kings 19.4–8 Related

Elijah's contest with the prophets of Baal (1 Kings 18.20–39) should have been a mighty victory. But when Queen Jezebel heard of it she was furious, and threatened his life. So Elijah fled beyond her jurisdiction. Once he was safely out of reach, depression overcame him; what use was he if his response was to run away (v. 4)? The incident related in this reading is one of the stories which (like the manna the Israelites received in the wilderness) is about God miraculously feeding his faithful people in time of need. Like the manna, it is physical food for a physical journey. Like the manna, it is also 'the bread of angels' (Psalm 78.25), since the miraculous manner of its bestowal points to a God who sustains us in every sense.

Ephesians 4.25–5.2

One of the enemies of Christian faith is surely 'moralism', which looks and sounds so much like the real thing that many people cannot tell the difference. For them Christianity can be equated, in its entirety, with 'living a good life' or 'keeping God's laws'. They then look at Christians and conclude that, since we manifestly do not always practise what we preach, they too can live a good life, but without bothering with all that nonsense about going to church, which doesn't seem to do much good anyway! Beginning today's reading at 4.25 can reinforce this impression, because what follows seems like a list of rules for living the good life. But what do the words 'So then' (4.25) mean? They refer back to what Paul says in 4.22–24, where he writes about putting away our 'old self', being 'renewed' and 'clothing' ourselves with the 'new self'. All this is quite crucial: Christian existence is about acquiring a 'new self', which is what happens when a person turns to Christ. Without that we only have moralism, which can do quite well without Christ. So it is important that this passage is presented in its proper context. Why then do we need these admonitions about our conduct? Because being renewed, and clothing ourselves with the new self, is a lifelong task involving our wills and our constant turning to Christ who gives us the victory (Romans 7.21–25). And this passage is about relationships within the community (4:25), spelling out specific ways in which Christians should seek to be 'imitators of God' (5.1). They are not hard to understand – though some of them may be hard to do! We should speak truthfully with one another because we belong to one another in the body of Christ (4.25), observance of which would transform many a church meeting. If we are angry (as we may well be) we are not to nurse it or let it become an obsession (v. 26), which says something to churches where people have running feuds with each other. Those whose former way of life was thieving should work hard so as to be able to give to others (v. 28), which is as effective a demonstration as you could find of what the 'new nature' is about. We must say only good things not evil ones, so that our conversation is positive and helpful (v. 29), which may have been in the mind of the minister who put up a notice in the church hall which read, 'No Gossiping'. Other things too must be 'put away' (mostly 'sins of the tongue', v. 31 – compare James 3.1–10), in order that we do not cause pain to the Holy Spirit who is the bond in our life together (v. 30). When the final positive qualities are listed (v. 32a), it is with the reminder that we must live 'as' Christ has forgiven us and 'as' Christ has loved us (5.2) – we are back to the 'new self' again.

John 6.35, 41–51

Last week's Gospel ended, as this week's begins, with Jesus' self-disclosure: he is the 'bread of life', and those who 'come to' him will find all their spiritual hunger and thirst met (v. 35). This causes further grumbling among his hearers (v. 41). John may well intend his readers to recall the way in which the children of Israel grumbled against Moses and Aaron (Exodus 25.24; 16.2, 12). But on the face of it, the complaint is a reasonable one (v. 42), heard in a different context in Mark 6.2b–3. It is not hard to imagine that this question was often asked about Jesus during his earthly ministry, but here it has a sharper edge. If Jesus claims to be the bread of life (v. 35) and that bread comes down from heaven (v. 33), what has that to do with someone whose family is well known locally? Only those who have, as it were, understood John 1.14 could begin to work this out. The complaint gives Jesus the opportunity to explain some of this: God is already at work in this very conversation, if they did but realize it, because those who 'come to' Jesus are drawn by God, so to be open to Jesus is to be open to God (v. 44a). More, the prophecy of Isaiah 53.13 quoted in v. 45 is being fulfilled in this very moment; they are, if they did but realize it, being taught by God through this sermon/conversation. But it is belief which makes this a reality (v. 47). In v. 48 Jesus reiterates what he has already said in v. 35 and then in v. 49 returns to the quotation from Psalm 78.24 (v. 31), which is, as it were, the 'text' for this sermon. Yes, the Israelites did indeed receive bread from heaven in the wilderness, but they died nonetheless. What he is offering is better than manna because it is the bread which prevents death by giving eternal life (v. 50). The point is reinforced by v. 51a, which restates and underlines vv. 33, 35 and 48. But then comes the surprise. Just as, following the request in v. 34, Jesus offers them not some teaching or heavenly wisdom but himself, so now he tells them that what he will give is not just himself, but his flesh. For the moment (oh, the frustrations of Lectionary divisions!) we learn no more, but if we are stunned, even offended by such a statement, so were his original hearers. This verse is no easy stopping place, but we should notice two things. First, he will 'give' (see the comments on the Gospel on p. 76). Second, what he will do is for the whole world (compare John 3.16).

SUNDAY BETWEEN 14 AND 20 AUGUST

Twentieth Sunday in Ordinary Time (Proper 15)

1 Kings 2.10–12; 3.3–14 Continuous

The statement in 2.12, that Solomon's kingdom was 'firmly established', glides rather smoothly over a court purge involving a number of political murders, understandably not included by the Lectionary. But once those were over and done with his occupation of the throne was indeed secure. The story of Solomon's dream, and his request to be given 'wisdom' rather than the more obvious riches and honour for which he might have asked, raises as many questions as it answers and appears puzzling to us when set against the historical narrative. The 'wisdom of Solomon' became proverbial, so much so that when a later 'wisdom literature' arose in Israel his name was associated with a good deal of it (see 4.32). The folklore story of the two prostitutes demonstrates this wisdom (3.16–27), and the Queen of Sheba was famously impressed by it (1 Kings 10.1–10), though not she alone (1 Kings 4.34; 10.24). But there were many things about Solomon's character and conduct which we would hardly regard as wise, and which indeed come in for some criticism from the writer. As early as 1 Kings 3.3b, the statement that he 'loved the Lord' is somewhat qualified; by 1 Kings 11.1–13 this has turned into open condemnation and the reason why his son will not be king over the whole nation. Allowing his foreign wives and concubines (more than one thousand of them according to 11.3!) to worship their gods, and doing so himself, strikes us as extremely foolish. We need to recognize that 'wisdom' here does not mean what we would normally mean by it. We think of wise people as possessing sound judgment in all areas of their lives. In Solomon's case it was more limited, and directly related to his task of running the country as ruler and judge (3.28b). During his reign the nation enjoyed a period of unparalleled peace and prosperity, and all the people shared in this (4.20–21; 8.66). Solomon's 'wisdom' was of a very practical kind, demonstrated by his governing justly and well. At the same time, it was more than simple human shrewdness; the point of the story in this lection is that it is God's gift. If, like Solomon, we pray for wisdom in our daily lives, we ought also to make sure that, unlike Solomon, we remain close to God.

Proverbs 9.1–6 Related

Wisdom is here given a (female) personality, and thus personified as Lady Wisdom. This was later developed in the books of Sirach/ Ecclesiasticus and the Wisdom of Solomon (see the comments on the reading from Sirach on p. 18). The Jerusalem Bible heads this section, 'Wisdom as hostess'. She is depicted building a house (v. 1), preparing for a banquet (v. 2) and sending out the invitations (v. 3). Who are invited? Those who are 'simple' and 'without sense' (v. 4). By sharing in Lady Wisdom's banquet of bread and wine (v. 5), even such foolish people will begin to acquire true wisdom. Wisdom here is more than the down-to-earth practical understanding we see in Solomon. It amounts to nothing less than the knowledge of God, which gives life (v. 6). This imagery may remind us of Isaiah 55.1–2, where God offers a similar invitation. The full depth – and cost – of it is not seen until John 6.51, 53. The lection ends at v. 6, but the passage as a whole involves a contrast between this banquet with Lady Wisdom, and a different kind of banquet – leading to different results – with Lady Folly (vv. 13–18). This actually forms quite a good link with today's Epistle.

Ephesians 5.15–20

This reading also starts by saying something about the contrast between wisdom and folly (vv. 15, 17). Wisdom here is an attitude to life which involves specific choices, and discernment of the will of God. It is set against the background of a pagan environment, whose way of life is 'folly'. The admonition to 'be careful' suggests that the Christian community's way of life is under scrutiny and must be able to stand up to it. As contemporary Britain becomes more secularized, being a Christian may involve a lifestyle more distinct from that of other people than once seemed to be the case. The lifestyle of the Christian community therefore needs to have an integrity which will stand up to scrutiny. In v. 16 the GNB translation catches the sense rather better than NRSV does: 'Make good use of every opportunity you have . . .'; the thought is about seizing all occasions of doing good. Drunkenness is singled out in v. 18, not because it is worse than other things, but as an example of 'folly' and one which, since it loosens inhibitions, may lead to other kinds of 'debauchery'. It also enables Paul to make the contrast with what it means to be filled with the Holy Spirit. Larry Kreitzer points out that both verbs in v. 18 are in the passive voice, so the thought could be expressed as, 'wine does the controlling, or the Holy Spirit does the filling' – the choice is ours, but one is foolish and the other wise. With v. 19 the passage turns to consider worship. The NRSV translation 'among yourselves' obscures one of its most interesting features: 'speak to one another' is better (so NEB, REB, NIV and GNB). Paul is saying that we should communicate *with one another* even as we sing and make melody *to the Lord*. In other words, what are sometimes called the horizontal and vertical dimensions of worship are both present here. Worship is, of course, offered to God and in praise of God. By engaging in it as a corporate activity we encourage one another. Verse 20 fittingly reminds us that our Christian thanksgiving is not confined to times of formal worship. As Horatius Bonar expressed it:

> Fill thou my life, O Lord my God,
> In every part with praise,
> That my whole being may proclaim
> Thy being and thy ways.

John 6. 51–58

Jesus says he will give his 'flesh' and will give it for the 'life of the world'. Since this is his description of 'living bread' and he has invited people to 'eat', it is a shocking and offensive remark so far as his audience are concerned (v. 52), though 'disputed' is a rather weak translation – the word means 'argued angrily'. We need not suppose they understood his words literally: talk of eating someone's flesh is offensive even as metaphorical language. It is, of course, a reference to his eventual death on the cross which is indeed for the whole world and is also Jesus' 'gift', a willing offering to the Father (10.17–18), the benefits of which they are being invited to make their own by 'believing' in him now. The angry argument has its usual function of moving the discourse on. But in his reply Jesus offers no explanation, and does nothing to soften the force of what he has said – indeed he strengthens it. He adds a reference to drinking his blood, strictly forbidden in Judaism, and tells them that such eating and drinking is the only way of sharing in eternal life (vv. 53–57). To have eternal life, we now learn, is to receive the benefits of the death of Jesus. Those who eat his flesh and drink his blood are those who see him and believe in him, and so receive him into themselves by faith. This is what is meant by 'abiding' in him (v. 56). Augustine's famous epigram, *Crede, et manducasti* ('Believe, and you have eaten'), makes the point very well. This is, of course, eucharistic language.

Paul tells us that the Eucharist is a proclamation of the Lord's death (1 Corinthians 11.26), by which he means not just that it reminds us of the cross, but that it makes the benefits of the cross available to us. So, when we take the bread and wine, and intend by that act to receive Christ into ourselves and claim the benefits he has won for us through his death, we are indeed doing what John's Gospel here tells us is necessary for eternal life (v. 58).

SUNDAY BETWEEN 21 AND 27 AUGUST

Twenty-first Sunday in Ordinary Time (Proper 16)

1 Kings 8.(1, 6, 10–11) 22–30, 41–43 Continuous

It would be a pity to omit the bracketed verses. They are skilfully selected to give a sense of the solemnity of this occasion. Verse 1 indicates the national importance attached to the act of moving the ark to its new home and v. 6 tells of its arrival. In vv. 10–11 the cloud is the sign of God's presence, as it was at Sinai (Exodus 24.15–16), and at the tent of meeting (Exodus 40.34–35). The message is unmistakable: God is now here and has taken possession of the new temple. Solomon's prayer before the altar begins by acknowledging that Israel's God is literally beyond compare (v. 23a). Even if the gods of the other nations were thought of as in some sense real, they could not compare with the God of Israel who had 'kept covenant and steadfast love' (v. 23b). God's greatness is located not in displays of power and might (though the Israelites sometimes looked for those too), but in faithfulness and blessing. This insight is one which Christians can accept, and we can find our own examples of the steadfast love. Verse 27, perhaps the best-known part of the reading, is widely regarded as a later addition to the text because it breaks the flow of thought. No matter, it is an insight as important now as it was then. Of course we know that our churches do not 'contain' God, but we often act as though they do. When we are in danger of domesticating God, this verse has much to say to us. Nevertheless, a God who is everywhere has to be sought somewhere, and Solomon's prayer for the temple (like our prayer about our churches) is that it will be such a place (vv. 29–30). There is a special importance to the petition in vv. 41–43. The 'foreigners' concerned are not the resident aliens (a different Hebrew word), but those who come deliberately to Jerusalem because they have been attracted by Judaism and its worship. A true house of prayer, now as then, must always be for all who seek God (Isaiah 56.7). It is never the exclusive possession of any one group.

Joshua 24.1–2a, 14–18 Related

Even if for many of us life moves along fairly routinely, we know that from time to time we need to make major decisions. They are most often about careers, relationships and children. They may also be about religion. We may be stirred into decision and action by something we read in the Bible, or perhaps something which is said in a sermon or by a friend. At such moments we sense that we have to make a commitment, or a re-commitment to the faith journey, or possibly to some new avenue of Christian service. Not to do so would be to regress, to turn away from that which gives life, which changes and transforms us. In this reading Joshua faces the whole nation with just such a moment of decision. Are they prepared to renew their relationship with their God? Not to do so would be to regress back to the gods their ancestors used to worship (this information about Abraham is not given in Genesis, but it is found in the late Jewish apocalyptic book *Jubilees*, and in the Qur'an), or to the native – but not life-giving – gods of the land in which they live (vv. 2b, 15a). Joshua both issues the challenge and, significantly, gives the lead: he has made his decision and invites others to follow (v. 15b). The outcome is not in doubt: they will serve the God who has so faithfully looked after them (vv. 16–18). As the Christian hymn-writer puts it:

> We'll praise him for all that is past,
> And trust him for all that's to come.

Ephesians 6.10–20

As Paul comes to the end of his letter he warns his readers against spiritual complacency. They will need to be strong (literally, 'be strengthened') by sharing in God's power (v. 10). The picture of the 'whole armour of God' which follows owes much to the picture of God as the Divine Warrior who brings salvation and remedies injustice (Isaiah 59.17; compare the Wisdom of Solomon 5.17–20). The whole passage is governed by the idea 'stand against' (v. 11); this is about the Church defending herself against evil. This evil, and its source, is described in vv. 11b–12. Many people have found difficulty here, because Paul appears to suggest that our fight against evil is a purely spiritual one ('not against enemies of blood and flesh', and 'in the heavenly places'), whereas in fact Christians have always found it necessary to fight against very tangible evils. The issue is a little complicated, but what Paul seems to be arguing is that our struggle is not merely against evil as a human construct. Though we are good at explaining away evil it is unwise to do so. It is not to be underestimated, because its origins are supernatural and its range cosmic. Human history, including that of our own times, suggests this is a correct assessment. When, for example, a Rwandan nun is convicted of supplying the petrol used for setting fire to a convent building in which people had sought sanctuary, do we not find ourselves forced to acknowledge that evil is a 'spiritual' reality though, of course, it manifests itself in enemies of blood and flesh? Paul's related point is that if evil is indeed this kind of phenomenon, material weapons alone are not sufficient to resist it: we fight by proclaiming the gospel of peace which transforms (v. 15b). The pieces of armour (vv. 14–17) may be summarized thus: 'belt of truth' = integrity and sincerity; 'breastplate of righteousness' = uprightness of character; 'shield of faith' = the Church's abiding trust in God; 'helmet of salvation' = claiming God's saving help; 'sword of the Spirit' = the word God gives us to hear and speak in time of need (see Hebrews 4.12). We omitted v. 15, the NRSV translation of which is slightly odd; better, 'let the shoes on your feet be the gospel of peace, to give you firm footing' (REB). Prayer in the Spirit, for all the saints and Paul himself (vv. 18–20), is not another piece of the armour but the field on which this spiritual battle takes place. So for example, both private and public prayer need to be well informed about where in today's world the forces of evil are at work. Our prayer will then engage them and will in turn inspire our daily living to do likewise.

John 6.56–69

We have learned from this synagogue sermon that to have eternal life is to receive the benefits of the death of Jesus. Those who eat his flesh and drink his blood are those who see him and believe in him, and so receive him into themselves by faith. There are many ways in which we feed on Christ by faith, including worship, prayer and reading the scriptures. But pre-eminently we do so when we share in the Eucharist, for that is the means which Christian tradition tells us Christ himself ordained and commanded (Luke 22.19; 1 Corinthians 11.24–25). However, the language of all this is difficult and it is not just Jesus' immediate hearers who are offended by it. It also proves a stumbling block for some who are described as 'disciples' and eventually results in their 'turning back''(vv. 60, 66; compare Mark 10.22; Luke 9.62). In v. 61 Jesus wonders how they would react if they were to see him revealed in his true glory. If many have now left him, what is going to be the reaction of those whom he has specially chosen? In a passage which parallels the confession of faith at Caesarea Philippi (Mark 8.27–29), it is Peter who gives the reply on behalf of all. They have journeyed with him and have 'come to believe' (v. 69). Significantly, Jesus is addressed here as the 'Holy One of God', a true enough description, but one which occurs in Mark where a demon-possessed man blurts out the 'messianic secret' (Mark 1.24). Peter's response is the one which John hopes all his readers will want to give too. 'I can think of dozens of good reasons for leaving the Church, and only one for staying in it,' a church member once said, and added, 'but that one is enough.' So it is here: if Jesus has the words of eternal life, that is exactly what we risk losing if we are foolish enough to turn back.

SUNDAY BETWEEN 28 AUGUST AND 3 SEPTEMBER

Twenty-second Sunday in Ordinary Time (Proper 17)

Song of Solomon 2.8–13 Continuous

We can be glad to lay aside all those ingenious but misplaced attempts, common throughout Christian history, to interpret this book as an allegory. Instead, we can recognize it for what it so clearly is, a joyful celebration of the gift of sexual love. We probably need this little book as much, or more, than ever before. Some Christians of the past found some of its language and imagery daring and even shocking and therefore assumed it must really be 'about' something else. In twenty-first-century Britain we encounter more explicit sexual imagery, both visual and verbal, almost every day, in broadsheet as well as tabloid newspapers and in mainstream television programmes. The problem is that so much of it is demeaning and exploitative, casual or 'knowing', and therefore unhealthy. Far from promoting open and enriching attitudes to sexuality, it simply makes us into voyeurs, as when the first television series of *Big Brother* was shown in 2000, and the British public became very interested in watching for sexual intercourse among a group of comparative strangers. But Christians must not react to all this with prudery or a denial of sexuality. On the contrary, we need to celebrate sexuality that is life-enhancing rather than demeaning, exploitative or casual. The Song of Songs can certainly help us to do that. It offers us poems which express frank and healthy emotion (even if the imagery is sometimes a bit obscure to us today). Moreover, we hear the voices of both the male and female partners in this relationship; today's passage is the woman's dream of being with her lover. It requires little detailed comment – indeed, that would spoil it. As she thrills to the voice of her lover she imagines him leaping and bounding towards her, 'on top of the world' as we say (v. 1). When he comes, he sings a sweet song inviting her to live with him and be his love (v. 10) for it is spring (vv. 11–13a) and, as the Pages sing in Shakespeare's *As You Like It*, 'Sweet lovers love the spring.' Further comment seems superfluous, but if we are to preach on this passage we must indeed take care not to spoil it.

Deuteronomy 4.1–2, 6–9 Related

When something we do or say turns out to have unexpected results we comment, 'That is not what I intended.' We cannot always be responsible for what others have made of our words or deeds (though sometimes we can!). Intention is important, and this passage expresses the original intention behind the Law which God gave Israel through Moses. These laws are the basis of the covenant relationship with God which is such a vital feature of Israelite religion. Moses says that he is 'teaching' them to the people in order that they may 'observe' them (vv. 1, 5b–6a). The intention is that they will enable Israel to live wisely and well, so wisely and well that they will attract the admiration of other nations (v. 6). They will be a distinctive people because of their covenant relationship with God (v. 7a) and the purpose of the Law is to express that distinctiveness for its source is none other than God (v. 8b). It is very understandable, therefore, that they should be instructed neither to add anything to it nor take away anything from it (v. 2). However, one of the problems with law (any law) is that it requires interpretation. The Law may say, for example, that you must 'love your neighbour as yourself' (Leviticus 19.18b). That seems clear enough, but it does not stop people asking to whom it applies or, in other words, 'who is my neighbour?' (Luke 10.29). When sufficient definitions have been offered, a body of case law may be built up which, in practice, obscures the intention of the Law and makes its observance both difficult and burdensome. This is certainly one way of 'adding to' it and is the charge that Jesus makes in today's Gospel.

James 1.17–27

All good things come from God and they come as gifts (v. 17). The greatest gift is that God 'gave us birth by the word of truth' (v. 18a; compare Colossians 1.5; Ephesians 1.13). This is James' way of describing the new birth, salvation in Christ. Note that since men are not capable of giving birth this is a feminine image for God, used here quite naturally. Throughout his letter, James is emphatic in insisting that those who have been 'brought to birth' should recognize the consequences of it in the way they live and he does so here (vv. 19–21a), while also recognizing that we cannot deal with our shadow side ourselves. We need the power of the 'implanted word' to help us (v. 21b). In vv. 22–23 we meet a view, common among James' contemporaries, that moral and religious teachers are like mirrors. If you look carefully into their teaching you see yourself as you really are, and thus recognize your own need for improvement. In James' illustration those who carefully observe their features in a mirror but promptly forget what they look like, stand for those who look into moral or religious teaching but fail to do anything about it. James is concerned that we should not only hear the message, but also act on it. Until hearing has become action the message has not been fully accepted. As we look into the Christian message we too must recognize how it challenges us on our need for spiritual improvement. Prayer, Bible reading, discussion groups and courses are not ends in themselves. We need to use them to grow in our understanding of what it means to be Christian. The proof that we have done so will be that we are willing to put our faith to work in practical ways in daily life (vv. 26–27).

Mark 7.1–8, 14–15, 21–23

'Have you washed your hands?' is a question adults ask children before meals. It is a matter of basic hygiene, so familiar that the casual listener to vv. 1–5 (including most of our congregation) may understand them in this way without further thought. Mark recognizes the problem; vv. 3–4 are his attempt to explain the issue to Gentile readers. These ritual requirements are said to be observed by the Pharisees and scribes (Mark's addition of 'all the Jews' in v. 3a means that the Pharisees and scribes would ideally have liked everyone to behave in this way). Such rituals are not laid down in the written Law which came from Moses. They had grown up over the centuries as ceremonies to ensure appropriate purity, but were additional to the Law of Moses (see today's related Old Testament lection). When asked the question, Jesus responds by alleging hypocrisy on the part of his questioners (vv. 6–8). These are people who act outwardly to impress others, but who have missed the real issue about cleanness and uncleanness. By using the phrase 'human tradition' of such ceremonies, and contrasting it with 'the commandments of God', Jesus clearly rejects the oral law. Mark's first readers, for some of whom the question of how far Christians needed to observe such ceremonies was important, would find an answer here. Verses 14–15 are addressed to the crowd; Jesus calls them, thus underlining the importance of the issue. The question of whether a person is clean or unclean goes much deeper than rituals and ceremonies. It cannot be dealt with by whether or not you wash your hands. It cannot even be dealt with by whether or not you observe the written food laws themselves (note v. 19b which, though not in the lection, is where Mark makes the issue crystal clear). This is very radical teaching. The food laws were important in Judaism (Leviticus 11; Deuteronomy 14.3–21), as they still are. There had been martyrs for this in the fairly recent past. But Jesus now says that the whole notion of what is clean/unclean must be sought in the human heart, which is the source of moral action. Holiness is not to be found in the realm of things, but of how we behave (vv. 21–23). We might be tempted to think that this issue, so thoroughly disposed of by Jesus, is now of merely antiquarian interest to us. That would be too comfortable a conclusion. We are wonderful at turning the teaching of Jesus back into law, and at inventing Christian ceremonial laws, especially denominational ones ('Methodists don't gamble' – but I will leave readers of other traditions to decide what theirs are!). The lesson of vv. 21–23 needs constant re-learning: true holiness is about what is in our hearts. Only God's implanted word can help us deal with that (see today's Epistle).

SUNDAY BETWEEN 4 AND 10 SEPTEMBER

Twenty-third Sunday in Ordinary Time (Proper 18)

Proverbs 22.1–2, 8–9, 22–23 Continuous

We do not need any more sermons on our Christian duty to help relieve world poverty and fight injustice. Too many of them have left our congregations feeling guilty and rather helpless. We may, though, need more sermons about how we *become* the kind of people who fight injustice and relieve world poverty as a matter of course, because of who we are and what we believe. These verses may provide some modest help with that and there are some obvious links with today's Epistle. In some families children's names are still chosen to express a (hoped for) character. This was so in Israel, and a 'good name' (v. 1) means a good character and reputation, which is preferable to great riches. Some contemporary rich scoundrels, whose deeds have been publicly exposed and who have thereby lost their reputations, might even agree with this! Verse 2 is innocent enough, apparently uncontroversial, but it has deep implications. The Lord is the same Lord for both rich and poor people. We are made by the same hand of God. Rich and poor alike share a common God-given humanity. To perpetrate injustice is a denial of that very important fact. Those who see the poor as easy targets because they lack the means to resist, and deny them justice (this is the meaning of v. 22b; see Ruth 4.1–12; 2 Samuel 15.1–6), will reap their reward (vv. 8, 23). The generous, by contrast, are blessed (v. 9). These verses from Proverbs ground our concern for justice and for the world's poor not in an abstract notion of duty, still less in a sentimental response to the plight of those in distress, but in God who gives us our common humanity. This is part of what it means to be a believer.

Isaiah 35.4–7a Related

There is much in Isaiah about God coming powerfully in vengeance against a sinful people (e.g. 34.8). Here God still comes powerfully but his vengeance now appears, paradoxically, as salvation (v. 4). The writer has already described how nature will be transformed (vv. 1–2); now he turns to what will happen to people when this salvation appears (vv. 5–6a). This is almost certainly a description of miracles and physical healings, not a series of metaphors for spiritual blindness and deafness. The start of a 'new age' will inevitably involve healing and life-giving energy (compare 33.24). After all, the blind, the lame and the deaf are the people in greatest need of it. Some of this passage is quoted in today's Gospel when its significance will become apparent.

James 2.1–10 (11–13) 14–17

The Christian assembly into which the two contrasting people come (vv. 2–4) is meeting to decide about something, possibly a disciplinary matter, rather than for worship. The community is instructed not to treat them in a manner which means the wealthy person will be listened to with more respect than will the poor person. At first this appears no more than common sense: the rich have no monopoly on wisdom. But James takes it out of the realm of good advice into the realm of good news. He insists that Christians are those who believe 'in our glorious Lord Jesus Christ' (v. 1). The REB translation is better and makes the point more forcibly: '. . . you believe in our Lord Jesus Christ who reigns in glory.' Favouritism towards the rich is not only foolishness, it is a denial of the reign of Christ whose Lordship is for all, rich and poor alike. This gives a new dimension to the thought in Proverbs 22.2. Verses 5–7 provide additional reasons for not favouring the rich, and it would appear that the Christian community here has experienced some rich oppressors behaving in the manner of Proverbs 22.22b. By so doing they have blasphemed the name of Jesus, invoked in baptism (v. 7). When James writes about fulfilling the 'royal law' (v. 8), and being judged by the 'law of liberty' (v. 12), he is thinking of the way in which the Law of Moses was reinterpreted by Jesus. Jesus saw it not as a means of salvation, but as a way of walking in God's wisdom. This is especially true of the famous 'love command' (Leviticus 19.18), which James quotes here and which Jesus quotes on no fewer than five different occasions. Our practical love for others will indeed be a measure of our faith, perhaps the most important measure of all. Verses 14–17 presuppose the example in vv. 2–4, but go on to add another one. Real faith demonstrates its reality in loving deeds. Verses 15–16 offer an example of a hollow profession of faith. It is so strongly drawn it is almost caricatured: the needy person is given a verbal blessing, 'Go in peace', but no real blessing at all. This helps us recognize the absurdity of professing faith but then failing to live it out. Verse 17 has often been thought to contradict Paul (e.g. Romans

5.1; Ephesians 2.8–9) but this is not really so. James is not offering a choice between faith and works, but demanding that the two be linked. Any so-called faith which makes no difference to us is no true faith at all. The preacher might well ask questions about what practical difference faith has made to our conduct, provided she includes herself!

Mark 7.24–37

Last week we found Jesus abolishing the traditional way of regarding things as clean or unclean. In today's Gospel he meets with an 'unclean' Gentile woman, and then with a man in an 'unclean' territory. First *things* are declared clean, then *people* are. In vv. 24–30, the focus is not so much on the exorcism, as on whether it is right for Jesus to perform it. The text suggests a struggle, though one with a decisive outcome. Jesus has not come to the region of Tyre with the intention of performing miracles, but he cannot escape notice (v. 24b). A woman in this particular place would obviously be a Gentile, but Mark goes out of his way to emphasize the fact (v. 26a). The conversation (vv. 27–28) is not an unreal one, where Jesus is merely seeing what response he gets. He is represented as being genuinely uncertain about whether such a sign of the reign of God should be given to a Gentile. He is not being asked to alter the priorities of his mission: he is still sent 'to the lost sheep of the house of Israel', as Matthew's version adds (Matthew 15.24). Even if the dogs (Gentiles) eat the crumbs under the table, the children (Jews) have still been fed (v. 28). Her answer convinces Jesus: Gentiles are to be added in. Verses 31–37 narrate a different sort of miracle. Here Jesus is in the Decapolis region where there was a sizeable Jewish population in each of the towns, but the territory as a whole had strong Gentile associations. By contrast with the preceding story Mark gives us many details about the healing (vv. 33–35). Though they are interesting it would be unwise to attach any deep significance to them. However, NRSV's description of the man's condition, 'a deaf man who had an impediment in his speech', is precise and accurate. The rare Greek word which Mark uses describes someone who has great difficulty in speaking, not someone who is unable to speak at all: after the miracle he 'spoke plainly' (v. 35b). But something more is implied. The rare Greek word is so rare that it is not found anywhere else in the New Testament and is used in the Greek translation of the Old Testament only at – Isaiah 35.6! Mark characteristically describes the onlookers as being astonished, but here they give a very precise reason for their astonishment (v. 37b). Through what Jesus has done God has brought salvation to this man and in this place the 'new age' has dawned. We cannot fail to note that in neither story is there any mention of faith (it has often been read into vv. 28–29, but without any evidence). Jesus heals a Gentile woman and a man in an 'unclean' territory simply in response to need. In so doing he breaks down barriers of religion and race and ignores the conventions. At the very least this invites us to reflect on the Church's task of serving women and men across conventional barriers, simply in response to human need, and without any thought of 'results', other than to declare by so doing that God's reign is present. It is also a rebuke to our tendency to put up barriers and to regard some people (those with AIDS, drug addicts etc.) as unclean or beyond the scope of God's love.

SUNDAY BETWEEN 11 AND 17 SEPTEMBER

Twenty-fourth Sunday in Ordinary Time (Proper 19)

Proverbs 1.20–33 Continuous

We have met 'Lady Wisdom' before (see the comments on the related Old Testament lection on p. 149), though this is her first appearance in Proverbs. She is found in the midst of a crowded, bustling city street, shouting her wares like a street trader (vv. 20–21). She calls on simple ones, scoffers and fools, to turn from their folly and learn true wisdom (v. 22). The 'simple' are those who lack judgment and are easily led into wrong ways (see 14.15). The 'scoffers' are trouble-makers who know wisdom when they meet it but proudly spurn it because they know better (see 21.24). The 'fool' has no time for truth at all, is stubborn and stupid, so best avoided (see 14.7–8). None of these people have to be what they are, it is their choice to (respectively) love being simple, delight in their scoffing and hate knowledge (v. 22). And so, despite Lady Wisdom's offer to enlighten them (v. 23), she does not appear to have much hope that they will accept it. So the offer turns to denunciation, with the threat of eventual disaster (vv. 24–28). In v. 29 we learn the root cause of all this: they have not chosen the fear of the Lord. There is nothing very easygoing about this passage. It probably reminds us of some of the fierce denunciations of the prophets. But whereas some of those are tied to particular sins, this is more timeless and non-specific. It has a contemporary ring about it. Christian mission always needs both to invite and to warn. However, there is a danger that we indulge ourselves in the popular Christian pastime of looking with lofty superiority on the majority of our fellow citizens, the great spiritually unwashed. They are rushing headlong to their own destruction, while we, with our fear of the Lord, are secure. The need with this kind of passage is to apply it not to others, but to ourselves. First and foremost we are intended to ask whether Lady Wisdom here addresses *us* and, if so, what we are going to do about it.

Isaiah 50.4–9a Related

For this reading see the comments on the Old Testament on p. 62.

James 3.1–12

James here identifies himself as a teacher ('we who teach', v. 1b) and urges that others should show restraint in following his example. His role as a teacher leads him to recognize that words have great power, for good or ill, and we human beings who handle them make many mistakes (v. 2a). This tirade against the tongue (vv. 2b–12) contains some pretty strong language. If we were able to control our tongues, he says, we could control the rest of our bodies (v. 2b). If this seems like an overstatement we may reflect how often we say something 'without thinking', as we put it, and later wish it unsaid. Sins of the tongue occur frequently just because of the ease with which speech happens. The illustrations in vv. 3–4 are all intended to make the same point: little things can have huge consequences. So the tongue, a little enough thing, is capable of wreaking havoc (v. 5). Verse 6 is extremely difficult. It appears to mean something along the lines of: each and every part of human experience can be 'set ablaze' or ruined by what the tongue does. James follows this up by pointing out that we are quite skilled in subduing (so REB, a better translation than 'taming') even savage wild animals, but not the tongue (vv. 7–8). So far we have heard nothing good about the tongue at all! But now he mentions the highest and purest function for which the tongue can ever be used, the blessing of God (v. 9a). He is referring not just to the singing of God's praises in formal worship but the way in which, in the Jewish tradition, the whole day was permeated by such praises. At once we are reminded that we also use our tongues for cursing those made in God's image (v. 9b; incidentally, does James include himself in the 'we' here? Very probably – see v. 2). Clearly, when we behave like this there is something wrong. Even in the world of nature we expect consistency and reliability from such things as springs of water (v. 11). Plants produce what they are genetically pro-grammed to produce, as we might express v. 12a, but human beings produce first one thing, and then another. Preachers need to take James' warnings about the sins of the tongue with some seriousness, because there is sometimes a Christian blind spot about this. We would never think of committing murder, but we may quite enjoy the kind of gossip which murders someone's reputation. In this area we have a great capacity for self-deception. Few things can as quickly destroy good relationships in a congregation, or its ability to display the winsomeness of the gospel, as failure to control our tongues. What is more, speech is one of the things which indicates, as Jesus told us, what is really in our hearts (Mark 7.20–23).

Mark 8.27–38

'Who is Jesus?' is a central question for Mark's Gospel. Jesus asks the disciples this question, perhaps because he realizes it is time they answered it for themselves (v. 27b). His first question is about other people's opinions and, in reply, they refer to popular speculation (compare 6.14–15). When asked the more direct question it is, not surprisingly, Peter who answers: 'You are the Messiah' (v. 29b). The reader of Mark's Gospel has known this all along (1.1) but in the context of Jesus' ministry it is important that the disciples reach this point. We have no means of knowing whether Peter is here seen as the spokesperson for them all or whether this is his personal insight. The former seems more likely; they have all journeyed with him, seen his works of power and heard his teaching. They have come to realize that he is God's messenger in a very special way. The acknowledgment that he is Messiah is, then, natural enough. But it is not at all clear that they actually understand what this means. Indeed, in a very short time we will learn precisely that Peter does *not* fully understand this. For this reason they are sternly told to keep quiet about it (v. 30). Nevertheless, they have now achieved sufficient insight into who Jesus is to be told more plainly what his mission will involve, and this Jesus proceeds to do (vv. 31–32b). We have already encountered the opposition from the teachers, but the rest will await him in Jerusalem. In telling them this Jesus refers to himself as 'Son of Man' (for some notes on this term, see the comments on the related Old Testament lection on p. 124). Peter probably understands it to simply mean 'I', and he cannot cope with Jesus saying such things about himself. Is Jesus not Messiah? And is the Messiah not the one who will drive out the Romans? How could Jesus, thinks Peter, predict the failure of his mission? No, Peter does not yet fully understand what kind of a Messiah Jesus is. Jesus' rebuke is stinging (v. 11). It needs to be, because essentially Peter is offering Jesus the same temptation as he was offered in the wilderness, to use worldly methods or force to achieve his mission (Matthew 4.8–10). No, his mission will involve his suffering and death. All who want to follow him must understand this. So Jesus calls the crowd as well (because this applies to all believers, not just the Twelve), and tells them about the need to take up the cross (v. 34). This was no metaphorical language: his hearers would be used to the sight of condemned criminals carrying the crosses on which they would die – they must be prepared even for that. Verses 35–37 express a supreme paradox which contrasts saving 'now', with saving 'for ever'. Some of his hearers were forced to make that choice, as some Christians have been ever since. We, in twenty-first-century Britain are not, though there are other ways of denying Jesus and so losing our real life, than refusing martyrdom. These things have eternal consequences. Lamar Williamson Jr's comment on v. 38 says almost all that needs saying: 'Whoever is ashamed of Jesus now in the common pressures of life will feel the shame of Jesus in the end, when those who wanted to save themselves stand before one who did not.'

SUNDAY BETWEEN 18 AND 24 SEPTEMBER

Twenty-fifth Sunday in Ordinary Time (Proper 20)

Proverbs 31.10–31 Continuous

From the writer's perspective this passage affirms women. For us today, however, it raises more questions than it answers. It begins by asking, 'A capable wife who can find?' and the added comment about such being 'more precious than jewels' (v. 10) suggests she is fairly rare! This is a portrait of a very busy woman. Every waking moment is occupied (vv. 15a, 18b). Her management of each aspect of house-hold life is impeccable (v. 27a). She is not, though, merely 'her inside'. She has a life outside the home, as a capable businesswoman who buys land, plants a vineyard (v. 16), and makes and sells clothes (v. 24). In short, she is a paragon of virtue, whose husband and children are extremely happy with her, as well they might be (v. 28). The secret of all this is that she is a woman who 'fears the Lord' (v. 30b). To be positive, we might recognize that there have always been women whose industriousness and commitment has sustained family life, even when married to feckless and dissolute men (though that is not an issue here). We should be deeply grateful for them. On the negative side, this reading shows us a paragon of virtue whose aim is to please her husband (vv. 28b–29). We might have fewer problems with this if there was a matching passage about a perfect husband whose aim is to please his wife. Even so, paragons threaten us, for we know we cannot match them. It is more realistic to look for a mutual commitment which acknowledges imperfections. We cannot preach on this reading without, in some sense, subverting it.

Wisdom of Solomon 1.16–2.1, 12–22 Related

This reading puts words into the mouths of the ungodly. They have made a 'covenant' or pact with death, because they believe that this life is all there is (1.16; the verse is probably based on Isaiah 28.15 where God condemns just such an attitude). In 2.12–22 the ungodly plot against the 'righteous man', resentful of his claim to know what God requires of people (2.13a). The very existence of the righteous is an affront to their own evil thoughts, because his holy way of life marks him out as different from other people (2.14–15). Therefore their evil intention is to put the righteous person to the test, both to see if he can endure it, and also to see whether God will, as he claims, uphold and save him (2.17–20). But their evil way of life has also corrupted their reasoning (2.21). They do not understand anything of the secret purposes of God (2.22a). In fact, although they scorn it, God will ensure that the holy and blameless receive an appropriate reward (2.22b) – after death is probably meant. This reading may have originally referred to wealthy apostate Jews persecuting fellow Jews who had refused to abandon their faith. The early church soon realized that it also described the way the powers of evil conspired to bring about the death of Christ, and the vindication God would give him after death. It is illustrative, not prophetic, material.

Jeremiah 11.18–20 Related

This passage reads like an extract from Jeremiah's spiritual diary. It tells us what it feels like to be the focus of anger and resentment of an entire community. We do not know the precise reason for this, but it does not matter. We do know that it had something to do with Jeremiah's faithfulness to his prophetic calling, and we also know that the opposition came from the people of his birthplace Anathoth (v. 21); so family, and those he might have counted as friends, were involved (compare Matthew 10.36). They are in fact plotting to kill him (v. 19b), though Jeremiah was unaware of that fact (this is the meaning of the 'gentle lamb' image in v. 19a) until God revealed it to him (v. 18). Whereas from earliest times Christians have used the 'lamb' picture of Isaiah 53.7 as a prefiguring of Jesus at his trial (see Acts 8.32), this earlier picture in Jeremiah, on which Isaiah may have drawn, is less amenable to such an interpretation. Jeremiah certainly does not suffer in silence! But he does look to God, who alone reads the heart, to vindicate him (v. 20). As with the related reading from the Wisdom of Solomon the point is not predictive prophecy, but the recurring themes of the persecution of the righteous by the ungodly, and of the vindication which God will provide for the righteous. Both these are supremely seen in the death and resurrection of Christ.

James 3.13–4.3, 7–8a

Our way of life demonstrates whether we are motivated by wisdom which is from 'above' (3.13b, 17a), or by the evil which lurks in the human heart (3.14–16; the use of 'wisdom' in 3.15 to describe such conduct is heavily ironic). To live by the evils of the human heart creates conflicts and disputes, both within the Christian community, and without (4.1, 2b). It even causes us to misuse the gift of prayer for our own ends (4.2b–3). There is even the suggestion that it might lead to murder (4.2a), which might refer to Christians becoming involved in violent political struggles. Life does not, however, need to be like this: there is an alternative way. Guidance by divine wisdom means living as those who both love and create peace. The end result is that, in NJB's vivid translation of 3.18, 'The peace sown by peacemakers brings a harvest of justice.' This reverses what we think of as the usual order of things, where peace can only flourish when justice and righteousness are in place (see Isaiah 32.17). Here James echoes Jesus, referring not to those who *seek* peace (and especially not peace at any price, see Jeremiah 6.14), but to those who *make* peace (Matthew 5.9). To make peace in our world, or our church, involves laying aside the vices of 3.14–16, seeking out the root causes of conflict and injustice, and working to put them right. In order to do this we need to resist evil and submit our whole way of life to the will of God who, by drawing near to us, will strengthen us (4.7–8a).

Mark 9.30–37

Verses 31–32 record Jesus' second open prediction of his death. NRSV's laudably inclusive translation, 'into human hands' (v. 31), unfortunately conceals a significant word-play in the original Greek. What Mark wrote is: 'The Son of *Man* is to be betrayed into the hands of *men*' (my italics). This was historically the case: all those involved in the death of Jesus were men, though there could have been women among the crowd who bayed for his death. However, that is not Mark's point. Rather, he seems to be saying that God has sent Jesus the 'perfect Man' to save us, but 'men' ranged themselves against him, betrayed him and put him to death. The prediction of *betrayal* is new, not present in the first open prediction of the passion (Mark 8.31). Verses 33–37 introduce a different, though related, topic. Sometimes when we get out of our depths we change the subject! Perhaps that is what the disciples did here, in a conversation in which Jesus evidently took no part (vv. 33b–34). Some people find it hard to credit that the disciples should have argued about who was the greatest. But they had now realized that Jesus was in some sense the Messiah (8.29), and could well have been arguing about their respective places in a 'messianic glory' which they only half under-stood (which is what we find later at 10.35–37). The teaching recorded in v. 35 is found a number of times in the Gospels, usually by way of contrast with what takes place in everyday life. The values of God's reign in this, as in other respects, turn ours upside down. At first sight Jesus' action in v. 36 seems unrelated to what has gone before. But as Dennis Nineham points out, in Mark's version (as distinct from Matthew 18.1–5), the emphasis is on the attitude of the disciples *towards* the child (as also in Luke 9.46–48). In both Aramaic (in which Jesus spoke), and in Greek (in which Mark wrote), the word for 'child' can also mean 'servant'. Jesus' action is therefore an acted parable on the saying in v. 35. The disciples are to welcome and treat each other (and others too, as the story which opens next week's Gospel will show) as fellow children/servants of the kingdom, and not squabble about who is the most important within it. This still has a number of lessons for today's Church, which can cherish status and hierarchy as readily as the disciples do here.

SUNDAY BETWEEN 25 SEPTEMBER AND 1 OCTOBER

Twenty-sixth Sunday in Ordinary Time (Proper 21)

Esther 7.1–6, 9–10; 9.20–22 Continuous

The story told in Esther is set in the time when many of the Jews were living in exile, and Israel was a vassal state of Persia. It concerns a young Jewish orphan who becomes the wife of the Persian King Ahasuerus, who does not know that she is a Jew. Under the guidance of her guardian Mordecai she foils a plot by Haman, who is the king's advisor and Mordecai's bitter enemy, to exterminate all the Jews in Persia in a single day. On the king's orders Haman is hanged on the gallows he had prepared for Mordecai (7.10). Esther and Mordecai direct that the Jews should keep an annual festival (called Purim), to celebrate this great deliverance (9.20–22, 29). Though the book is evidently written in the form of a short story it is quite likely that some historical event inspired it; we know too little about the life of the Jewish community in Persia to be sure. The book is difficult for us in several ways. It never mentions God, displays no obvious theological interest and (though this is not included in the Lectionary reading), its gloating over the destruction of enemies is unpleasant (9.5ff). Nevertheless, its presence in the canon of Christian scripture is of considerable importance. The story of Christianity's relationship with Judaism is one of the darker aspects of the Church's history. When, in the twentieth century, Adolf Hitler behaved towards European Jews much as Haman planned to do, too many Christians were silent or compliant. If nothing else, Esther ought to remind Christians that anti-Semitism is unacceptable.

Numbers 11.4–6, 10–16, 24–29 Related

At first sight it looks as if the story in vv. 4–6, of how some of the Israelites grumbled about having nothing to eat but manna, raises the main theme of this reading. In fact, it merely provides the reason why Moses is so irritated by them. He complains bitterly to God about the people's specific grumbles at the lack of meat, but also more generally that he is having to act like a mother to a miserable and ungrateful people. He cannot do this any longer without some help (vv. 10–15). God's reply addresses both concerns, but the response to the grumble about the lack of meat disappears in this selection of verses. The story of the sharing of God's spirit with seventy 'elders' (vv. 16, 24–25) is God's response to Moses' more general plea for support and help. The significant fact is that they 'prophesy' (v. 25 – though its final sentence has never been satisfactorily explained). Exodus 18.25–26 records Moses appointing other people as officers and judges. The fact that the elders in this story prophesied suggests that they had another role. Presumably they were intended to share the spiritual leadership with him, though the text does not actually say so. However, the main interest of this reading (taken in conjunction with today's Gospel) lies in vv. 26–29. Eldad and Medad are still in the camp when they receive their share of the spirit and so prophesy (v. 26). Joshua is alarmed by this and asks Moses to stop them (v. 28). Moses' reply is a strong reminder that God's spirit is sovereign and free (v. 29). Where something is happening which is clearly of God it should be welcomed even if it comes from an unexpected quarter.

James 5.13–20

This passage is often understood to be about healing and is a focus of interest for those concerned about the ministry of healing. However, it is just as much about prayer and it tells us something about the nature of Christian community. In v. 13a, NRSV's 'suffering' is not a happy translation; 'in trouble' is better (so JB, REB, NIV, GNB). Since sickness is mentioned separately, the troubles here are either those which come to everyone at some time or those caused by the wrong attitudes of some fellow Christians (3.14–16; 4.11–12). In any case the remedy is prayer. Conversely, those who have something about which to be thankful should sing songs about it (v. 13b). Those who are sick should ask for a pastoral visit from the church's leaders, and the purpose of the visit is again prayer, accompanied by anointing with oil (v. 14). It is not clear whether this anointing is for medicinal purposes (in which case it illustrates the undoubted truth that both medical techniques and prayer have their part to play in what Christians understand by healing), or whether it is a purely religious act, symbolizing God's favour and presence with the sick person (see Isaiah 61.3; Psalm 45.7). Since its administration is confined to the elders the latter seems more likely. Either way it is not magic; it is the prayer which is envisaged as the effective agent of healing (v. 15a). The statement that the Lord 'will' act in response to this prayer is difficult for us: that is not always our experience. It is sometimes said that if people are not healed it is because they (or those who pray) do not have sufficient faith. James says nothing whatever about faith here. He does, though, continue by saying that anyone who has committed sins (we need to note that it is not assumed that the sick person has necessarily done so), will be forgiven (v. 15b). This leads James into another thought which we find difficult (v. 16a). Mutual confession of sins has been characteristic of some revival movements but it presupposes a higher degree of mutual trust than perhaps exists in most of our congregations. Praying for one another (v. 16b) is something we are more accustomed to, but we need to note its purpose. It is so that 'you' (that is the whole community) might be healed. In all this we sense a high level of care and concern for one another's welfare which is illustrated further in vv. 19–20. The encouragement to pray is reinforced by the example of Elijah (where James draws on traditional interpretations of Elijah's actions such as Ecclesiasticus 48.3 rather than the text of 1 Kings 17–18). The interweaving of prayer, confession/ forgiveness, healing and concern for each other which we find here gives us a picture of congregational life against which we might measure our local church.

Mark 9.38–50

Last Sunday's Gospel showed how the disciples are to treat each other. The incident recorded in v. 38, together with Jesus' response (vv. 39–40), broadens the picture. This man too is a fellow child/ servant of the kingdom. The disciples have tried (unsuccessfully) to stop him because he does not 'belong'. It is a pity that Mark 9.14–18 is not in the Lectionary, because it forms a wonderfully ironic contrast with this passage: the unknown exorcist succeeds where the disciples failed! By declaring that the deed of power was done in his name (v. 39), Jesus is saying that because of his opposition to Satan's grip on people's lives, this exorcist is united with Jesus, whose mission is about God's reign in people's lives. Like Joshua in today's related Old Testament lection, the disciples want to control what God can do and through whom it can be done. There is a lesson here for the Church: we are not the only ones through whom God's work is accomplished. Wherever we see healing and wholeness coming to broken lives God's Spirit is at work. Far from being jealous or resentful, we should welcome this with open arms. Verse 41 is an independent saying, though it has links with v. 37 (hospitality) and v. 35 (humble service). Is v. 42 also an independent saying? Most commentators think so, but William Lane advances a good case for it as a further comment on v. 38. If so, 'the little ones' are other followers of Jesus, like the exorcist. Failure to recognize this is a serious matter. Verses 43–48 employ vivid oriental imagery about how anything which tempts us to be untrue to God must be discarded, even at great cost, just as a surgeon amputates a limb in order to save life. It is just possible that actions such as those described in these verses were used as punishments for various crimes (as in some Islamic societies today). If so the imagery would be familiar to the disciples: it is better to lose a limb than a whole life, and 'life' (meaning a right relationship with God) is exactly what is at stake. We can no longer recover the meaning of v. 49, but v. 50a is a command to make sure they preserve the true qualities of disciple-ship, and v. 50b to share in fellowship and be at peace, so rounding off the teaching begun at v. 35.

SUNDAY BETWEEN 2 AND 8 OCTOBER

Twenty-seventh Sunday in Ordinary Time (Proper 22)

Job 1.1; 2.1–10 Continuous

This is the first of four Sundays where the Lectionary gives us a taste of this difficult but important book. The storyteller begins abruptly with the equivalent of 'Once upon a time'. We must take the statement in v. 1 about Job's goodness and uprightness with total seriousness or else the rest makes no sense. When ch. 2 begins Job has already undergone an incredibly severe testing in which he has lost his children, his servants and all his possessions (1.13–19). None of this persuades Job to curse God (1.22). Satan now says that if Job himself is touched by affliction his piety will quickly be shown up as false. He is then permitted to test Job further (2.4–6). We have no means of knowing what disease is being described in vv. 7–8, but it was clearly serious. More importantly, it would be regarded as a direct punishment from God. Job's afflictions, in contemporary thought, proclaimed before all the world that he was a sinner, even though Job knew that he had done nothing to deserve his sufferings. Job's wife thinks he should admit his faults and curse God so that God will strike him dead; that would at least put an end to his sufferings (v. 9). She earns a very harsh rebuke (v. 10), the narrator adding a comment that Job preserved his integrity. The lesson thus far seems to be: whatever sufferings come your way, do not lose your faith in God; rather accept them as a test of your character and you will be brought through. At one level there is a very precious truth in this, and some of us will be able to think of wonderful Christian people who have lived like that and whose faith puts ours to shame. At another level it does not deal with the problem of innocent suffering in anything like a realistic way. What is more, the writer knows that it doesn't, because he will proceed to add forty chapters to this story, and not until we reach the end can we see the extent of his exploration. The only way to deal with this would be to preach a four-part sermon over this and the next three Sundays, though that assumes a regularity of attendance at worship which might not be the case.

Genesis 2.18–24 Related

Even reading this passage in church may cause embarrassment or amusement. It is often cited to prove how deeply the Judaeo-Christian tradition subordinates women (the 'spare rib') to men. It may be important to preach on it precisely for this reason. It begins with God's declaration that the human he has created was meant for community, not aloneness; he needs a helper and partner (v. 18). The animals are created next and, in a tender scene, brought before 'the man' to receive a name (vv. 19–20a; if you have all-age worship to lead you can have some fun with this!). But he finds no 'partner' among them (v. 19b). So God 'makes' a new creature out of 'the man' and brings her to him. Verse 23 is a joyful cry: here 'the man' recognizes what he had not recognized in any of the animals, one who will be the *partner* and *equal* that he so much needs. Three times in this verse we find the little Hebrew word *zō'th*, which means 'this one'. The feminist joke about woman being God's second attempt to get it right is not entirely wrong! He refers to her in v. 23a as 'bone of my bones/flesh of my flesh', which is an expression used elsewhere in the Old Testament to indicate deep and lasting relationship (see Genesis 29.14; Judges 9.2; 2 Samuel 5.1; 19.12–13). The man and the woman belong to each other as true partners (the pun in the Hebrew on *'īsh* and *'ishshāh*, indicated in the NRSV footnotes, is just about reproducible in English by *man* and wo*man*). The narrator's comment in v. 24 lays down this partnership as the basis of human society. We are rightly sensitive to the wide variety of family units which exist in Britain today. Without demeaning any of them, we still need to say that a relationship of trust and commitment between a man and a woman is the ideal foundation of family life.

Hebrews 1.1–4; 2.5–12

For 1.1–4 see the comments on the Epistle on p. 14. These verses consider Christ's superiority to the whole created order, including the angels. In 2.5–12, the writer says that the 'coming world' was subjected not to angels, but to human beings. His quotation from Psalm 8.4–6 states that God has given a very exalted status to humans, seen as the crown of creation, with all else in subjection to them. The problem is that this does not correspond with the reality we experience; we do not see it to be so (v. 8b). Indeed we do not! Even the physical world can be a source of danger and disaster over which we have no control. Hebrews also has in mind those spiritual powers which can wreak a different sort of havoc in human life (compare Ephesians 6.12). No, we do not yet see human dominion over these things, 'but we do see Jesus' (v. 9a). And in seeing Jesus we see the one who *has* achieved the victory and the dominion, at the cost of suffering and death (vv. 9b–10). In Jesus we see the promise of Psalm 8 fulfilled, because in the course of achieving his victory he became truly human, lower than the angels (v. 9a) and his victory is now ours. Jesus now has 'human brothers and sisters' (v. 11b). For all the complexities of the Epistle to the Hebrews its essential message can often be very simple, as here: when overwhelmed by the immensity of human sin or misery, look to Jesus and see the victory which will one day be ours too.

Mark 10.2–16

Pastoral sensitivity is demanded from all who preach on this lection, since vv. 1–12 seem to forbid all divorce and remarriage. In a country with one of the highest divorce rates in Western Europe few of our hearers will be unaffected by this, either personally or through some family member. Jesus is asked about what is permitted (v. 2), but the answer he gives is about what is commanded (vv. 3–4). In v. 4 the questioners refer to Deuteronomy 24.1, which allows a man to divorce his wife (though not the other way round). The meaning of this was subject to much discussion among the rabbis. His questioners may have expected Jesus to join in that discussion. Instead he tells them that such permission was a concession to the hardness of the human heart (v. 6), and appeals straight to God's original intention for marriage (vv. 6–9, quoting Genesis 1.27 and Genesis 2.24). Divorce forms no part of God's intention: marriage should be permanent. In vv. 10–11 the disciples ask him again about the matter, and Jesus repeats his uncompromising teaching, though in different words (adding that a wife should not divorce her husband, unthought of in Jewish law, so giving women equality, though equality in what is forbidden!). What he states so uncompromisingly is an ideal, and a very important one. Those who marry must intend their marriage to be lifelong. Divorce may be (we might even say, 'must be') tolerated and permitted because of the hardness of the human heart, but it is always in some sense a falling short of God's intentions. What we must not do is to turn Jesus' words back into law. Both in Matthew (19.9) and Paul (1 Corinthians 7.12–15) we find the need to work out the implications of all this in new contexts, and that has gone on being the case throughout Christian history. People who have been through the pain of divorce do not need a lecture from the Church about their failure. If they find a new relationship they may need help to discover how that can become a new ideal, untainted by guilt or cynicism. Verses 13–16 make the simple point that the only way to receive God's kingdom is 'as a little child', that is, trustingly. But we must not miss Jesus' real concern for children and their well-being. He was 'indignant' (a strong word and the only time in the New Testament it is used about Jesus) at his disciples for trying to turn away the parents who were bringing them (vv. 13–14a) and deliberately blessed them (v. 16). We should care for children as part of the Church now, not as is sometimes said, as the Church of the future.

SUNDAY BETWEEN 9 AND 15 OCTOBER

Twenty-eighth Sunday in Ordinary Time (Proper 23)

Job 23.1–9, 16–17 Continuous

Between last week's reading and this, Job's three friends have arrived (2.11). They have made speeches about how Job should interpret what has happened to him, and Job has, in turn, responded to them. Eliphaz has just finished appealing to Job to repent and return to God who delivers the guilty but humble (22.21–30). Job's reply virtually ignores what Eliphaz has said. Instead he gives voice to his wish to meet with God (v. 3) in order to present his case and convince God that some dreadful mistake has been made (v. 4). He would listen to what God would say to him (v. 5) and believes that God would not simply overwhelm him (v. 6a), though earlier he had feared that God might do exactly that (9.34; 13.21). He is still confident that in God's court he will be acquitted (v. 7; here we remember the importance of taking 1.1b very seriously). But meeting with God is easier said than done! Some people seem very sure that they can never get away from the presence of God (Psalm 139.7–12), but Job's experience is the opposite (vv. 8–9). Verse 17 is so difficult to translate (NRSV footnote indicates one possible alternative rendering and there could be others), that it is best ignored. It is, in any case, not needed. There is enough in this passage already to establish where Job is in his argument with God. He has rejected all attempts to persuade him that he is a sinner who deserves his sufferings (because he knows he does not), and wants to meet with a God who is hidden. Perhaps we too readily speak of the presence of God. In our times it is often, in the words of the poet R. S. Thomas, a presence that is 'like an absence'. Job helps us see that those times when we cannot find God, even though we desperately feel that we want to, are part of an authentic spiritual journey. And in rejecting the well-meant, though rather bookish, arguments of his friends, he reminds us that for faith to have integrity it has to stand the test of our own deepest experiences.

Amos 5.6–7, 10–15 Related

Amos prophesies at the shrine of Bethel, threatening complete destruction (v. 6b). Verses 6a, 14a and 15b suggest (unusually for

Amos) that it might be averted. Justice is demanded above all (vv. 7a, 15a) since it alone can protect the vulnerable. Righteousness is also required (v. 7b), and here it refers to right relationships between people. Verse 10 refers explicitly to the sin of undermining justice; the 'gate' is the place where the local court sat, the only way in which the poor and vulnerable could be protected. To undermine it was therefore an especially serious matter and involved a deliberate breaking of the ninth Commandment (v. 10b). Verses 11–15 show Amos denouncing specific exploitations of the weak and poor by the rich and powerful. They will learn that the punishment (from God) will fit the crime (v. 11). Whereas we tend to think first in terms of charitable relief for the needy, the Old Testament offers us a strong corrective by stressing the need for justice. An impartial and accessible judicial system is fundamental to human rights. One of the first things would-be dictators do is to undermine the independence of the judiciary. But justice can be denied in more subtle ways than that: by being made too expensive or complicated for the poor, for example. Since Amos reminds us that a denial of justice is an affront to the humanity of others, and thus to God, it is a proper subject of Christian concern. Quite why this passage has been chosen as a related lection for today is a puzzle. A good part of today's Gospel is concerned with wealth, but none of it is about the wealthy denying justice to the poor.

Hebrews 4.12–16

Verses 12–14 present the challenge and vv. 14–16 provide the encouragement! What is this 'word of God' described so vividly in v. 12? In some Christian circles the phrase denotes the *written* word, the Bible. It is also used to describe the *incarnate* Word, Jesus himself. Sometimes we use it to describe the word *spoken* through preaching. The writer probably means primarily the written word of scripture (the Old Testament for him of course), since he has just quoted a call to hear God's voice from Psalm 95 (v. 7). But all three meanings are bound up with each other, and in v. 13 he moves straight into 'before him' (meaning God) as if God and the word of God cannot be separated, which indeed they cannot. Verse 12 is a piling up of terms denoting 'every part of human nature'. We can hide parts of who we really are from other people and even from ourselves, since we are practised in self-deception – but not from God. Before God, who and what we really are is naked and laid bare. This truth can have a comforting aspect (1 John 3.20), but not here: we must render an account. Now for the encouragement, as v. 14 takes up where 2.18 left off. The risen and ascended Jesus, God's Son, is our 'high priest' who intercedes with God on our behalf. He understands what we go through in the way of trials, temptations and weaknesses, since he too has been tested (NRSV footnote 'tempted' is better). 'Yield not to temptation, for yielding is sin' runs the old hymn. In v. 15b, 'yet without sin' must mean just that: Jesus was tempted, as we are, but did not yield to it. From time to time sections of the British press take great delight in reporting comments from some hapless judge, unwise enough to admit in court that he has not heard of a pop singer or TV soap character, and therefore presumed to be out of touch with, and unable to understand, those with whom he is dealing. Hebrews here tells us that Jesus is not out of touch with, or unable to understand, us and what we experience. This gives us confidence to approach God from whom we find not judgment and punishment, but mercy and grace when we most need it (v. 16).

Mark 10.17–31

Today's passage is about the cost of discipleship. A rich man comes to Jesus with a question about what he has to do to inherit eternal life (v. 17). The question itself tells us that he sees the acquisition of eternal life as being rather like the acquisition of anything else. It is presumably acquired by doing something, and he wants to know how much he has to do. Jesus gently probes his commitment to the Commandments (a representative sample, though with 'You shall not defraud' instead of 'You shall not covet'). Yes, he has kept these ever since he became responsible for his own actions (v. 20). This is not arrogant, just a statement of fact. Jesus' reply (v. 21) is an invitation to discipleship with its cost spelled out. It is too great a cost for the man, who will kneel before Jesus (v. 17) but not follow his demand (v. 22). There is no happy ending; the man is too attached to his possessions and Jesus lets him go. Verses 23–27 spell out the significance of what has happened. Affectionately addressing the disciples as 'children', Jesus quotes a proverb about a camel and a needle (v. 25). Attempts to turn the camel into a rope (a similar Greek word), or the eye of the needle into a narrow gateway, are entirely fanciful: the whole point of the illustration is that it is ridiculous and impossible. But God can release people from a dangerous attachment to what they have (Francis of Assisi is a notable example), and make possible what is otherwise impossible (vv. 26–27). Peter then asks about the cost of *their* discipleship. They have actually done what the man in the story could not bring himself to do; what is to be their reward (v. 28)? Jesus' reply has humour, covering relationships as well as goods. What are they going to do with a hundred houses each, or a hundred sisters? In giving up these things they will in this age receive relationships and hospitality within the Christian community richer than they can ever imagine – though persecutions too. In the next age they will receive nothing less than eternal life (v. 30). What is the cost of our discipleship as Christians today? Many make real sacrifices of time, money and other things. Does the Church always value that and use those things well? And is the support and fellowship within the Church such as to constitute a true 'reward'?

SUNDAY BETWEEN 16 AND 22 OCTOBER

Twenty-ninth Sunday in Ordinary Time (Proper 24)

Job 38.1–7 (34–41) Continuous

Last Sunday's reading found Job unsuccessfully searching for God, confident that in a 'fair trial' he would be found not guilty and therefore not deserving of his sufferings. Since then there have been some more speeches and arguments, none of which take Job's situation as a good man who suffers unjustly with proper seriousness. In this chapter God breaks his silence to answer Job 'out of the whirlwind' for the first time (v. 1). For comments on vv. 1–7 see those on the related Old Testament lection on p. 117. Verses 34–41 rather detract from the grandeur of the passage and add nothing to the meaning, so are better omitted. We need to return to the question raised in the comments on p. 117 but not pursued there because it was not relevant to the context: how satisfactory an answer is this? It has been described as God 'pulling rank on Job'. What can Job possibly understand of the great scheme of things? How many of God's questions can Job answer? And so matters continue until 40.3–5, where Job simply says that before such a mighty God he is utterly insignificant and has no more to say. This is not quite the end of the matter because God will address Job again. Next week's reading will give us part of Job's reply and indicate the final outcome. But Job has no answer to his questions. God has done what Job always feared he would do, overwhelmed him with power and magnificence. How satisfactory an answer is this? At the level of minds which want, above all, to know the answers to their questions, not at all. But this passage invites us to recognize that even when we do *not* know the 'answers' to the deep questions which human existence throws at us, we are not excluded from the presence of God who, even though now disclosed to us in the person of Christ, is unfathomable mystery, or else not God at all. Whatever else the book of Job does or does not do, it prevents us from domesticating God or pretending we know all the answers.

Isaiah 53.4–12 Related

For this reading see the comments on the Old Testament on p. 74. It has presumably been chosen as the related Old Testament lection for today's Gospel because it has often been thought to lie behind the images of service and ransom in Mark 10.45. However, it is by no means certain that it does so. It would have been more appropriate if the Gospel had begun at Mark 11.32 rather than 11.35, thus including the third open prediction of the passion.

Hebrews 5.1–10

Last week's Epistle touched on the theme of Jesus as our 'great high priest' and argued that because he has been tempted as we are, we are able to come to God and find grace and mercy when we most need it. The writer now continues to reflect on the theme of priesthood, though initially in its form under the old covenant. He is not interested in the social or political role of the high priest, though this was of considerable importance (see Mark 14.60–64 and parallels). The high priest here is a cultic figure, concerned with the offering of worship and sacrifice and the representation of people before God (v. 1). It is said that his awareness of his own humanity is a qualification for dealing gently with those in spiritual need (v. 2), and the fact that he is only human means that the sacrifices he offers are to deal with his own sin as well as that of others (v. 3). The final qualification is that he must not have taken the role upon himself but, like Aaron, have been selected by God (v. 4 – see Exodus 28.1). The writer now proceeds to demonstrate – in reverse order – that Jesus possesses these qualifications. Jesus was selected by God as 'high priest' (vv. 5–6, 10) and his experience of being human enables him to deal gently with those in spiritual need (vv. 7–8). Many have found these verses rather difficult. But if Jesus was truly human, even if without sin, he had to experience what it is like to be a sinful human being with all the shame and guilt that involves. And if we are to believe that he can help us now we have to know that he experienced it. Most commentators point to Jesus' time in Gethsemane, where the response of obedience comes only as part of a prolonged personal struggle (Mark 14.32–36). It is in this sense that Jesus had to learn obedience through what he suffered (v. 8b). If, as is probable, some of the readers of this letter were tempted to renounce their faith in order to escape suffering, even martyrdom, then knowing that Jesus had been there before them and won through would be very important. So it is for us when we are tempted and tested and prayer seems unanswered. Sometimes the Church has presented the risen and ascended Lord as a remote figure, so distant from us that it has then been found necessary to put intermediaries, often the Blessed Virgin

Mary or one of the saints, between ourselves and him. Very many Christians find no problem about asking the saints to pray to God for them, but it depends why it is done. If it is an expression of a fellowship within the body of Christ which transcends death that is one thing. If it is because Jesus is felt to be too distant to approach directly it is quite another, and Hebrews here offers a necessary corrective.

Mark 10.35–45

We sometimes think of the disciples as rather stupid, and perhaps sometimes they were. But the incident recorded here is not so much an example of dimwittedness as of having got the wrong idea into their heads and being stuck with it. The story was seen as embarrassing to James and John, so Matthew attributes the request of v. 37 to their mother (Matthew 20.20–21). The request indicates the kind of expectation about the Messiah common in contemporary Judaism. Despite all Jesus has previously said to disabuse them of it, they have not understood. With Peter (and occasionally Andrew), these two form part of an 'inner circle' (Mark 1.16–20; 5.37; 9.2; 13.3; 14.33–34). They want to be sure that this continues and that when Jesus sets up his kingdom they will have the chief places on the governing council. Jesus' reply refers to the cup and baptism that will come his way (v. 38). The imagery comes from the Old Testament. The cup is a frequent image for God's anger (Psalm 75.8; Isaiah 51.17; Jeremiah 25.15–28 etc.). The baptism image is rather less obvious, but immersion in water often represents being overwhelmed by disaster (Psalms 42.7; 69.2b; Isaiah 43.2). James and John, their minds filled with their own thoughts, do not realize that Jesus is asking whether they are able to share his coming suffering. They respond positively (v. 39a) and Jesus tells them that their expectations will be fulfilled. Even so, places at his right and left hand are not his to grant (v. 40). Is there an ironic hint here of the two who were crucified with Jesus, by which time brave James and John were well out of sight? The others are angry when they learn what is going on (v. 41) and the following verse makes it plain that they are angry because they too are thinking of status and are resentful about James and John getting their requests in first. Patiently, Jesus explains all over again what true leadership among his followers is all about (vv. 42–44; compare 9.33–37). But this time he makes a significant addition to his teaching. In v. 45 he says that he (the Son of Man) has come to serve, not to be served, 'and to give his life a ransom for many'. While at one level this continues the thought that true leadership is service, and is the kind he himself offers, it also goes far beyond it. His death will be a gift to others, a ransom 'for many' (a Semitic idiom which does not exclude anybody else). We must not read too much into the word 'ransom' and start asking questions such as, 'to whom is it paid?' (though theologians later did so). Jesus is not laying down a theory of the atonement, or even an explanation of it, but is making the clear statement that his death will be redemptive for the world. He will give his life in service for others, not seek to save it (see Mark 8.35).

SUNDAY BETWEEN 23 AND 29 OCTOBER

Thirtieth Sunday in Ordinary Time (Proper 25)

Job 42.1–6, 10–17 Continuous

Last week's reading from Job gave us part of God's first awe-inspiring reply to Job, and we looked ahead to 40.3–5 (though it is not included in the Lectionary), where Job offers God his submission and his silence. This is followed by a second challenge from God 'out of the whirlwind' (40.6–41.34), then Job's further reply, and finally the story of how it all turned out. The second challenge is essentially 'more of the same'. Job's further reply begins by acknowledging God's omnipotence (v. 2), then recalls some of the things which have been said during the course of the debate (vv. 3–4). Verses 5–6 are the heart of all that has happened. God has revealed himself to Job in the midst of Job's suffering and anguish. What he had formerly known by report and repute he now knows personally and certainly. The problem of why he has suffered when he has done nothing to deserve it is still completely unanswered (it never could be answered in that sense and perhaps it was never the writer's intention to do so). But that no longer matters if Job can know himself in the presence of God. Verses 10–17 are a problem, and those who think they have been added by a later editor may well be right. We can see why they were added: the original folk tale of chs 1–2 rather requires that Job be restored to his original prosperity and that Satan is shown to be wrong in declaring that Job's goodness rested only on self-interest. But our problem with them is that they read to us like a fairy tale, a 'God will put it all right' add-on, which is simply untrue to human experience. We cannot preach on vv. 10–17, but we can return to v. 5 and learn well what it says. There is no intellectual answer to the question about why human existence is often as awful as it is, but there is the insistence that a real relationship with God is the most important thing for any human being, whatever their circumstances. Let H. H. Rowley have the last word, from the General Introduction to his fine 1970 commentary on Job: 'It is of the essence of its message that Job found God *in* his suffering, and so found relief not *from* his misfortunes, but *in* them. God was to him now far more precious than he had ever been.'

Jeremiah 31.7–9 Related

For this reading, see also the first part of the comments on the Old Testament lection on p. 18. It is included here primarily because of the reference in v. 8 to the 'blind and the lame' being included in this great song of triumph as the people return from captivity. Today's Gospel tells of a blind man who receives deliverance from his affliction and becomes a disciple. We take it for granted that caring for the blind or the deaf is a mark of a 'civilized society'. It is easy to forget that this has not always been self-evident. Many primitive societies regarded those with such afflictions as cursed by the gods, and therefore excluded from proper care and concern. They had no mechanism for dealing with people with such special needs, who were a hindrance when life was harsh, food scarce and enemies plentiful. It is striking that the Judaeo-Christian tradition takes such a radically different attitude. Care for people in need is commanded (Leviticus 19.14); looking after them is a sign not only of a civilized society, but of one which is obedient to God.

Hebrews 7.23–28

The writer continues his reflections on the high priesthood of Christ and its contrast with the Levitical priesthood of Israel, which he started in last week's reading. The 'former priests' of v. 21 are the high priests of Israel who died and had to be replaced. By contrast, Jesus is risen and ascended and therefore 'continues for ever', with the corollary that his priesthood also exists for ever and is permanently effective (vv. 24–25). Of course, the intercession which Jesus makes for us is not the humble supplication of someone who seeks a favour. This high priest is risen and exalted and seated at the right hand of God. We might allow the thought in this verse to put a question to some of the hymns, songs and prayers we use in worship. Many of them are directed solely to Jesus, who is praised for things and asked for things. While this can certainly be defended as permissible it needs watching. The norm of Christian prayer and praise is that it is offered *to* the Father, *through* the Son, who always lives to pray for us. While this may seem trivial, it is one of the things which cause some Muslims (for example) to misunderstand Christian faith and claim that we worship three Gods. The main emphasis here is not so much on Christ's prayer for us as on his offering for us. Verse 26 is saying, in effect, 'This is just the kind of high priest we need', and the five characteristics which are listed add up to an ideal portrait. We should perhaps note that the phrase 'separated from sinners' does not imply remoteness (he was, after all, known as 'friend of sinners' during his earthly ministry), but that he was not contaminated by our sin. The writer then makes another comparison in v. 27. The old priesthood had to offer repeated sacrifices, but Jesus offered just one – himself on the cross. This never needs repeating: it stands as done and valid for ever. In v. 28 this part of the story is complete: God has appointed by 'oath' (if this seems puzzling, it refers back to the way God established the priesthood of Melchizedek in Psalm 110.4, referred to at 7.21 but not read in the Lectionary passage) the Son who has been made perfect for ever. As so often in Hebrews, we struggle with somewhat complicated thoughts but reach a simple and encouraging conclusion. Christ has offered a perfect sacrifice, permanently valid, and lives for ever to pray for us. It is in this very important sense that he is our living Lord. This, surely, is worth a sermon!

Mark 10.46–52

The story of blind Bartimaeus is told very vividly, with probable eye-witness touches. This blind man has a name. The Aramaic name means 'son of Timaeus'; Mark offers a translation, not additional information, in v. 46. Bartimaeus has heard about Jesus and his powers of healing. This is scarcely surprising, despite Jesus' frequent instructions to people not to say anything. Earlier reports in Mark indicate the spread of his reputation (e.g. 1.28; 3.8; 4.1; 5.21; 6.33 etc.). So when Bartimaeus learns that Jesus is nearby he begins to call out persistently (vv. 47–48). We cannot quite be sure what else Bartimaeus knew about Jesus or what the term 'Son of David', which is found nowhere else in Mark, means on his lips. It is likely that it was intended, and received, as some kind of messianic title. If so, Jesus does not rebuke him: the cross, through which alone Jesus' messiahship will be properly understood, is drawing near. The title points forward to the triumphal entry into Jerusalem which follows it. Another notable thing is that Jesus takes the initiative (v. 49). When Bartimaeus learns that Jesus wants him he rises hastily and goes (v. 50). One of the little 'eyewitness details' is that he threw off his cloak. Some argue that this is purely symbolic, since oriental beggars normally spread their cloaks on the ground to receive money. But a seated blind beggar would presumably spread his cloak over his legs and feet, so that he would feel, as well as hear, any coins thrown into it and be able to retrieve them easily. This detail is not invented but

Mark does intend us to see a deeper symbolism: Bartimaeus has faith, and knows he will not require his cloak, an aid to begging, in the future. He addresses Jesus as 'Rabbouni' – rather more reverential than 'Rabbi' – and asks for his sight. Jesus tells him his faith has made him well, but the word means both 'healing' and 'salvation', which points to the final statement, that Bartimaeus followed Jesus 'on the way' (v. 52). This means both 'along the road' and 'in the way of salvation'. The physical healing he has received is the sign of an inner healing. All who come to Jesus with faith that he can help will be set in the way of salvation. Ahead lies the cross which will make this true beyond the limitations of Jesus' earthly ministry.

ALL SAINTS

Wisdom of Solomon 3.1–9

This beautiful passage expresses the notion of the 'immortality of the soul' rather than what some have judged to be the more Hebraic and biblical idea of the 'resurrection of the body'. However, to put the issue in that way makes it sound as if the two ideas are not only distinct from each other, but also incompatible with each other. It might be wiser to see them as dealing with the same reality, though approaching it from differing backgrounds. How or whether we preach from this passage may depend on our view of the status of the Wisdom of Solomon, for not all churches accept it as canonical scripture. Verse 1 states a firm conviction about the place of the righteous in the afterlife. The reference to being untouched by any 'torment' is primarily to torment after death: no punishment awaits the righteous. The wider application, that they are now beyond the reach of the torments of this life, is clearly also true. The 'foolish' are those who do not understand the ways of God. They therefore believe that those who have died have perished utterly, and nothing is left to such people except their mourning and loss (vv. 2–3a). The wise, who have learned from God, know that the departed are 'at peace' (v. 3b). All this is very comforting and reassuring. We do, though, have to be careful not to deny the reality of physical death. Humanly speaking, when people die it is indeed often a disaster for those who love them and we must not pretend otherwise. But the perspective of faith here is about those who have died, not those who remain behind. For the righteous departed peace awaits, not destruction. Verses 4–6 seem to refer to the tests and trials we experience in this life. To the 'foolish', the sight of human suffering indicates that the person is being punished for sin (v. 4a – compare Job). But those who come through their trials (and thereby show that they are righteous) receive their reward from God. Again, true though this is, we need to be careful not to preach as though the reward of eternal life somehow makes up for the inequalities of this one. It is far from clear how any reward could ever compensate for the agonies some people experience. Nonetheless, as the passage concludes by saying, eternal life is indeed God's gift to the 'holy ones' (v. 9b) and on All Saints' Day we rightly celebrate that.

Isaiah 25.6–9

For this reading see the comments on the Old Testament lection on p. 82.

Revelation 21.1–6a

Perhaps slightly oddly for All Saints' Day, this reading requires us to put out of our minds all notions of heaven as the sphere of existence to which we go when we die, or to which we are raised. In John's vision here the movement is the other way round. He sees first a new heaven and earth, replacing the old (v. 1). Scholars cannot agree as to whether he envisages this as a totally new creation or as a radical renewal, but perhaps it does not greatly matter. Even more startling is the imagery of v. 2, which sees the holy city *descending* from heaven to earth. It is this holy city which fills the vision, providing the context for the glorious fellowship between God and the redeemed. The whole point of the city descending as it does is expressed in the opening words of the loud voice from the throne: 'the home of God is among mortals' (v. 3a). The NRSV footnote points out that the word 'home' here, and the word 'dwell' in the next sentence, both refer to 'tabernacle'. Since John 1.14 famously says of Christ that he 'tabernacled' (or 'pitched his tent') among us, the Seer appears to be saying that what was begun in the incarnation is here brought to completion. We are familiar with the Old Testament phrase so often used of Israel, 'and they shall be his people'. Here we find a plural version, 'peoples' (the NRSV footnote rightly states that some manuscripts have the singular, but although people copying the text might well alter the unfamiliar plural to the familiar singular it would be most unlikely to happen the other way round, so 'peoples' is almost certainly original). This is a reminder of the universality of God's final salvation; no longer does God dwell only with one people. Verse 4 clearly announces the fulfilment of the promise which is recorded in today's Old Testament reading at Isaiah 25.8. Those things which belong to the old order, such as mourning, crying and pain, will be no more. This applies to death itself, the 'last enemy' (1 Corinthians 15.26), already defeated through the cross and resurrection of Christ, now finally seen to be vanquished. God announces that he is making all things new (v. 5a). Again, this is an idea familiar to us from elsewhere in the New Testament. Paul often writes about those who are 'in Christ' as being already a 'new creation' (2 Corinthians 5.17; Galatians 6.15) and of the way in which the wasting away of our physical bodies is matched by the renewal of our inner nature (2 Corinthians 4.16–18). What the Seer writes about here is the same process, but on a cosmic scale and now brought to completion. From start to finish this is the work of God who is beginning and end (v. 6a), not just in the sense that he was there at its beginning and will be there at its end, but in the sense of an active involvement in the whole process of transformation. Whether or not this is a particularly appropriate reading for this particular feast, it does at least have the merit of reminding us that heaven is not just about 'us and our loved ones' but about the final transformation of all things by God's grace. That, of course, is the reality to which the true saints point by their lives on this earth.

John 11.32–44

We sometimes forget that this is not the only account in the Gospels of Jesus raising someone from the dead (see Mark 5.35–42; Luke 7.11–15). But the raising of Lazarus lingers in our minds as a story of great power, magnificently told. To call it a 'story' does not mean that it did not happen, but John's manner of telling makes a great piece of creative literature. Indeed, its power as a story is so considerable that the most effective way of preaching on it may well be to tell it precisely as a story, adopting the perspective of Mary, Martha, one of the onlookers or even, if we are feeling particularly bold, Lazarus himself. Whether we adopt that approach or some other, we still have to consider what issues the story raises, which would need to be brought out in any kind of sermon. The Lectionary rightly recognizes the problem of length with a story which really begins at 11.1, and so gives us only part of it in the reading. Our preparation for preaching should involve reflection on the entire narrative. The heart of its meaning is, of course, in the conversation which Jesus has with Martha, and particularly 11.25–26 which, we may say, the story of the raising of Lazarus puts into dramatic shape. Barnabas Lindars rightly calls it 'a sort of dress rehearsal for the Resurrection of Jesus himself', and points to the similarities with John's account of that: the mourning women, the rock-hewn tomb with a stone across it and the grave-clothes, with a separate mention of a cloth which wrapped the face. If we are inclined to ask why John wants us to understand the story in this way, Professor Lindars supplies a convincing answer: as an allegory of the death and resurrection of Jesus the story relates these things to the experience of ordinary human beings, whom Lazarus represents. In other words, just as Lazarus experiences first death, then resurrection through Jesus, so everyone who believes in him, though they die, will live (v. 25). This 'life' is not an add-on reward type of afterlife. It begins now through our present relationship with Jesus, and it is that relationship which will continue through and after our death. That promise is already true for the faithful departed. Here in the Fourth Gospel, Jesus promises that it can be true for all of us.

SUNDAY BETWEEN 30 OCTOBER AND 5 NOVEMBER

Thirty-first Sunday in Ordinary Time
(Fourth Sunday before Advent)

Ruth 1.1–18 Continuous

We may initially wonder why the book of Ruth is in the Bible, since the events it relates do not seem to be of any great religious or political importance. The Lectionary passages give us the heart of the story, the full significance of which only becomes clear next Sunday. Verses 1–5 set the background: because of famine in Israel, Elimelech moves to Moab with Naomi and their two sons. Moab and Israel were occasionally allies, more often enemies (1 Samuel 14.47; 2 Samuel 8.2; Psalm 60.8a). This story comes from a time of peace. The deaths of Elimelech and her sons leaves Naomi desperate, a lone foreign woman without protector or breadwinner. She is too old to marry and have more children (vv. 11–12a). But she is blessed by the close bonds she has with her Moabite daughters-in-law Orpah and Ruth. They at least have the option of going back to live with their own mothers (v. 8), which is what Orpah eventually does, settling for the way of life, the religion and the security she knows (v. 15). Ruth, however, protests her determination to keep her mother-in-law company in all circumstances, up to and including death, and this commitment involves taking Naomi's God to be her own (vv. 16–17a). The sincerity of her religious commitment is underlined by sealing her promise in the name of Israel's God (v. 17b). This is no casual or easy decision. It involves a journey back to Israel where Ruth will then be the foreigner. What kind of reception will she, an economic migrant, find there? Thus far the story speaks to us of ordinary women who, when faced with harsh conditions, take brave decisions, care for each other and trust in God. In an age when refugees, asylum-seekers and economic migrants are hotly debated political issues, especially in 'host' countries such as Britain, this tale from long ago provides an important perspective.

Deuteronomy 6.1–9 Related

In vv. 1–3, Moses tells the children of Israel what matters most in their future life in the promised land. The purpose of the commands

196

is that everyone might reverence the Lord their God (v. 2a). This will bring prosperity and blessing (v. 5). Central to this is the *Shema'* (vv. 4–5), which sets out the nature of God and the response required from human beings. NRSV translates the opening as: 'The LORD is our God, the LORD alone', but in the footnote indicates three alternative translations, the second of which is the one found in today's Gospel (Mark 12.29) and is probably preferable. The Israelites discovered the uniqueness of their God when they were led out of Egypt, whose gods could do nothing to prevent it. That the Lord must be called 'our God' was a matter of experience. But other nations could say the same about 'their' gods, and more than that is meant here. 'The LORD is one' is a statement that Israel's God is not merely one among others, but is rather the only true God there is. As Peter Craigie comments, 'when he spoke there was no other to contradict; when he promised, there was no other to revoke that promise; when he warned, there was no other to provide refuge from that warning.' Only a God like that is worthy of being loved with all a person's heart and soul and might, which is the response that is called for (v. 5). But, as we know, although obedience can be commanded, love cannot. This is why the commands were to become part of the texture of everyday living, to be meditated upon and remembered at all times and in all places (vv. 6–9). Thus do people learn to love the Lord from whom they come. There is plenty of material here to provoke reflection on the ways in which we, as Christian people, learn to love the Lord our God through the way we live our daily lives.

Hebrews 9.11–14

We have never imagined that we could be made holy by somebody doing something with goat's blood, bull's blood or the ashes of a heifer (v. 13). That is one of the difficulties we find in drawing spiritual sustenance from Hebrews. The writer's world is not always the one we inhabit. He is deeply concerned to prove the superiority of Christ to the sacrificial system of Judaism, from which his readers had converted to Christianity, but to which some of them were being tempted to return. Neither the experience nor the temptation is ours. However, it may be worth making the effort to understand what he is saying in order to discover whether it still has meaning for us. For the last three Sundays Hebrews has dealt with the theme of the 'high priesthood' of Christ, and now moves towards its climax. The passage begins with the writer seemingly at his most obscure. Much scholarly ink has been expended on working out his precise view of the heavenly sanctuary in vv. 11–12a, but the emphasis is on Christ's entering the 'Holy Place' (v. 12a), not on how he arrived there, and we can be content with that. He is there to offer 'his own blood' (v. 12b). We cannot understand what this means unless we remember in general terms that the sacrificial system of the Old Testament was designed to take away sin, but we do not need to know more than that. The writer contends that such sacrifices might make people ceremonially clean (v. 13), but insists that the blood of Christ (that is, his self-offering), does something much more, it gives us eternal salvation (v. 12b), purifying the conscience so that we are set free to worship the living God (v. 14). In some way which our writer is not in the least concerned to explain, what Christ has done on the cross supersedes all the ways in which we humans might attempt to earn cleansing from sin. That is what we need to concentrate on in this difficult passage. It speaks to us whenever we make our rituals, prayers, sacraments, acts of Christian service, or any of the things which make up our Christian existence, into ways of persuading God to give us eternal life. They are not and do not need to be: Christ has done that already.

Mark 12.28–34

Although in the New Testament scribes and Pharisees frequently appear among Jesus' opponents, there were many who were good and godly. Today's story concerns one such. It is evident that he asked the question about which commandment was the most important (v. 28b) not to trap Jesus, but because he was impressed by the things he had heard him say (v. 28a). The question was frequently asked among religious people; it was, and is, very important. The Law of Moses includes many commandments of various kinds (613 is the usual reckoning), all of them said to have been given by God. Are they all of equal importance, or are some more important in the sense that they shape and direct the way we interpret the rest? Jesus is only asked about which is 'first', but his answer involves two and we are meant to understand that, although separate in the Old Testament, they are actually inseparable in importance. Jesus turns first to the *Shema'* of today's related Old Testament lection (see the comments). To the text from Deuteronomy is added, 'with all your mind'. Whether that comes from Jesus, Mark or a later copyist, it is intended to show that loving God with your 'heart' also involves using your mind. What about a sermon on the importance of having the courage to think about our faith? Then Jesus adds Leviticus 19.18, the command to love our neighbours. Morna Hooker's comment cannot be improved upon: 'The command to love one's neighbour arises from the command to love God, and the love of God is empty unless it issues in love of neighbour.' A sermon about how both 'all-worship-and-prayer' Christians and 'all-good-works' Christians miss something crucial, might be helpful. Or, since these commandments are not only inseparable but also 'first' (and must therefore shape how Christians interpret the others), we might preach about how they help us in Christian living. What does it mean to place love of God and neighbour at the forefront of our minds in dealing with questions of, say, economic justice, human sexuality, race relations or abortion? That would be the 'brave' sermon! To return to Mark: the scribe approvingly repeats what has been said (vv. 32–33a), adding, in effect, that it is also the heart not of the commandments alone, but of all religion (v. 33b). Does he follow Jesus, so coming 'into' the kingdom rather than being 'not far' from it? Tantalizingly, we are not told.

SUNDAY BETWEEN 6 AND 12 NOVEMBER

Thirty-second Sunday in Ordinary Time (Third Sunday before Advent)

Ruth 3.1–5, 4.13–17 Continuous

If last Sunday's readings were replaced with those for All Saints it would be pointless to use this reading today and the reading from 1 Kings should be used instead. The Lectionary omits what is probably the best-known part of the book, the story of Ruth gleaning 'amidst the alien corn', thus coming to the attention of Boaz who is evidently attracted to her. At the start of today's reading Naomi has a plan for Ruth's future security (3.1). It depends partly on the fact that Boaz has already taken favourable notice of Ruth, but also on the fact that he is a 'kinsman' (v. 2a), in fact of Naomi's deceased husband Elimelech (2.1). There are two pieces of background information which partly explain how the story works out. The first is the institution of levirate marriage, which laid down that a man should marry his dead brother's wife in order to raise children in his brother's name, and so continue the line (Deuteronomy 25.5–10). The only other recorded instance of it comes in Genesis 38 (referred to in Ruth 4.12). The second is the idea of the 'kinsman', or 'redeemer' (Hebrew, *gōʾēl*) whose task is to keep the family name and property intact. In effect Ruth, at Naomi's instigation, asks Boaz to fulfil both these roles (the story contains the complication of another man whose responsibility these things really were, but the Lectionary does not trouble us with that). What we have not learned from the Lectionary passages is that this is also a love story. No reader of the entire book can doubt the genuineness of the relationship between Ruth and Boaz. It is much more than a story about a legal provision. The close of the story (4.13–17) shows real happiness, the miseries and uncertainties of the past now just a distant memory. God's blessing rests on Ruth, who acted with loyalty and faithfulness. This might seem quite sufficient, but there is more: the little genealogy in 4.17 is not accidental. Ruth's son Obed, turns out to be the grandfather of King David! The Christian reader of this book then realizes that this makes Ruth, a Moabite woman, an ancestor of Jesus according to Matthew's reckoning (Matthew 1.5). Truly, those who act in loyalty and faithfulness in their own humble circumstances may have no idea how, in God's providence, all that will turn out.

1 Kings 17.8–16 Related

Although the reading starts at v. 8, we need the information given in v. 7. The river from which Elijah had been drinking had dried up, indicating a period of drought and therefore famine. It also provides a reason for Elijah to move on, and the command is given to go to Zaraphath, in Phoenicia (v. 8) where he will be fed by a widow. He duly meets a widow whose poverty is indicated by gathering sticks (v. 10). In the ordinary way of things no help could be expected from her. But Elijah makes a double request, for water (v. 10b) and then for bread (v. 11). She cannot supply bread and explains why: the little she has is barely enough for a meal for herself and her son. It would, in any case, be the last meal either of them would eat (v. 12). In Israel, where caring for widows was laid down by the Law (Deuteronomy 10.18; 14.29; 24.17–21), we may suppose that they would not have been allowed to die of starvation, but this story is not set in Israel. Her plight is as desperate as it could be. Into this situation comes God's command through Elijah: she is to return home, make what she has into a little cake and bring it to the prophet. Only after that should she make something for herself and her son. She will be able to do so because the supply of meal and oil will be miraculously renewed until the drought ends (vv. 13–14). The widow does as Elijah commands, and the prophecy is fulfilled (vv. 15–16). The story is primarily about God's unceasing provision for his prophet, who had previously been fed by the ravens (17.6), and in this story must be fed first. But this feeding comes through the obedience of a destitute widow who, despite living in heathen territory, answers Elijah in the name of his God (v. 12a) and unhesitatingly obeys the prophet's commands. It is a waste of time looking for naturalistic explanations. Both the miraculous feeding and the widow's generosity are important components of the story.

Hebrews 9.24–28

This reading consolidates much of what has been said over the past few weeks about the sacrifice of Christ our great high priest, and what it means for us. Verse 24 reminds us of what we have already learned: the risen and ascended Christ has entered into heaven itself (9.11) in order to appear in God's presence 'on our behalf', that is, as the one who makes intercession for us (7.25). As already stated at 9.12, Christ's sacrificial offering of himself took place just once (v. 25a), and a new reason for this is now advanced. Since his sacrifice involved his death, it would be palpable nonsense to think in terms of his having to die repeatedly (v. 26a). But in any case that is not an issue, since his death did everything needed to deal with sin and its consequences are eternal (v. 26b). Nothing therefore remains to be done, sin has been dealt with. Human beings also only die the once, but for us death is followed by judgment (v. 27). The implication (though the writer does not spell it out) is that because of what Christ has done we no longer need to fear that judgment. If Christ's death was also once and for all what, as it were, remains for him? Not dealing with sin (that has been done), but a second appearance (v. 28), which will usher in the world's final salvation. But that is not yet: for the present, believers may live in the knowledge that Christ's sacrifice has brought them freedom from sin and that his ministry of intercession keeps them even now in the grace of God. For readers who shared the writer's assumption that death is followed by judgment, and who lived in fear of it, all this is unqualified good news. But few Christians today seem to live in fear of God's judgment and it is therefore genuinely difficult to know how this passage might be helpfully preached from.

Mark 12.38–44

Last week we read about a good scribe. In today's reading Jesus condemns some others. A scribe's job was to study, preserve and interpret the Law of Moses and the 'case law' which had grown up concerning it. A religious society values those who interpret the faith which undergirds it, and so that scribes could be recognized and honoured they wore distinctive long white linen robes. At important gatherings they were honoured guests. They lived on what we would call 'freewill offerings', good Jews being encouraged to show their piety by offering scribes hospitality and gifts. For some the status had become all-important (vv. 38–39). Worse, some used their status to prey on vulnerable people and feather their own nests (v. 40), thus turning their sacred calling inside out and drawing Jesus' stinging condemnation. The Christian leader who is overly concerned about status, or who treats the church as a means to a comfortable living, is certainly thus condemned. But so are we all if we think of our 'status' as Christians as a means of securing a reputation for respectability and goodness. That turns our calling to discipleship inside out. The widow of vv. 41–44 had no worldly goods worth a bad scribe's attention; she had only two of the smallest unit of currency. Jesus does not criticize the rich for putting in large sums; all that was properly calculated according to the law of tithe and tradition. The widow had virtually nothing, so was not expected to put in anything, yet she did. And a calculating prudence might have led her to give one coin but keep the other for herself. She does not, and it is her extravagant generosity and total commitment which calls forth praise from Jesus (v. 44). The contrast is both with the hypocrisy of some scribes (v. 40a), and the calculation of the rich givers (vv. 44a). Her action is neither calculated ('How little can I get away with giving?') nor self-seeking ('What benefit will this bring me?'). Unlike the scribes she understands what it is to live in grateful dependence on, and total commitment to, God. In recounting Jesus' response (v. 44a) Mark intends us to understand that faithful discipleship involves a like commitment.

SUNDAY BETWEEN 13 AND 19 NOVEMBER

Thirty-third Sunday in Ordinary Time (Second Sunday before Advent)

1 Samuel 1.4–20 Continuous

It is not obvious why this lection was chosen as the 'continuous' option for today. The record of Samuel's early ministry is the Old Testament reading for the First Sunday of Christmas in Year C, but that is some six weeks away. Today's reading is about the conception of Samuel. The family situation is presented briefly but tellingly (vv. 4–8). Polygamy was legal in Israel, though not widely practised. If Elkanah had two wives he was probably a wealthy man. The friction between Peninnah and Hannah is depicted as coming entirely from the former (v. 6), and Hannah's childlessness offered either a reason for it or a convenient excuse. Within the social structure of ancient Israel childlessness was regarded as a severe misfortune, in some cases as a punishment. This, of course, forms no part of Christian thinking and we need to be sensitive to the pastoral issue. Some people are unable to have children and it is a source of great sadness; others deliberately choose to be childless and it is a valid Christian choice. The writer characteristically ascribes Hannah's situation to the direct action of God (vv. 5b, 6b), the counterpart of which is that God is able to change the situation in due course. The narrative is at pains to emphasize Hannah's genuine distress (vv. 7b, 10, 15–16). Prayers which begin, 'O Lord, if you will . . .' are not uncommon and usually involve some kind of unacceptable bargaining with God for something we want. Hannah's prayer, though, was fundamentally unselfish: if God would give her the son she longed for he would be dedicated to God for the whole of his life (v. 11) and so it proved (v. 20). For the writer of 1 Samuel, God miraculously provided Hannah with a son, and the nation with a great leader for the future.

Daniel 12.1–3 Related

This short but important passage has been a happy hunting ground for many sectarian groups. It is important when reading 'apocalyptic' material such as this, not to over-interpret the details, when what matters is the overall picture. The Seleucid monarch Antiochus IV was known as 'Epiphanes' (God made manifest) and was notorious among the Jews for his desecration of the Jerusalem temple and his attempts to suppress Jewish identity by barbarous methods. It might have been hoped that his death would bring the time of terrible tribulation to an end, but this passage envisages the worst anguish as yet to come (v. 1b). In such a dreadful time the Jewish people's guardian angel Michael would arise and defend them (v. 1a, c). Daniel has previously referred to Michael at 10.29. In neither place is it judged necessary to explain who he is; the first readers were presumably all familiar with an angelology which saw God as assigning each nation its guardian angel. The outcome will be deliverance for everyone who is 'written in the book' (v. 1c). But what of those who have already been martyred in the struggle or, indeed, those who have been particularly wicked? The question of justice for them is dealt with by the only clear reference in the Old Testament to the resurrection of the dead (v. 2; compare Isaiah 26.19, also a 'late' passage). This is not a general resurrection, it is of the righteous (presumably the martyrs) who deserve the reward of which they appeared to be deprived by death, and of the wicked who deserve the punishment it appeared that death had allowed them to escape. Though we must not press the details too much, it looks as if the rest are envisaged as staying in Sheol (for which, see 2 Samuel 12.23; Job 7.9; Ecclesiastes 9.5, 10). This passage is, as it were, the seedbed for later beliefs about resurrection and life after death which were only to flower fully in the New Testament. Its important message is that God takes evil seriously and will deal with it comprehensively. Out of the greatest imaginable anguish God brings good for the faithful. God will not allow evil to triumph. It is this which gives us the confidence to be faithful and active in standing up for righteousness and truth now.

Hebrews 10.11–14 (15–18) 19–25

Verses 11–18 by and large represent the writer's final summing up of what he has written since 7.1 about the priesthood of Christ. There are a few new ideas, especially that in v. 13, though it is not certain who Christ's 'enemies' are; probably they are those who oppose the Christian faith or apostatize, so there could be a warning to the readers here not to put themselves in that position. As often in Paul's writings, 'therefore' (v. 19) alerts us to the fact that the consequences of the preceding teaching will now be set out. In Paul's case the consequences are generally ethical; here they primarily concern our worship and life as a Christian community. Verses 19–25 are a single sentence in the Greek, as if the writer is anxious to show the inter-relatedness of his thoughts. What Christ has done for us through his accepted sacrifice is to give us 'confidence' to enter the 'sanctuary' (the presence of God). In our worship we share in the worship of heaven itself. Jesus has opened a 'new and living' way into that presence. That the way is new is clear enough; 'living' is slightly puzzling, but probably means that because Jesus lives for ever, the way into God's presence which he has made possible is also permanently available. We can approach God, not grovelling and apologizing, but with 'full assurance' of faith because our 'hearts' are genuinely made clean (though Christ's sacrifice) and our bodies washed (through baptism). It is important that we 'hold fast' to our hope, and give thought to how we 'provoke' (a strong word) each another to 'love and good deeds'. The familiar triad of 1 Corinthians 13.13 has been now been used in three successive verses, and in the same order. We cannot 'provoke' one another, a mutual activity, unless we meet together, so the writer urges people not to neglect Christian worship and fellowship. This becomes all the more impor-tant as the 'Day' (the Day of the Lord, associated by the early Christians with the return of Jesus) draws near. A sermon about the nature of Christian worship and its importance in the life of disciple-ship would be very fitting.

Mark 13.1–8

Even more than the reading from Daniel, this passage (and much that follows in this chapter) is the focus of attention by those whose chief interest in the Bible seems to be to use it as a kind of long-range religious weather forecast. It begins with a disciple remarking on the magnificence of the Jerusalem temple (v. 1). It was indeed a fine structure, recently restored and extended by Herod, which attracted the admiration of many travellers. Jesus predicts that it will be destroyed, which happened in the August of AD 70. We cannot be sure whether Mark was writing before or after its destruction. Prophecies concerning its destruction were not uncommon, but never popular, since the temple seemed like a guarantee of God's presence (Jeremiah 7.4). At the very least this prediction makes it plain that the temple can no longer be the focal point for the kingdom of God. In characteristic Marcan fashion, the disciples ask for further expla-nation of what Jesus has said, posing two questions, one about when it will happen, the other about the signs which will precede it

(vv. 3b–4). Jesus' reply runs as far as v. 23, after which the second section of the discourse deals, in apocalyptic language, with the signs of the end times. Of the first part of the discourse we read just four verses. They seem designed to dampen down the excitement and speculation we can sense in the disciples' questions. They must not be misled into thinking that the final judgment is imminent. There will be messianic pretenders: they will mislead many but believers must not allow themselves to be so deceived (v. 6). War, earthquake and famine (all typical apocalyptic imagery) will happen, but 'the end is still to come' (v. 7b). Paul uses the same terminology when persuading his readers that they must not believe the day of the Lord has already arrived (2 Thessalonians 2.2). This is a slightly frustrating reading because it gives us only part of the picture (some of the remainder was read almost a year ago on the first Sunday of Advent). As Mark presents it, Jesus is concerned that the disciples should not be 'alarmed' by what they see around them, but hold a steady course of faith. In preaching we may need to stress the 'still to come' aspect, especially for those who become excited about these things.

SUNDAY BETWEEN 20 AND 26 NOVEMBER

Sunday before Advent (Christ the King)

2 Samuel 23.1–7 Continuous

The 'last words of David' are not the last words he ever spoke, nor necessarily the last poem he ever wrote, but a summing up of what his life had been about. The opening verse breathes a sense of amazement: he is the son of humble Jesse (1 Samuel 16.11) yet one whom God exalted and anointed, victor in his battles because favourite of 'the Strong One' of Israel. All that has been accomplished has been through God's choosing and empowering. Verse 2 refers to the Psalms (an example of which has just been given us at 22.2–51 = Psalm 18). They are songs through which the spirit of the Lord speaks. Although not all the psalms attributed to David are likely to be by him, there is no reason to doubt that a good many are. Considering their almost constant use in Jewish and Christian worship and devotion, David's psalms, and the tradition they inspired, constitute his most lasting personal legacy to the world. Verses 3–4 turn to his kingship over Israel. The most important thing is to be a just ruler (v. 3), which for the most part David was. The beautiful images from the natural world which we find in v. 4 depict the blessings that come to a nation whose rulers fear God. In democratic societies there is an issue for some Christian voters about whether those who stand for election are men and women of faith themselves. This is an important question, but not a simple one. It is profoundly unhelpful when self-proclaimed Christian politicians lack humility and espouse repressive or discriminatory social programmes. Leading or ruling 'justly' in a pluralist society requires considerable wisdom. In the final section (vv. 5–7) David's thoughts turn to the future. The 'everlasting covenant' which God has made with David will have astonishing outcomes that even he cannot know (see the readings, and comments on them on pp. 8–9). Perhaps the writer of 2 Samuel, who knew that David's successors were sometimes more like the godless of v. 6 than the just ruler of v. 3, is inviting us to look forward to the time when the covenant will be fulfilled in the Messiah.

Daniel 7.9–10, 13–14 Related

The context of these verses is judgment. The details of the description in vv. 9–10 must not be pressed: here is an attempt to put into words what is ultimately indescribable, a vision of God at work. The misery and oppression which had been suffered by the Jewish people from the time of the exile onwards is symbolized by the succession of 'beasts' seen earlier in the dream (7.1–8). But in faith Daniel sees that God is passing sentence on them (v. 10b). Then the vision changes to 'one like a human being' (v. 13), which the NRSV footnote rightly points out represents the Aramaic phrase, 'one like a son of man'. It is impossible to know with certainty whether this is an individual figure, or whether it represents the saints who have suffered in the persecutions; most commentators incline towards the latter. At any rate, he is presented to God (v. 13b), and to him is given dominion, glory and kingship, of which it is thrice said that it shall be without end. Whatever else this means it represents a total reversal of fortune. The evil rulers who have oppressed God's people are destroyed and punished. The one who will have a kingdom for ever comes from, and represents, the saints of God. It does not seem that Judaism associated this figure with the coming Messiah, but Jesus used 'Son of Man' to refer to himself, combining it with the idea of the Suffering Servant in order to define the kind of Messiah he was to be.

Revelation 1.4b–8

> 'My name is Ozymandias, king of kings:
> Look on my works, ye Mighty, and despair!'
> Nothing beside remains. Round the decay
> Of that colossal wreck, boundless and bare
> The lone and level sands stretch far away.

So wrote Shelley in his poem, 'Ozymandias'. Throughout history, including in our own times, tyrants and oppressors always think themselves invincible and that they are answerable to nobody. But there is only one 'ruler of the kings of the earth' (v. 5a; compare 19.16), even though the tyrants do not yet know it. The reign of Christ is a very different kind of reign from anything experienced in the empires of this world. It is founded on justice and truth and on Christ's freeing of human beings from the power of sin and evil (v. 5b), and we are sharers in it (v. 6a). Like Daniel, John is writing for persecuted believers, and it is important that they grasp that God is the Lord of everything, past, present and future, the one 'who is and who was and who is to come' (vv. 4a, 8b), for this will put their sufferings into the perspective of eternity. The time will come, John insists, when those who do not presently recognize the Lordship of Christ will do so (v. 7). He who is Alpha and Omega ('the A–Z of everything') is 'the Almighty' (REB: 'sovereign Lord of all', v. 8b). This is the description of God as 'Lord of hosts', familiar to us from the Old Testament. But as G. B. Caird says: 'John uses it with a difference; for he has learned from Christ that the omnipotence of God is not the power of unlimited coercion but the power of invincible love.' This is the reason why Christians can, and must, challenge and oppose all tyrannies, oppressions and abuses of power, and must strive to make the life of the Church reflect the values of God's kingdom rather than the power structures of this world.

John 18.33–37

In John's description of Pilate's interrogation of Jesus, the issue for Pilate is whether or not Jesus is 'King of the Jews'. That is in itself a Roman way of putting things (compare John 1.49; 12.13), and shows that Pilate is primarily worried about the political aspects of any claim Jesus might have made and the threat to Rome's authority which might be involved in this. Jesus' counter-question (v. 34) forces Pilate to reveal that he is acting on information received (v. 35; see Luke 23.2). Pilate is not interested in any 'religious' charges, but presses Jesus further. The reply Jesus gives (v. 36) accepts the idea of kingship, but redefines it. This is a repudiation of a claim to political kingship such as Pilate would need to be concerned about. Instead, Jesus' kingship is 'not from this world', which is to say it does not derive its authority, effectiveness or legitimacy from the structures and organization of human society but (it is implied) only from God. It follows, therefore, that this kingship cannot be defended with means which are only appropriate to this world, such as physical violence (see Matthew 26.51–53). Pilate is not interested in a religious discussion: he is a politician. He seizes on the fact that Jesus has accepted the description of himself as a king (v. 37a), but Jesus says, in effect, 'It depends what you mean by king', now defining his kingship in terms of truth (v. 37b). The whole purpose of his ministry has been to open up the way of truth for people (compare John 14.6). The way of truth is not, of course, just about the hereafter, but about how we live in the present. The old AV translation of part of v. 36, 'My kingdom is not of this world', gave the unfortunate impression that Jesus was saying his kingship had nothing to do with this world. Quite the opposite is true: Jesus' kingship is not *from* this world, but it has everything to do with it and with how women and men live within it. Jesus comes from, and brings knowledge of, that other world where the supreme reality is God. For God to become the supreme reality in this world, we must 'listen' to the voice of the one he has sent. This phrase reminds us of John 10.16, 27, which is probably deliberate on John's part because, as Barnabas Lindars puts it, 'The allegory of the shepherd beautifully illustrates the meaning of the kingship of Jesus.' If some find talk of Christ's 'kingship' difficult because the word is sullied and, in the contemporary world, outdated, at least let today's Gospel remind us that it is a 'kingship' utterly different from, and standing in deliberate contrast to, anything Pilate here understands.

CHURCH ANNIVERSARY

Genesis 28.10–22

At the time of this incident Jacob is running away from his brother Esau whom he has cruelly wronged (Genesis 27.41–45). He has an amazing dream. The 'angels of God' (v. 12b) are a link between heaven and earth and a sign of the holiness of God, with the traffic between heaven and earth taking place on some kind of ramp. The meaning is clear, and Jacob afterwards names it very precisely as 'the gate of heaven' (v. 17b). In his dream he hears the voice of God using the time-honoured formula (v. 13a), and then making to him the same promises as were made to Abraham and Isaac (vv. 13b–14). Since Jacob is fleeing to another land, God promises to protect him and bring him back again (v. 15). Jacob's response of astonished awe has all the marks of genuine first-hand religious experience; he has been completely overwhelmed by the presence of God (vv. 16–17). And so, in response, he sets up the stone as a shrine, known as Bethel (vv. 18–19). Verses 20–22 show Jacob bargaining with God, despite the fact that he has already been promised all that he is demanding. It will take more than one religious experience to fully convert Jacob! Religious experiences do not have to happen in church, but sometimes they do, and so do significant life experiences, when we mark birth, marriage and death. Sometimes the ordained are too dismissive about what they call 'bricks and mortar' and people's attitude to churches. Our churches are meant to be 'the house of God' and 'the gate of heaven' where, in worship, we are enabled to meet, not just once but many times, with the living God. That is why we celebrate their anniversaries.

2 Chronicles 7.11–16

This reading recounts God's response to Solomon's prayer at the dedication of the temple (2 Chronicles 6.14–42; compare the continuous Old Testament lection for the Twenty-first Sunday in Ordinary Time). God appears to Solomon privately (v. 12), to assure him that his prayer has been accepted. Solomon had asked that the prayers offered in the temple would be answered. The solemn repetition of 'I have chosen' in relation to the temple (vv. 12b, 16a) indicates that this will be so. But there will be nothing automatic about it. Such prayer has to be an expression of a genuine turning to

God (v. 14). This passage points us to the question of 'sacred space' and what it is for. It makes no sense to think that God is confined to particular places. If God is everywhere we can obviously offer prayer to God anywhere. What, then, is the point of 'sacred space'? The answer involves the faith community. New Age thinking encourages us to choose individual sacred spaces which have meaning for us, perhaps only for us. But the question which then arises is who is this God that you find there? It is within the faith community that the tradition of what God is like and has done is preserved in scripture and liturgy. When as Christians we make our personal prayers in our personal spaces, we do so in the language learned from the faith community, to the God whose nature we have learned from the faith community. Churches (like the temple) are the sacred spaces where the community of God's people (v. 14a) worships and prays. Without the community celebration the 'story' would be lost and the faith would die. That is why we need our sacred spaces, whatever form they take.

Ephesians 2.19–22

For this reading see the comments on the Epistle on p. 133.

1 Peter 2.1–5

The first part of this passage is an exhortation to the readers to be rid of various evils which plague all human communities, even the Church (v. 1) and to long for spiritual nourishment just as a young baby longs for milk, i.e., frequently. The nourishment is not specified, but we do not have to choose between the hearing/reading of scripture and the Eucharist: all things which nourish our faith are commended and necessary. Christian people have already 'tasted that the Lord is good' (v. 3b, adapted from Psalm 34.8). If those who have 'tasted' continue to draw nourishment from the available sources, they will 'grow into salvation', a phrase which probably indicates full maturity as believers and does not imply they are not yet saved. With an abrupt change of metaphor, the writer refers to Jesus as a 'living stone' (v. 4a, see Jesus' application of this to himself at Mark 12.10 and parallels). If Jesus is a 'living' stone it is because he is risen, but we also are 'living stones' because we are in relationship with the risen Lord. As such we must let ourselves be built into a 'spiritual house', like a temple. This describes the *nature* of the Church. The writer now describes the *calling* of the Church, which is to be 'a holy priesthood'. We sometimes talk loosely about 'the priesthood of all believers', but that important doctrine does not mean that any believer can do anything in the Church. The priesthood here is corporate. It is the Church's vocation to present God to the world (in evangelism) and the world to God (in intercession). The Church does not exist for its own sake but for the sake of others. To offer 'spiritual sacrifices' is to offer the whole of ourselves, our corporate life as a believing community, to God in holy obedience (compare Romans 12.1–4).

Matthew 12.1–8

Mark's account of this incident is included in the Gospel for the Ninth Sunday in Ordinary Time, and the comments on p. 107 supplement what follows. The significant additions which Matthew makes to Mark come in vv. 5–7, which offer a further reason why the disciples should not be condemned for breaking the Sabbath laws. The Law itself commanded that sacrifices should be offered on the Sabbath, in fact more of them than on ordinary days (Numbers 28.9–10; Leviticus 24.8). Nobody condemned the priests for doing this work; they were not guilty of any breach of the Sabbath regulations. Now, claims Jesus, 'something greater than the temple is here' (v. 6). It is not absolutely certain what this means. Does it refer to Jesus himself, to the kingdom of God coming through Jesus, or to the community of the disciples who are the subject of the story? It is possible that all three ideas are implied. The overall argument of vv. 5–6 seems to be that if the rabbis recognize that some laws (those regarding the Sabbath) are subordinate to others (those prescribing the temple duties), then they should be able to recognize that same principle at work in this instance. The argument is capped with the quotation in v. 7 from Hosea 6.6, which places the 'law of compassion' firmly above the observance of ritual requirements. It is something of a mystery why this passage should be suggested for Church Anniversary.

John 4.19–26

This passage forms part of the story of the encounter at the well between Jesus and a Samaritan woman. Jesus has challenged her about her marital arrangements and she, changing the subject to a less embarrassing one, raises a major issue between Samaritans and Jews, concerning where worship should properly be offered (v. 20). The dispute was between Jerusalem with its temple, and Mt Gerazim, where for a while there was a Samaritan temple until its destruction about 108 BC. Jesus' reply confirms that the legitimate worship of God and 'salvation' (that is, the Messiah) indeed come from Judaism (v. 22). However, he goes on to say that such distinctions will come to an end because the true worship of God (which the Fourth Gospel wants us to understand is even now being brought in through Jesus) will no longer be restricted to one place or territory. This is because its centre will not be a physical temple but Jesus, who is the truth (v. 23; compare 14.6). Those who will be invited to worship in this way will not just be Jews and Samaritans, but all the world. They will do so in spirit and truth, precisely because God is spirit (v. 24). We should not read into this any disdain for forms of worship, ceremonies or sacraments. Rather, it is an insistence that the worship God requires always has to have at its heart a living spiritual relationship between the worshippers and God. The passage ends with Jesus' open disclosure to the woman of who he is (vv. 25–26). If other passages for today point to the importance of our church buildings, this one calls us to deep examination of what goes on within them week by week.

COVENANT

Exodus 24.3–11

This passage pictures the people's ratification of the covenant God offers to them. It takes place, as we gradually come to realize, in the context of a great fellowship meal. First, Moses tells the people 'all the words of the Lord', which in this context presumably means the contents of chs 20–23, and the people confirm their acceptance (v. 3). Moses then writes them down and builds an altar and twelve pillars (v. 4). First the sacrificial blood is dashed against the altar (God's side of the covenant, v. 6), then the covenant is read and accepted a second time (v. 7), and finally the remainder of the blood is sprinkled on the people (Israel's side of the covenant, v. 8). What follows in vv. 9–11 is utterly astonishing. Aaron, two of his sons and seventy elders, having previously been worshipping at a distance (v. 1), now join Moses who has been allowed nearer to God (presumably further up Mt Sinai, v. 2). All of them see the God of Israel (v. 10). Exodus 33.20 says flatly that this is not possible, a view which the whole Jewish and Christian tradition supports (Deuteronomy 4.12; Judges 13.22; compare 1 John 4.12). Perhaps the writer had difficulty believing this could have happened, since v. 11 has a note of incredulity – 'they saw God, and *lived*!' It is just possible that a vision of God is meant, since the word for 'saw' can indicate a vision. It is also just possible that the strange reference to the pavement that was 'like the very heaven for clearness', is meant to indicate that they looked through the pavement and saw (so to speak) the soles of God's feet. But when all is said and done, v. 10a is very emphatic and seemingly unambiguous. However we explain all this, the crucial thing is that at the moment they ratified the covenant they were intensely aware of the reality of God, as we hope to be as we renew our covenant. Christian readers can also see this passage as a prefiguring of the Eucharist, in which we meet with God, eat and drink, and live.

Deuteronomy 29.10–15

In the Old Testament there are a number of covenants between God and Israel. Each was made only once, though they might be renewed. This passage describes part of a renewal of the Sinai covenant, described in the other Old Testament lection. The renewal takes place on the plains of Moab (29.1). Moses enumerates those who are taking part (vv. 10–11). If we have a mental picture of ancient Israel as a racially exclusive society, we may be surprised by the inclusion of 'aliens' in this list and in this covenant. But Israel remembered what it was like to be aliens in a foreign land (Deuteronomy 10.19). For that reason aliens were entitled to the full protection of the legal system (Deuteronomy 1.16), and even included in the covenant which binds the whole nation. Moses uses the word 'today' five times within this passage, which tells us that this renewal of the covenant was not intended to be a merely formal act, but to accomplish something by revitalizing the relationship between God and the people. This is an important point to make about our renewal of our covenant with God. Verse 13 contains the heart of the covenant, that God will establish them as his own people, and undertake certain obligations towards them, to which they must respond by faithful obedience. This is also a corporate concept. Just as the original story has the people respond twice, 'All that the Lord has spoken we will do' (Exodus 24.3b, 7b), so here the enumeration of vv. 10–11 stresses that everyone is involved. When we renew our covenant with God we do so not just as individuals, but as Christian communities. We must also note the phrase in v. 15 about this covenant renewal being also made with 'those who are not here with us today'. This must mean those who would come after them, the generations not yet born. We have here a sense of sacred trust, that in this moment of renewal of our covenant we are pledging ourselves to the faith, in order to hand it on to future generations. It is for their sakes too that we undertake it.

Jeremiah 31.31–34

For this reading see the comments on the Old Testament lection on p. 58.

Romans 12.1–2

When we meet the word 'therefore' in Paul's writings we know that he is about to set out the consequences (usually the ethical consequences) of what he has just written. Here it refers to the previous eleven chapters, which have explored 'the mercies of God' in considerable detail. For Paul the 'old age' is on its way out and the 'new age', the age of God's mercy and grace made known in Christ, is on its way in. Christians are part of it, and must live as if they are (compare 2 Corinthians 5.17). The appeals here are not just addressed to individuals, but to the Christian community. Believers are to present their bodies as a 'living sacrifice'. By 'bodies' he means not just our physical bodies but ourselves as persons, who we are in the network of relationships and activities which make up our daily lives. There is no 'religion is only for Sundays' about this passage (nor indeed, anywhere else in the New Testament). What is envisaged is a total dedication to God in every part of life, offered in response to 'the mercies of God' which have been shown to us in Christ. In v. 2, Paul offers a contrast. We are not to be conformed to the ways of the world around us, the 'age without Christ' which is passing away. On the contrary, we are to be transformed, a transformation that is not just a matter of outward acts (though it will show itself in those), but of our minds, affecting what we think and feel, our motives and drives. The way into this is the 'spiritual worship', as Paul describes our self-offering. Our sincerity is taken for granted; without that everything would be a waste of time. But when we offer our spiritual worship and open ourselves to the needed transformation, we begin to discern the will of God, develop a discriminating judgment about what is 'good and acceptable and perfect' in each situation. We become those who can say to God: 'I am no longer my own but yours.'

John 15.1–10

For this reading see the comments on the Gospel on p. 93.

Mark 14.22–25

We are learning to see the 'Last Supper' not as an isolated act, but as part of a series of meals Jesus shared with his disciples and others, both during his earthly ministry and after the resurrection. It is striking how the post-resurrection meal accounts contain elements which reflect back on this particular meal (e.g. Luke 24.30; John 21.13a). Paul's account of the early Christian Eucharist (1 Corinthians 11.18–34) makes it clear even at that stage that it was no mere repetition of the Last Supper, for since then 'the Lord has risen!' Nevertheless, it derives its significance from what Jesus did at the last meal he shared with his disciples before the crucifixion. The four actions with the bread (taking, thanking, breaking and giving) and the three with the cup (taking, thanking and giving), are all interpreted by the words 'Take; this is my body' (v. 22b), and 'This is my blood of the covenant, which is poured out for many' (v. 24). Only the so-called 'longer text' of Luke has 'new covenant', though some manuscripts of both Mark and Matthew add it, and it is in Paul's account, which is the earliest of all. Jeremiah promised a 'new covenant' (Jeremiah 31.34) which would fundamentally change the relationship between God and human beings by enabling human hearts and minds to be fully open to God's grace. Christians believe that at this meal Jesus announced the fulfilment of that promise. Through the bread of his body and the wine of his blood, offered to God in sacrifice at Calvary, would come a whole new relationship to God, available to everybody. In an important sense, every time we share in the Eucharist we make a renewal of that covenant relationship with God, because we claim the benefits of Christ's death and resurrection. A Covenant Service has a slightly different purpose, but it would not be complete unless the Eucharist formed a part of it.

HARVEST THANKSGIVING

Genesis 8.15–22

The story of Noah and his ark speaks to us of how near God's anger and judgment are to each other. When God decides to destroy the whole of the human and animal creation, Noah and his family are the single exception (Genesis 6.6–8). By the end of the story we see that God's mercy is greater than God's anger, and when God smells Noah's pleasing sacrifice (v. 21) there comes the promise that makes this lection suitable for Harvest Festival. It concerns the continuance and regularity of the seasons, replete with their times of planting and reaping (v. 22). This reminds us that it was through Noah that God made a covenant with the whole of creation, long before any covenant was made with God's chosen people (Genesis 9.8–17; see the comments on the Old Testament lection on p. 46). If we read this passage in a British country church, looking out over recently harvested fields, it is comforting and reassuring. Even if the harvest is below average, we can remind ourselves, as farmers frequently have to do, that we must take the long-term view. But how might this passage sound in the ears of a congregation in Bangladesh, or sub-Saharan Africa, when there has been no rain for several years and when the farmers have been forced to eat their seed corn to stave off famine? In a world which is a global village we dare not leave that out of our Harvest Festival thinking. One response has been to argue that there is always enough food in the world to feed the world's population adequately; the problem lies not in God's provision but in the use human beings make of it. That argument may be dismissed by humanists as just a convenient way of letting God off the hook, but it is almost certainly true, even if sometimes oversimplified. However, we dare not employ it unless we are prepared to be God's agents, living more simply that others may simply live (as a charity slogan once put it), and campaigning for international justice on debt and fair trade.

Deuteronomy 26.1–11

The Harvest Festival in church is a fairly recent rediscovery. Rural communities have always celebrated the harvest, especially when it was good (as Breughel's paintings tell us!). Robert Hawker, Vicar of Morwenstow in Cornwall, revived the Lammas custom on the first

Sunday of October 1843, using bread made from the first ripe corn for the Holy Communion. From that sprang our modern harvest celebrations. It is ironic that this happened just as Britain was becoming the first industrialized country. By 1900 only a minority of the population had any real connection with the land, and the proportion has steadily decreased ever since. Quite rightly, we have now widened the scope of our harvest celebrations to include urban Harvest Festivals, and industrial ones. We have learned to give thanks for the 'God-given neighbours, unseen and unknown', who plant and grow, pick and transport the goods which we enjoy. We cannot celebrate that without becoming aware of our 'one-third, two-thirds' world, so issues of justice and fair trade have also come in. All these things are with us as we celebrate Harvest. Is there, then, anything which forms the essence of a harvest celebration? If there is, it is to be found in this reading, which records the 'first-fruits' ceremony. The Israelites had previously been a nomadic people with no land of their own to cultivate. Now, as they enter the promised land, they will become agriculturalists. The first produce is to be brought to the priest as an expression of gratitude for all that God has given in this new land (v. 3). The ceremonial words to be spoken (vv. 5b–10a) recall God's goodness in past history and look for its continuance in the present. As this special ceremony for entering the promised land became part of the annual cycle of worship, offered during the Feast of Weeks, the regulations spelled out the tithes to be given to those who cannot 'plough the fields and scatter' as an expression of the same gratitude (Deuteronomy 16.9–12). The essence of Harvest Thanksgiving is therefore: God gives, we are grateful. An exploration of what it means to be grateful in our own context needs to underlie all our Harvest Thanksgivings, whatever their character.

Ruth 2.1–23

Although the bulk of this reading is about Ruth gleaning in the fields, it is not an easy reading to preach from at a Harvest Thanksgiving since, in one sense, that is incidental to the rest of the story. Ruth, the Moabite widow, has come to Israel with her mother-in-law Naomi (see the comments on the continuous Old Testament reading on p. 196). Israelite law was extremely compassionate to the needy, especially to orphans and widows. Ruth's action in gleaning, collecting those sheaves which had been left by the reapers, was fully in accordance with the provisions of Deuteronomy 24.19–22 (see also Leviticus 19.9–10). Here is the possible link with a contemporary

Harvest Thanksgiving: the constant reminder throughout scripture that what God has given is to be shared with the poor and the needy, even to the extent that the Old Testament does not leave it to a charitable appeal, but builds it into the laws which are seen as reflecting the character of God and which must be obeyed. The chapter as a whole relates how Ruth acted in accordance with this provision (of which, no doubt, Naomi had told her). At the same time, we are made aware that Naomi was a thoughtful woman who had already begun to work out how to secure Ruth's future (v. 1; for the significance of this statement see the comments on the continuous Old Testament reading on p. 200). Boaz' interest in and concern for the young woman is marked throughout the chapter. We begin to sense not only that Naomi's plans for Ruth's future are likely to come to fruition, but also that Ruth and Boaz welcome a growing relationship.

1 Timothy 6.6–10

This passage strikes us as rather mundane and lacking in theological undergirding. Scholars find most of the sentiments in these verses paralleled in 'secular' Greek literature of the time, amounting in some cases to actual quotation. The usual conclusion is that the writer has taken over these thoughts, working them into his text without much reflection, because they voice sentiments broadly in line with Christian ethics. All that may be true, but is not necessarily a reason to ignore the passage. These may not be the most exalted sentiments in the New Testament, but there is practical wisdom here which ought not to be despised. Verses 6–8 extol the virtues of a combination of godliness and contentment. This means recognizing that 'you can't take it with you', as the popular proverb puts it (v. 7b), and that if a human being has food and clothing that, at least, should prevent us from being dissatisfied (v. 8). After all, those are exactly the things to which Jesus referred in one of today's Gospels as illustrating God's provision for us (Matthew 6.25–29). Verses 9–10 speak realistically of what can happen in a human life when discontent sets in and the drive for material prosperity becomes all-important. The observation of v. 10b is perfectly true. Most of us can think of Christian people of modest circumstances who have raised children caringly and lovingly, only to find those children 'bettering themselves' by making materialism the goal of their lives and, in the process, throwing away their spiritual inheritance. The real difficulty here is v. 10, which most translations render along the lines of 'The love of money is the root of all evil.' Such a statement falls ludicrously below the New Testament's great insights into the nature of evil. NRSV's translation makes the love of money 'a' root (rather than 'the' root) of 'all kinds of evil' (rather than evil itself). This stretches the Greek a little, but produces a defensible statement. In a society where for many years we have been encouraged to regard making money as the highest good, and where almost everything still has to justify itself in monetary terms, it needs to be heard.

Revelation 14.14–18

Perhaps judgment is an unavoidable theme at Harvest. If nothing else the image of reaping is an obvious image of death and judgment. The Old Testament uses it (Jeremiah 51.33; Lamentations 1.15; Hosea 6.11). In the Gospels we find parables which link the themes of harvest and judgment (Matthew 13.24–30; 21.33–41). That is certainly so here, though it is a difficult passage to interpret in detail. The Lectionary should not have omitted vv. 19–20 and they really must be read if this passage is to be preached on. However we are to understand them, they form the conclusion of the passage and vv. 17–18 do not make sense without them. At first reading it looks as if vv. 14–16 describe the reaping of corn, seemingly to gather in God's faithful ones to salvation, and that vv. 17–20 represent the reaping of grapes, seemingly to gather in others to the destruction so dreadfully described in vv. 19–20. Some commentators argue that both reapings are for salvation, and that the 'winepress . . . trodden outside the city' (v. 20) represents the martyrs whose blood has been spilled. Each reader must make his or her mind up about the likelihood of this. There are many difficulties with preaching about judgment. We can no longer frighten people into the kingdom (could we ever?) and it is not moral to try. And when we look at what many Christians have said about judgment (in some cases still do), we find them happily condemning human beings to destruction and punishment because of things which they cannot help (such as sexuality), ignorance of the Gospel (even if they have never heard it) and even, may God forgive us, differences of theological opinion! It is unedifying and unchristian. Most of all, we ought to have a profound sense that it is not our business to pronounce about judgment: it is God's alone. Thankfully, this passage says that much clearly, as should we if we really feel a need to preach about the subject.

Matthew 6.25–33

Sermons which merely offer good advice are not much use. Yet at first blush, this is exactly what Jesus appears to be doing here. Some of our congregation, if they are honest, will have problems with this familiar passage. They may not be openly critical, because it is part of the Sermon on the Mount, therefore the words of Jesus, but they do wonder whatever it is all about. It sounds like a recipe for irresponsibility: just leave it all to God! We need to make one careful distinction, between *worry* and *concern*. We may be concerned about a lot of things, and have good cause for it: our health or work prospects, the well-being of a loved one, discrimination against a minority group to which we belong, the government's educational policies, the effects of climate change on coastal communities etc. Those are legitimate concerns. In many cases it is our Christian duty to have such concerns and to act on them. No, what Jesus is speaking of is *merimnan,* a Greek verb for which a single English equivalent is not easy: 'to be over-anxious' is about right. It is primarily a state of mind (though often showing itself in what we do). It is about when we spend much of our time in a state of stress and anxiety about things such as food and drink, or clothing (v. 25). The illustration in v. 26 has an often-missed touch of humour: indeed the birds do not sow, reap or gather, but they do work very hard at finding their food! The point is that God provides it for them to gather. And there is a touch of humorous absurdity in the illustration in vv. 28–29 too: nobody wants to look like a flower of the field, but the fact that the world is full of beautiful flowers is a simple illustration of God's care and provision. Now we see the importance of the 'therefore' of v. 31: this is not good advice, it is an invitation to trust the God who graciously provides. But we will only know that from experience when we get our priorities right. Verse 33 is an invitation to do just that. It does not mean doing 'church work' all the time. It means constantly seeking the will and purpose of God in all we do (work, relationships, social concerns, politics etc.). If that is so, other things assume their proper place, will be there when we need them, and we need not be over-anxious.

John 6.24–35

For comments on this reading, see those on the Gospel on p. 142.

JOHN AND CHARLES WESLEY

Isaiah 12.1–6

This is a thanksgiving psalm which cannot be attached to any particular occasion or event and is appropriate whenever God's saving help is being celebrated. There are links with the opening of the psalm of triumph in Exodus 15.1–2, which celebrates the deliverance from Egypt. In v. 1 the singer rejoices that what has previously been experienced as God's anger is now experienced as God's comfort. This resonates with one aspect of the classic Christian 'conversion' story. So does the language of v. 2, which both acknowledges that salvation comes from God alone, and also involves the personal appropriation of that salvation. If we are celebrating the Wesley brothers we will think of the famous entry in John's *Journal* for 24 May 1738: 'I felt I did trust in Christ, Christ alone for my salvation; and an assurance was given me that He had taken away *my* sins, even *mine*, and saved *me* from the law of sin and death.' This verse even suggests two other possibilities for preaching. NRSV translates the end of the second clause, '. . . is my strength and my might'. In his commentary R. E. Clements suggests 'energy' or 'vitality' rather than 'might'. Whether or not John Wesley's experience at Aldersgate Street is best described as a 'conversion', or in some other way, is open to debate. What cannot be doubted is the immense energy which flowed from it. Until well into old age he travelled ceaselessly, preaching, establishing societies, writing etc. A number of other translations (e.g. AV, RSV, JB, NIV) judge that the Hebrew word comes from a different root and translate: '. . . is my strength and my song', which offers the opportunity to celebrate Charles Wesley's great contribution to Christian hymnody. Verse 3 contains a potent image: life depends on a reliable water supply, and in places where the only source of this is a well, it is a matter of constant concern that it should not run dry. The image of 'wells of salvation' from which all can draw freely is clear enough. Verse 4 reminds us that giving thanks to God and making known what God has done (i.e., worship and evangelism) belong together, the one springing out of the other. The members of the early Methodist societies gathered to praise God and listen to the preaching, and they shared with their neighbours the story of what God had done for them. Finally, we may note that this psalm climaxes with the assertion that God is 'in your midst' (v. 6).

As he lay dying, John Wesley twice cried out: 'The best of all is God is with us.' Such a conviction energizes and enables.

Isaiah 51.1–3, 7–11

This passage consists of three short units of prophecy. In vv. 1–3 there is an appeal to those who seek 'righteousness', by which is meant God's deliverance (v. 1a). Such seekers must recall their origins, and in particular Abraham and Sarah, through whom came God's great promise of blessing for the whole world (Genesis 12.1–3; 17.3–8, 15–16). To look back is not just to recall a past deed, but to affirm that through it God has brought blessing for the present, and will do so again in the future, when gladness and singing will be found where formerly there was wilderness and desert (v. 3). Christians of other denominations sometimes allege that Methodists are obsessed with their past and with the Wesley brothers in particular. There is some truth in this, especially when love of the tradition is used to resist necessary changes. Nonetheless, if we do not understand our history we shall not understand why we are the kind of people we are. In an age when, thankfully, denominational divisions mean less and less to people, many worshippers in Methodist churches may have little idea of that history or its significance. Wesley Day celebrations are an opportunity to look to those who were, under God, the inspiration for what became a worldwide renewal of Christian life and witness, and give thanks for them. We will do this best if we celebrate it not as a denominational story, but as part of universal Christian history. And just as the prophet rightly remembers Sarah along with Abraham, we should remember the remarkable Susannah Wesley, through whose ministry John and Charles learned much of the righteousness of God. Verses 7–8 are addressed to those who have righteousness in their hearts, and who therefore know that they have nothing to fear from their enemies or persecutors. The early Methodists were often persecuted, and had many enemies. In contemporary Britain there is no open persecution, but Christians of all persuasions have many enemies whose weapons are mockery, ridicule and intellectual snobbishness. Verses 9–11 again recall God's past deeds and affirm that God's people will have reason to sing because their joy comes from God. The 'everlasting joy' of v. 11b is described by George Knight as 'an outrageous kind of joy that is shocking to the faithless' (compare Acts 2.13). What are the reasons why a church which was 'born in song' should still be singing now?

Romans 5.1–11

This classic exposition of the Christian understanding of salvation through faith in Christ is appropriate to Wesley Day because the life and work of John and Charles was devoted to bringing people into just such a relationship with God as Paul describes here. Paul begins by saying that we are put into a right relationship with God through faith in Christ, and this gives us 'peace' with God. Peace here carries the overtones of the great Hebrew word *shālôm* which, as is often said, conveys much more than the absence of conflict and war. If we feel at peace with God that is because we have good grounds for doing so: the stress in this verse is not on how we feel, but on the reality of what God has done. We have not only peace, but a present access to the grace of God – there is no waiting list (compare Ephesians 3.12)! And because of our acceptance by God now we shall share God's glory hereafter (v. 2b). Even our sufferings (which almost certainly here refers to persecutions) are not meaningless, as we might suppose. However, the statement that 'suffering produces endurance' must be taken in its context; as an absolute or unqualified statement it is untrue. But Paul here means that bearing persecution in faith makes us tried and tested veterans (v. 4). We are, despite out-ward appearances, not living in a fool's paradise; our hope for the future rests on what God has done for us and the Holy Spirit is evidence of this (v. 5). We are, after all, incapable of saving ourselves (v. 6), but do not need to because God has done this for us in Christ, who loves the unlovely (v. 8). Paul does not attempt to explain how the death of Christ saves us. It is sufficient to know that it does. In v. 10 Paul moves from the language of 'justification' to that of 'reconciliation'. The enmity was on our side, not God's. We are reconciled to God, not God to us (compare 2 Corinthians 5.18–20). But, 'if God loves sinners, sinners must be won to love God' (Kenneth Grayston), a process which is only possible once enmity is ended and a state of reconciliation and peace has come about. God's action has made this possible and our response is to 'boast' (better 'exult', REB) in what God in Christ has done for us (v. 11). We are most faithful, not just to the legacy of the Wesleys but (much more importantly) to the imperative of the Christian good news, when we see it as our task to encourage people into a state of reconciliation with a God who loves them.

2 Peter 1.1–11

This reading describes the qualities which should mark out the people of God. The opening greeting refers to 'our God and Saviour Jesus Christ' (v. 1b). The NRSV footnote indicates that there is another way to translate it, but the text is probably right. Calling Jesus 'Saviour' causes us no surprise today, but it is fairly rare in the New Testament, occurring only in the Pastoral Epistles and – five times – in this letter as a direct title. The writer uses it because he wants to remind his readers that they have a 'Saviour' who will help them achieve the virtues he will soon outline. In v. 2 it is the knowledge *of* God (not just knowledge *about* God) which brings grace and peace, and in vv. 3–4 comes the assertion that the 'divine power' has given us all that we need in order to live in a godly way. These are 'precious and great promises' (v. 4a), which enable us both to escape the moral corruption of the world around us, and to 'become participants in the divine nature' (v. 4b). This last phrase gradually developed, through a group of theologians known as the Cappadocian fathers, into a whole theology of salvation which has had great influence in the Eastern Church. Known as 'divinization' it claims that the process of salvation involves humans being gradually made one with God, a process in which prayer and sacraments play their part. This passage in 2 Peter will hardly bear so much weight, yet it is interesting that the aspiration for union with God is a notable feature of some of Charles Wesley's hymns:

> Send us the Spirit of thy Son,
> To make the depths of Godhead known,
> To make us share the life divine.
> (*Hymns and Psalms* 300, v. 2)

Christians must therefore live as those whose destiny is to become participants in the divine nature. Verses 5–7 are a list of virtues. Each of them helps to produce the next one in the list, which is not very obvious from NRSV's translation. Verses 8–9 remind us that we must not rest content with what we are (let alone regress), but should be 'eager' to confirm our calling and place in God's kingdom, in which we have a place both now and in eternity (vv. 10–11). The passage challenges us to take seriously the living of a holy life. This was the aim of Wesley's so-called 'Holy Club' at Oxford and later of the Methodist 'bands'. We might ask what there is today which helps us to take the challenge to holy living seriously.

Mark 12.28–37

For this reading see the comments on the Gospel on p. 198.

Luke 10.1–12, 17–20

In Luke 9.1–6 we are told about Jesus sending out the twelve disciples. In this passage, found only in Luke, we discover him sending out seventy (or seventy-two) on similar terms. The intention of the mission is to prepare the way for Jesus himself (v. 1b), yet the message is the one which Mark tells us Jesus himself preached (v. 9b; see Mark 1.15a, omitted by Luke at 4.14–15). There is a great sense of urgency about this mission, with no time for idle chit-chat (v. 5) and those who undertake it must travel light (v. 4). There is also a sense of danger (v. 3 suggests that the time for the fulfilment of Isaiah 11.6 has not yet arrived). When the seventy return and report their successes (v. 17) Jesus rejoices in what has been accomplished (v. 18). In imagery drawn from the Old Testament (e.g. Deuteronomy 8.15) he assures them not of their personal comfort or safety, but that the forces of evil and opposition will not ultimately prevail. Most of all, they should recognize that what has been accomplished is from God, and their greatest rejoicing must be in their own relationship to God (v. 20). Even granted that they are not sent outside the borders of Israel (v. 1b), it is probably right to see in this story the commissioning of the entire Church to be a missionary body to the entire world. A sermon on this passage would most appropriately concentrate on that central point, rather than dwelling on the details. John Wesley's assertion that he looked upon all the world as his parish might be set alongside the saying of the twentieth-century Sri Lankan Methodist Daniel T. Niles: 'The church exists by mission as a fire exists by burning.' There is always a temptation for us to think that there is 'some other' person or 'some other' group which bears the responsibility for the Church's mission. The fact is that the responsibility lies with all of us. Much recent research has shown that the most effective means of bringing people to a commitment to Christ is the daily witness of ordinary Christians and their willingness to talk to others about their faith. Of course, some of the methods envisaged in this particular passage would be highly inappropriate for our society. If evangelism in that context meant 'no chit-chat', evangelism today might instead involve the patient building of long-term relationships.

NEW YEAR: WATCHNIGHT

Deuteronomy 8.1–20

A Watchnight service inevitably has elements of reflection on the year that is dying and hope for the year that is being born. For most people those things will be closely interwoven. Reflection on the old year may include regret and loss, things we would prefer to forget, along with things which have enriched us and which we will long remember. Our hopes for the incoming year may be shaped by our memories. We may be looking forward to better times and be confident – or otherwise – of them. We may bring anxieties about the unknown future, or anticipate it positively. There may be expected events which have been long planned, perhaps marriage or a retire-ment. At Watchnight services we offer all these things to God who loves us. This reading appropriately mingles two sets of contrasting themes in much the same way. On the one hand there is the imagery of the past, which for the Israelites was the wilderness journey, and on the other hand there is the imagery of the future, which is the promised land. In connection with both wilderness and promised land there are the possibilities of remembering, or forgetting. As they look back they are to *remember* the wilderness journey which involved privations such as hunger (v. 3a) and snakes and scorpions (v. 15), but which also demonstrated God's care for them in the midst of their difficulties through the provision of manna (vv. 3b, 16), water out of the rock (v. 15b), and clear leading (v. 15a). As they look forward they are to hear the promise of God about the goodness of the future (vv. 7–9) and 'bless' the Lord for it (v. 10). Nevertheless, the future holds its perils too. They are different perils from the wilder-ness and they come in tandem with the blessings. For when they enjoy all these blessings (vv. 12–13), they must not *forget* to whom they owe them (v. 14) or the commandments they have been given (v. 11). If success, prosperity and 'better times' come in the future they must *remember* that God is the source of all good gifts (vv. 17–18). Although *forgetting* that God is the giver is bad enough, the worst thing of all is to *forget* God himself (v. 19). There is plenty here which will resonate with the mixed hopes and fears, joys and regrets, concerning both past and present, of a Watchnight congregation.

Ecclesiastes 3.1–15

This passage has acquired much popularity in recent years. The first eight verses have an almost mesmeric quality, the language and rhythm weaving a spell around us. Here, we feel, is 'timeless wisdom', something for all moods. Someone hearing v. 15 for the first time and asked to name its source might even suggest T. S. Eliot's *Four Quartets*. This reading will appeal to those who keep a copy of Gibran's *The Prophet* on their bedside table. But, to be prosaic, what does this passage actually mean? Verses 1–8 offer a conspectus on virtually everything in life. There are those things which choose us rather than us choosing them. How we respond is often the making – or otherwise – of us. So it is with birth and death (v. 2a), with falling in love and with falling out of love (v. 5b), with the routine which is set before us (v. 5a). There are those things which we choose to do or be, and our choosing will show what sort of people we are becoming. So it is with knowing when to speak and when keep silent (v. 7b), with knowing when to respond savagely and when gently (v. 3a), with knowing when the past matters most and when the future (v. 6b). There are those things which demand deep emotional responses and cool judgments. So it is when differences must be glossed over because they are secondary, or lived with because they run deep (v. 7a), when enmities must be dealt with one way or the other (v. 8). How magnificent it all is, and the idea that 'for everything there is a season' seems to suggest that all this (i.e., human experience) fits together into a magnificent picture, if only we could see the whole of it, and v. 11a seems to support this. But v. 11b tells a different story: what does all this mean? God only knows! Is there any ultimate purpose in life? God only knows. All we can do is to accept the mystery (v. 14) and get on with the business of enjoying life as best we can without too much thought about what it all means (vv. 12–13). The fact that Jesus, in one of today's Gospels (Luke 12.19–20), suggests that this won't quite do, should give us pause for thought. But the passage mirrors the mood of many today, including some who will be in church. And it is an antidote to the kind of cheap Christian optimism which does not correspond to life as it is for many people. For that reason alone we need it more than we may realize.

Revelation 21.1–6a

For this reading see the comments on the Epistle on p. 193.

Matthew 25.31–46

This story is a vision of the Last Judgment. It comes immediately before the start of Matthew's passion narrative where we see the king identifying himself with those in the greatest need of all. The whole of humankind is gathered before the judgment seat, not just Christians (v. 32). They are gathered as nations but judged as 'people', i.e., individuals (v. 32). The separation into sheep and goats mirrors the practice in Palestine of having mixed flocks, separated at night because the goats had to be kept warm while the sheep preferred the open air. The sheep are placed on the king's right-hand side, probably because they were more commercially valuable (v. 33). What is the basis for the separation? The 'sheep' are told that they have ministered to Jesus himself when he was in need (vv. 35–36). The statement takes them by surprise, as well it might; they have never self-consciously thought of themselves as doing any such thing (vv. 37–39). Then they are told that they have ministered to Jesus whenever they have responded to the plight of the poor and needy by doing something to help. There is no discrimination here between those who 'deserve' help and those who do not. In fact the phrase 'least of' in v. 40 may imply 'least deserving' in the eyes of others, those most likely to be ignored by the official welfare structures. We may note in passing that one interpretation sees 'the least of these' as Christian missionaries, and NRSV's paraphrase leans towards this, but in view of Matthew 5.43–48 it is unlikely. The acts of mercy which are listed are only examples of the kind of thing which might be done. Such acts were truly performed for Jesus himself (v. 40). The judgment is strictly impartial, and when the 'goats' are consigned to damnation (v. 41) it is not because of anything they have done but because of what they have failed to do (vv. 42–43). The goats are equally surprised; they might have realized they had not cared for the needy, but they had no idea that they were thereby failing to minister to Jesus (v. 44). At first sight this reading appears to teach that we are saved by what we do, which is in flat contradiction of much of the rest of the New Testament. However, the key is in vv. 37–39: the 'righteous' do not keep a record of their good deeds, to show them to God and earn salvation. The good deeds are a natural outcome of the kind of people they have become. And if we ask how we may become the kind of people whose lives manifest such unself-conscious goodness, becoming 'new people' (2 Corinthians 5.17) will lie at the heart of the answer.

Luke 12.13–21

We sometimes call the story which forms the principal part of this reading the Parable of the Rich Fool. He was not a fool because he was rich, he was a fool because of his attitude towards his riches, and the distinction is important. The story is occasioned by Jesus being asked to arbitrate in a family dispute over inheritance (the rules for dealing with such matters can be found in Numbers 27.1–11; 36.7–9; Deuteronomy 21.15–17). Jesus' reply (v. 14) is slightly condescending in tone: the questioner is asking something unworthy of him. He responds by saying that we must guard against greed (v. 15a). Possessions are of course necessary, but an abundance of them does not constitute our real life. This saying is for those who have more than they actually need – which is most of us. The story which follows is both vivid and straightforward. The man is already rich (v. 16). The fact that his lands yielded a bumper harvest would be seen as a sign of blessing. The problem comes with what he decides to do with his good fortune. His actions (vv. 17–18) are all directed towards himself. He stores his wealth against his own future, not even in order to provide for his dependants, and certainly not in order that he might be a help to others. Indeed, his only concern is his hedonistic lifestyle (v. 19; compare Ecclesiastes 3.12–13). Then God enters the story and utters the judgment. The man is a 'fool', and the description is used here as it is in the Old Testament wisdom literature: the man rejects the wisdom of God (Proverbs 1.22–23). The concluding comment says that storing up treasures for ourselves is foolish, we must be 'rich towards God' instead (v. 21). In this context, being 'rich towards God' is not about cultivating a deep devotional life or giving significant time to 'spiritual things'; it is about using what we have wisely, for the benefit of others. New Year is a good time for reflecting on how we use our resources, and resolving to be wiser in this respect in the coming year than we have been in the one that is past.

Luke 12.35–50

This reading turns our attention to themes which are normally associated with Advent but which are appropriate to New Year, especially as Luke presents them. After the instruction to be ready (v. 35), the passage contains three parables, with the thoughts of 'returning' and 'being ready' running through all of them, though with different emphases. Matthew offers this kind of material largely in relation to the end of the age and the return of Christ (Matthew 24.43–51) but Luke wants us to think of judgment not just as something still to come but as operative among us now. God knows how 'ready' we are and how we are discharging our responsibilities, which speaks directly to our expectations of how we will live in a New Year. The first parable is in vv. 35–38, where the emphasis is on the unpredictability of the master's return. They must be ready now, even though he may return late (v. 38). The startling note in this parable comes in v. 37, where the roles of master and slave are reversed, as a reward for the faithfulness of the slaves. In a world which prized hierarchy even more than we do this is astonishing. Yet in Luke's Gospel we find Jesus saying this about himself at the Last Supper (22.27; compare Mark 10.45a). The second parable is in vv. 39–40, and here the emphasis is first on the vigilance of the master of the household, though the unexpectedness of the burglar's arrival is also part of the picture. The parable is so vivid (and, sadly, so true to the experience of many people in today's Britain) that it needs no elaboration. The third parable is in vv. 42–48 and it is here that we see most clearly how Luke has presented the material to be directly relevant to the life of the Christian congregation. The steward of such a household, though a slave, held a position of some authority, being responsible for ensuring that the other slaves did their work properly and for managing it. At the same time he was responsible for ensuring that they were properly looked after and that their needs were met. What in Matthew is a message of impending judgment (Matthew 24.51) is here a stern warning to those who hold authority about what is expected of them (vv. 46–48). It is probable that Luke has in mind those who hold office in the Church (see 1 Timothy 3.1–10 for the kind of personal qualities which were looked for). Authority consists in serving others. It is seen in a particular context in relation to the disciples' role (which is the point of Peter's question in v. 41), but applies more generally within the Christian community. Verses 49–50 are a slightly odd conclusion to this reading and could be omitted.

REMEMBRANCE SUNDAY

Note: It is significant that three of today's eight lections occur else-where during Year B (on Easter Day, Christmas Day III and the Sixth Sunday of Easter), but in no case has it seemed possible merely to refer to the previous sets of comments. The use of scripture on Remembrance Sunday can be a delicate and difficult business, as can the day itself, so far as worship at the beginning of the twenty-first century is concerned. In the comments that follow I have tried to indicate how the lections might be used on Remembrance Sunday, but it must be admitted that this often means paying less attention to what a reading is really about than we would normally expect to do.

Isaiah 25.1–9

In the first part of this reading, the prophet rejoices in the wonderful works of God (v. 1). God is seen as having reduced the cities of ruthless enemies to rubble (v. 2), thus displaying a power which will cause even strong and ruthless foreigners to fear God (v. 3). The way in which God is thought to have done these things is not specified, but it does not need to be. The usual understanding in the Old Testament is that God's people are delivered from oppression by winning victory in their battles (conversely, when they lose their battles it is because they have been sinful and are being punished). This is not how the overwhelming majority of contemporary Christians would interpret the way God works. It is easy to sneer at the 'God is on our side' thinking in which, for example, some Christians on both sides of the conflict in World War II indulged. But we do have to answer the question as to whether some things (Naziism?) are not so intrinsically evil and contrary to God's will that it is quite proper to say God is 'on the side' of those who oppose them. The problem is that it is very far from being a simple issue. For vv. 6–9, see the comments on the Old Testament lection on p. 82. Verse 8 will have resonance for those who still mourn the loss of comrades.

Isaiah 52.7–12

For comments on vv. 7–10 see also the Old Testament lection on p. 14. On Remembrance Sunday the emphasis will be on the welcome announcement of peace which introduces the reading (v. 7). War is at best a necessary evil: no sane person wishes their country to be involved in armed conflict. When we read accounts of how ordinary British people received the news of the cessation of hostilities after both the World Wars of the twentieth century, we are made aware of wholehearted rejoicing. Of course, it was the rejoicing of those who had won! But there is more to it than that: there is the deep-down rejoicing of those who know that they (and perhaps especially loved ones) are no longer in daily danger and that life can return to normal. That, of course, is true for ordinary people on the 'losing' side as well. So this passage can point us to what a proper celebration of the victory might be. It is a celebration of the fact that 'we' have won (with the implication that justice has done so too), but it is also a celebration of the fact that the bloodshed is over and human life as God intends it to be can be resumed. And the passage contains a warning against forgetting God in the new context of peace: if we are faithful to what God requires, God will be both behind and before us (vv. 11–12).

Micah 4.1–8

This reading consists of two distinct prophetic oracles, the first of which (vv. 1–4) is of greater interest for Remembrance Sunday. It also appears in Isaiah 2.2–4 and the fact that it is used twice testifies to the attractiveness and importance of the situation it depicts. It is a visionary oracle describing 'days to come' (v. 1). Its fulfilment involves the 'mountain of the Lord's house' (Mt Zion, or Jerusalem) being seen as the 'highest of the mountains', not literally of course, but in esteem and importance. People from all over the world will come to it (v. 2a) so as to learn the ways of Israel's God (v. 2b). The wisdom which Israel had always known as God's gift through the Law of Moses will continue to go out from Jerusalem (v. 2b), but what is now different is that the whole world will acknowledge it. God will act like an international court of justice, and directly arbitrate in disputes between 'strong nations far away' (v. 3a). As a result, those nations will abolish their weapons of war and warlike ways (v. 3b) and there will be peace over the whole earth. The oracle concludes with a down-to-earth and traditional picture of what it means to ordinary people when *shālôm* prevails (v. 4; compare Zechariah 3.10). We all long for our world to be like this. Remembrance Sunday is a good day to pray for those human institutions which work for it to come true.

Romans 8.31–35, 37–39

This passage only makes sense in the light of what has preceded it. Paul has set out the way in which God has acted, through Christ, to bring men and women out of their state of sin and disobedience into a new relationship with himself. If God is 'for us' in this sense (v. 31), then what Paul says here flows from it. Nothing and nobody can undermine it, since God has accepted us (v. 33). With Charles Wesley we can sing, 'No condemnation now I dread', because Christ has died for us and now pleads our cause (v. 34). Paul produces two lists of things which might superficially appear to be able to separate us from God's love. The first list is of hardships and deprivations (vv. 35–36), which seem to summarize what he had experienced in following his calling (see 2 Corinthians 6.4–5). Human beings are not spared these things, but they do not ultimately determine our fate. The second list is of less tangible but even more fearsome things (vv. 38–39a). They include death itself, the 'last enemy' (1 Corinthians 15.26), and the mysterious 'powers' of various sorts. We are to think of those who believe themselves to be at the mercy of fate, astrological forces and the like. Reverting to his question of v. 35a, Paul is emphatic: there is nothing at all which can separate us from God's love now revealed to us in Christ our Lord.

Revelation 22.1–5

Here is the Seer's vision of the new Jerusalem with the throne of God, shared by the Lamb, as the focal point (v. 1b). It draws its imagery from the garden of Eden in Genesis 2.8–14 and the vision of the new Jerusalem in Ezekiel 47.1–12. This is the restoration of the former and the fulfilment of the latter. Eating of the tree of life brought banishment from the garden, but here its leaves are for the healing of the nations (v. 2b). In Genesis the ground is cursed because of human sin (3.17–18) but here curses have been lifted, all is clean, creation has been renewed by God (v. 3). The servants of God will worship and see God's face (vv. 3b–4; compare Matthew 5.8). Fulfilling the promise of Revelation 3.21, the servants of God will 'reign for ever and ever' with God. As G. R. Beasley-Murray says, 'That is an extension of the grace of God in Christ beyond the grasp of the human mind.' On this day, some will be recalling the horrors of war in which they participated, the blood and pain, the smashed bodies and the ruined homes. All of us see such sights regularly on our television screens, and are almost immune to them.

John's picture here is set against all pictures of carnage and destruction (and against such pictures in his own writing), as God's final and sure intention for creation.

Matthew 5.1–12

The primary focus of interest today is v. 9. The Christian story can be described in terms of 'God as peacemaker', since God's action in Christ is intended to make peace between different groups of human beings as well as between human beings and God (Ephesians 2.14–18). Those who engage in peacemaking therefore share in something which is (if we may so express it) at the core of God's being. That is why they are called 'children of God'. And, we note, it is peace*making* that is in question. Everybody, except tyrants and megalomaniacs, loves and wants peace; those who make it are in a special category (compare James 3.18). The more we reflect on peacemaking, the more we realize what a complex thing it is. We never make peace by simply smoothing things over. Hearts and minds have to be changed, emotionally charged issues which may go back centuries have to be negotiated (as in Northern Ireland or the Balkans), injustices have to be righted. Peace is not real peace unless it allows freedom and justice. Sadly, the conclusion is sometimes reached that the only way to establish real peace is first to have war, though Christians have always disagreed about the rightness of that. Remembrance Sunday is not the day for settling that question. It is the day for honouring those who gave their lives that peace with justice might be established.

Matthew 5.43–48

This is a hard but necessary reading on Remembrance Sunday, though it is really a hard reading on any Sunday. Where are we told to hate our enemies (v. 43b)? Not anywhere in the Law of Moses, though it certainly commands us to love our neighbours (Leviticus 19.18). But human beings know how to hate and are clever at finding acceptable motives for doing so (e.g. Psalm 139.21–22). Jesus is here dealing with a popular interpretation of the Law: we are commanded to love our neighbour, we are not commanded to love our enemies, therefore it is permissible to hate them. But it is not, and for two reasons. Loving (that is, doing good to) those who love you, or who belong to your 'group', is not very difficult; even people who don't have the benefit of God's Law generally manage that much

(vv. 46–47). More significantly, living as God wants us to means reflecting the character of God who, as we can plainly see, shows the same love to good and bad alike (v. 45). If we want to be 'perfect' (v. 48) we must love our enemies (v. 44), but no blueprint is provided; this is an ideal, not a law. Something will have to be said, sensitively, about how we often demonize enemies and former enemies (what do some newspapers say about the Germans every time a difference of opinion arises within the European Community?). Loving enemies is a radical thing to do. It calls for special grace and is a distinctive mark of faithful Christian discipleship.

John 15.9–17

A large number of war memorials in British cities, towns and villages have v. 13 inscribed on them. It is understandable, but it is in some ways unfortunate. As an absolute statement it is questionable (in the light of the reading from Matthew 5.43–48, might not a greater love be to lay down one's life for one's *enemies*?). And, of course, in the context of the Fourth Gospel it is not intended as an absolute statement. Jesus is saying something about the sheer goodness of God, about God's forgiveness, acceptance and love, which makes the unlovely lovable and, in turn, loving to others (vv. 15b, 17; see the comments on the Gospel on p. 95). And in that context he is calling his disciples 'friends' and telling them that he will make the supreme sacrifice for them. If we use this passage to suggest, in some simplistic way, that all those who have died in armed conflict have laid down their lives for their friends as Jesus did, and are therefore blessed as Jesus was blessed, we come close to a drastic misuse of scripture. We also come close to a romanticizing of war, which is intolerable. As the First World War poets told us, war is always a bloody business. Nor can we exclude from Remembrance Day the insight that many of those who are killed in it lose their lives not out of some noble idea of self-sacrifice, but because they have no choice but to be involved. In that sense they too were victims. And yet we most certainly do want to honour those who gave their lives in order that we might not be subject to tyranny. In the end, whether they were victims or noble idealists is not the most important thing. They (and those who loved them) made a sacrifice which we recall and value. We must say that clearly, but this is a very dangerous passage of scripture from which to do so.